CLASSIC REPRINTS

"Truth" as Conceived by Those Who Are Not Professional Philosophers

Arne Ness (Naess)

an exact reproduction of the text
originally published in 1938

reprinted with kind permission from
Springer Science + Business Media B.V.

Advanced Reasoning Forum
P. O. Box 635
Socorro, NM 87801 USA
www.ARFbooks.org

ISBN 978-1-938421-08-2

"TRUTH" AS CONCEIVED BY THOSE WHO ARE NOT PROFESSIONAL PHILOSOPHERS

BY
ARNE NESS

Skrifter utgitt av Det Norske Videnskaps-Akademi i Oslo
II. Hist.-Filos. Klasse. 1938. No.4

OSLO
I KOMMISJON HOS JACOB DYBWAD
1938

Fremlagt i fellesmøtet den 3. mai 1938 av A. Aall

Trykt for Fridtjof Nansens fond

A.W. BRØGGERS BOKTRYKKERI A/S

Preface.

For the development of the statistical parts of this monograph, I owe much to the ready and careful assistance of Mr. H. Simonsen, Miss Eva Anje, and Miss Else Hertzberg, who also assisted as test-leader.

My indebtedness to the many test-persons spending hours on my intricate questionnaires is so great that I wish to dedicate this monograph to them.

J. Hertzberg. Principal, Stabekk komm. h. almenskole, kindly let me use his pupils as test-persons. - Among others, Mr. E. Tollefsen and Miss Fougner have tried to make me write better English, for which my best thanks.

Oslo, July 1938. A. N.

Contents.

Introduction.

Sect.	Page
1. The Aim of the Treatise. Genesis of the Idea	11
2. What Is a Theory of Truth?	12
3. The Non-Philosopher's Idea of Truth according to the Philosophers	14
4. Explicit and Implicit Opinions	16
5. The Questionnaire-Method	19

Chapter I.
The Questionnaires.

6. General Classification	22
7. Questionnaires of Class A	22
8. Questionnaires of Class B	24
9. Questionnaires of Class C	28
10. Questionnaires of Class D	30
11. Some Remarks on the Examination Technique	30
12. A Selection of Typical Replies to Questionnaires	32

Chapter II.
Fundamental Formulations among the Replies.

13. Definition of A-, B-, and Other Fundamental Formulations	39
14. Reproduction of a Part of the ABfrl	42
15. Age and Sex of the ps	44
16. Social Groups Represented	45
17. Education of the ps	45
18. Duration of Examination	46
19. Ps having Considered the q.c.c. before being Examined	47
20. Number of Formulations in the ABfrl	47
21. Mean Variability of the ABf	48
22. Tendency to Produce Several ABf	49
23. Number of ABf and Duration of Examination	50
24. Spontaneity of the Answers to q.c.c.	54
25. Adequacy of the ABf as Expressions of Opinions	56
26. The D-Formulations	57
27. Questionnaires concerning the Ambiguous Df	58
28. The F-Formulations	59
29. The M-Formulations. Moral Conceptions of Truth	59
30. Statistical Analysis of the Mf	60
31. Moral Views and Age, Education	62
32. Moral Views and Type of Questionnaire	62

Chapter III.
Typology of Fundamental Formulation-Roots.

Sect.		Page
33.	How to Group the ABfr	63
34.	The Gr1	65
35.	The Relative Homogenity and Consistency of the Different Gr1-groups	69
36.	Some of the Gr1-groups Contain a Multiplicity of Formulations	69
37.	The Gr2-principle of Grouping	73
38.	The Gr3-principle of Grouping	75
39.	Tendency of the ps to Adhere to One and Only One Group	76
40.	ABf on Positive and ABf on Negative Values. The Principle of Excluded Middle	78
41.	The Gr4-principle of Grouping	78
42.	The Size of the Gr4-groups. Distribution of Afr and Bfr	79
43.	The Gr5-principle of Grouping	80
44.	Relative Size of the Gr5-groups	80
45.	The Gr6-principle of Grouping	81
46.	Size of Gr6-groups	83
47.	Is there Any "Natural Classification" on ABfr?	84
48.	Concluding Remarks on the Size of the Groups	84
49.	Correlations between Age, Education, and Groups of Afr	85
50.	Correlation between Gr1, Gr2, Gr3, and Age, Education	86
51.	Low Age - and Low Education-Groups according to the Grouping Principles Gr1, Gr2, and Gr3	88
52.	High Age and High Education Groups according to Gr1, Gr2, and Gr3	90
53.	Gr4- and Gr5-groupes. Relation to Age, Education	90
54.	Relation between Gr6-groups and Age, Education	90
55.	Variability of ABf and the Factors Age, Education	91
56.	Development of ABfr	92
57.	Crude and Discerning Classifications	93
58.	Concluding Remarks	94

Chapter IV.
The Main Features of Amateur-Theories.

59.	Introduction. Ps who are Not Represented by Any Af.	96
60.	Ps who Deny, Doubt or Ignore the Existence of c. c	97
61.	A Possible Source of Suggestion	100
62.	Ps whose ABf do Not Picture Adequately their Opinions	101
63.	Do the Ps Understand the q. c. c.?	102
64.	The Aim and Scope of a "Qualitative List of Answers to q. c. c." . (ABfl.)	105
65.	Classification of Fundamental Formulations	108
66.	The ABfl	112
67.	The Subject Matter of Fundamental Formulation Roots and their Frequency Distribution	112
68.	Expressions used as Synonyms	114
69.	Frequency of the Different Standpoints towards Absolutes	118
70.	Standpoints towards Different Types of Absolutes	121
71.	Standpoints towards Absolutes. Correlations with Age, Education	121
72.	Standpoints towards Absolutes. Correlation with Sex	124
73.	Standpoint towards Absolutes. Correlation with Gr1-groups	124
74.	The Confidence-Test. Introduction	126
75.	Description of Test	127

Sect.	Page
76. The Q and C as Measures of Confidence-Suggestibility	128
77. Q, C and Standpoints towards Absolutes	128
78. Relation between C and Ga2, 1. Ga2. 2	131
79. Prognostic Value of Characteriological Traits. Can the Contents of Truth-Theories be Forecast?	131
80. Introduction to the Statistical Analysis of the Example of Something True (o.so.s.)	131
81. Instances of Examples	132
82. Classification of Examples	135
83. Frequency of the Different Gel-groups	136
84. Thing-Examples	137
85. Age, Education, and Gel	138
86. Choice of Examples and External Surroundings during the Examination	138
87. Certainty of Mathematical Statements in the Eyes of the ps	139
88. Introduction to the Discussion of the ps Attitude towards the Afr of Others	139
89. The qt DA	140
90. Asserting, Neutral, and Critical Evaluations (ae, ne, and ce)	142
91. Statistical Results of qt DA	143
92. Critics and Type of Afr	144
93. How Certain Distinguished Afr are Looked Upon	144
94. The qt DB	145
95. The qt DC	146
96. The qt DD	147
97. Attitude of the ps towards the Products of Professionals as Reflected by the Relative Frequency of ae, me, and ce	147
98. The ps' Arguments against Professional Af. Examples	149
99. Qt DE	151
100. Are the ps More Critical towards Afr of ps of Low Education than towards Those of ps of High Education	151
101. General Comparison between Attitude towards Professional and Attitude towards Amateur-Af	151
102. Correspondence between Arguments of Amateurs and Arguments of Professionals	153
103. Amount of Labour Necessary to Improve the Reliability of the Statistical Results of This Work	153
104. Problems Solved Wholesale to Avoid a Closer Touch with Facts	156
105. Main Theses Formulated in Programmatical Form	159

Chapter V.
The Theories of Philosophers on the Options of Non-Philosophers.

106. Introduction	163
107. General Views Imputed to the Amateurs	164
108. Alleged Thruth-Theories of the Non-Philosopher	169
109. Alleged Philosophers of the Non-Philosophers	171
110. Truth-Theories as Pseudo-Knowledge	173
111. Pedagogical Remarks	174
112. Philosophy versus Science	176
113. Scientific Problems Associated with the Truth-Problem	177

Abbreviations.

By the aid of simple abbreviations it has been found possible to save considerable space in this work. A great many statements deal, for instance, with definitions of "true, or truth, or the true, or the Truth, or not true, or the truest, or right, or not right, or "true or right", or correct or — — — or "opposite of fact"". Abbreviating 32 expressions of the indicated kind to "true (o. s. n.)" several pages have been saved. I therefore trust that the reader will accept the abbreviations although they are more numerous than is usual in psychological works.

Discussions with friendly critics have convinced me that some short, preliminary explanations of the terms abbreviated are desirable. These explanations cannot serve as definitions — they are only intended to make it easier for the reader to remember the significance of the terms explained at length in various sections of the book.

I

p	test-person.
l	leader of the tests.
q	questions.
a	answer.
a. s. n.	and similar notions (cf. IV.)
a. so. s.	and something similar (cf. IV.)

II

c. c.	Common characteristic.
q. c. c.	(1) Questions concerning the c. c. (or common specific property) of what is true (a. so. s.)
	(2) request to define truth (a. so. s.)

III

Af	A-formulations. Short general statements on truth (a. s. n.) except "fact", having the character of definitions (in the sense of presymbolic logics). "Af" stands both for "A-formulation" and "A-formulations".
AFr	A-formulation-roots. Neglecting the difference in kind of object-matter of the formulations (the differences with bearing on the definiendum) a certain kind of formulation-fraction is obtained, which is very adapted to the purpose of comparison. These fractions are called roots of the formulations.
Bf	B-formulations. Formulations corresponding to the Af, but dealing only with the notion of fact.
Bfr	B-formulation-roots. Roots of the last-mentioned formulations.
ABfrl	List of A- and B-formulation-roots. Partially reproduced in sect. 14.
ABfl	List of A- and B-formulations. Partially reproduced in sect. 66.
Mfs	Ethical or "moral" opinions on the notion of truth a. s. n. Opinions according to which these notions are ethical norms.

Mfrs	M-formulation-roots.
Mfrl	List of M-formulation-roots.
PAf	Af found in philosophic literature, "professional Af".
PBf	Professional Bf.
PAfl	A standard list containing c. 400 PAf.
G	Grouping principle.
Gr	Grouping principle applied to fundamental formulations on truth (a. s. n.) and their "roots".
Grn	The grouping principle No. n applied to fundamental formulation roots. Such grouping principles correspond to the arrangements of truth-theories as found in philosophic literature, for instance, correspondence-theories, coherence-theories etc. (Professional grouping principles proved, however, insufficient and too vague to allow the amateur-answers to be grouped).
Gr1	By means of Gr1 the amateur answers are gathered in small groups generally according to superficial verbal similarity.
Gr3.1	The group No. 1 according to the grouping principle No. 3 applied to fundamental formulations.
Ga	Grouping principle applied to answers to questions about "absolutes" (absolute truth etc.)

IV.

Some complex abbreviations, in which the following simple abbreviations are used:

a	and		n	notion(s)
o	or		+n	notions expressing "positive" values (truth, correctness)
s	similar		÷n	notions expressing "negative" values (wrong, erroneous etc.)
so	something		w	word
e	expression		+e	expressions of positive values
			÷e	expressions of negative values

truth (a. s. n.)	"truth and true and the true and the Truth and — — — and opposite of fact", i. e. the logical addition of all notions listed in the "list of S-expressions" of sect. 65.
truth (o. s. n.)	"truth or true or — — — or opposite of fact", i. e. the logical multiplication of the same notions.
truth (a.s.-⊦n) } falsity (a.s.÷n) }	Cf. the foregoing. As "+n" are reckoned the positive values found in the "list of S-expressions". The "÷n" are the remaining ones.
something true (a. so. s.)	"something true and something not true and something right and — — — and something opposite of fact", i. e. the logical addition of all expressions of the "list of S-expressions" in front of which "something" gives sense.
something true (a. so. +s)	The "+" denotes that only "positive values" of the "list of S-expressions" are considered.
something true (a. so. ÷s)	The "÷" denotes that only "negative values" of the list referred to above are intended.

Introduction.

Sect. 1. The aim of this study cannot be stated in a few words. As students of philosophy we once read with special interest the papers of philosophers on the notion of truth. We thought the subject very important when trying to understand what "science" is as well as when forming an "ideology" on scientific grounds. No "theory of truth" persuaded us. Reading pragmatic authors we found their opinions on the truth notion quite acceptable and their criticism of "intellectualistic theories of truth" splendid. Reading anti-pragmatic authors we found their "theories" quite acceptable and their "down with pragmatism" reasonable. The jargon and ideology of pragmatism appealed to us more than those of the anti-pragmatical authors, consequently we produced some "theories of truth" copying the pragmatic jargon and trying to neutralize the arguments of their criticisms. Unfortunately, we tried to test our own products in concrete cases. They proved wholly worthless. Our ordinary schoolboy "experiments" with chemicals seemed to us to be of higher scientific value. In spite of the defeat and the feeling of having deceived ourselves and having been led astray by the philosophical authors, we made up our mind to try to state the possible sound scientific problems involved in philosophical discussions of the truth notion, and to form an opinion on their (possible) practical solvability. We found it natural to start with the philosophical theories and discussions of "the opinion of the ordinary man (the "non-philosopher") on the notion of truth". In contrast with other questions classed under the heading "the problem of truth", this particular one seems to us to some degree capable of a solution. By this we do not intend that other questions are "deeper", but rather that they are less intelligible, more ambiguous, vague, and badly stated.

It very soon became apparent that the work necessary to fulfil our first intention was overwhelmingly large, if the result were to be at all satisfactory from a scientific point of view. A scientific institution of considerable dimension working by stimulating 5-years' plan would probably do. Without such aid we had to choose between giving up everything or publishing what we knew was incomplete, but still perhaps of interest. We chose the latter and a lengthy monograph has been the result of that choice. Its special subject is that which philosophers consider to be "the opinion of the notion of truth held by persons not being philosophers" or "the common-sense view on the notion of truth". The material collected as relative to this subject throws some light on the evolution of philosophical theories of truth and even on the deeper questions concerning the nature of philosophical ideologies.

Sect. 2. It is impossible to carry out the aim of this study without describing what are called "theories of truth" in philosophical literature. In this connection only very brief indications will be made. To control our statements and to judge the method employed, it must be presumed that the reader is acquainted with literature dealing with the "truth-problem".

"Theories of truth" are more or less systematically arranged statements concerning the word "truth" or the notion of "truth" of the following type: "The relation of truth is a relation between two things, a belief and a corresponding reality", "Truth, means nothing but this, that ideas become true just in so far as they help to get into satisfactory relation to other parts of our experience", "One must distinguish between several types of truths — —", "There are no common characteristics of what is true", "Mathematical truths are absolute, all others are relative". Sometimes notions as "correctness", "sureness", "consistency", are involved, e. g. "The only propositions that are certain are those which cannot be denied without self-contradiction, inasmuch as they are tautologies".

A very frequent opening of the discussion is to put the following questions: "What is the common characteristic of what is true?", "What does "true" mean?" or "How is "truth" to be defined?" But one may induce from the answers offered to these questions, that the philosopher does not comprehend them in the same way. A bewildering multiplicity of possible interpretations are given and their exponents indulge in acute polemics with each other. Some distinguish sharply between a criterion and a definition of truth, or between a sufficient and necessary criterion of truth and the essence of truth, others think that no such difference exists. Some speak about true beliefs, others about true propositions, and others of true things. Some speak about the truth, others about truths and others about true relations, all criticizing each others' standpoints. Some find the word true undefinable, others definable. Some find it contrary to scientific tact to use it, others find it impossible to leave it.

From a statistical point of view it is possible to select some subjects which are more important features of truth-theories than others. An inspection of a great sample of truth-theories (100—200) shows that some subjects are almost never lacking. To each of these subjects much space is generally devoted. The aim of this monograph makes it desirable to attack close attention to the more important features of a truth-theory and to leave out the rest. The following list contains the more important types of statements found in philosophic truth-theories according to our estimate. The point of view selecting just these types has been a statistical one. The papers of ca. 200 philosophers have been inspected.

1. Definition of the term "true", "truth" and (occasionally) similar notions or notions occurring as synonyms for "true" in the definitions. (The aims of definitions are naturally conceived differently, but that does not affect us here.)

2. Definitions of notions conceived as opposites to the notion of "truth" (o. s. n.).

3. Distinctions like that between "formal" and "materiral" truth, comments on mathematical truth, in short, classifications of "truths" and definitions of each type.

4. Examples of something "true" (a. so. s.).

5. Standpoints towards the distinction "true — absolutely true". Possible examples of absolute truth or proofs that there are no absolute truths or that the referred distinction is meaningless. Standpoint towards the existence of degrees of truth.

6. Conception of the process of verification.

7. Standpoint towards the law of excluded middle (formulated in a manner that makes this law relevant to truth-theories).

8. Critical remarks on the truth-theories of other philosopers.

What is the aim of a theory of truth? This question is seldom treated by the exponents of the theories, but if indications are made, they rarely agree. It is therefore impossible to state in a few words what the aims are. One has to guess by a systematical treatment of more or less doubtful symptoms. When a philosopher deals with the aim of a theory of truth at length, usually some critics declare the aim to be another. Some philosophers try to make out the meaning of the word "true", its "dictionary-meaning". Some try to give a formal definition suited to logical purposes. Others try to define the word true as it appears in science. Some try to find out what "truth" has meant to mankind until the present time, the common characteristics of belief held until now, others what it ought to mean from now on. Some seem to make no difference between these purposes, others sharply distinguish between them. The indication that most philosophers try to "define" truth does not say much: all main varieties of doctrines about definitions (cf. for instance the work of Dubislav on types of definitions) are at least tacitly implied in the discussions.

We shall now continue our brief description of the discussion on the notion of truth. The description consists largely of statements which cannot be defended in this monograph exclusively concerning a very special feature of the truth-theories. The statements are, however, easily controllable by statistical analysis of the truth-discussion.

Between the exponents of the different "opinions of truth" great controversies are set afoot. N holds that the standpoint of M is "untenable", "false", "bad", "impossible", "self-contradictory", "in conflict with the timeless laws of reason", "with the Bible", or "with the ideology of the state", "morally pernicious", "logic-shopping" or "typical of Yankees" and so on.[1] Some state that the whole controversy is idle, that the statements occurring there are meaningless, others that it is fundamental. The individual philosophers put forth their theories without much hesitation as "the solution of the problem". Doing this, it is not common to take into account a large sample of theories of others. Only some — *perhaps on the average less than 1%* — are explicity mentioned (generally very insufficiently and with slight tendency to caricature). Some *fancied* theories are labelled with technical names and put forth as theories "well known", "very common among philosophers of our days", "very often held", or as "the distinguished coherence theory", "the pragmatic theory of truth", "the cartesian criteria" etc. To make victory more easy, the real and fancied theories of other philosophers are on the whole unduly simplified. Systematic comparision between the main points of the theory of a particular philosopher and — let us say — 10 descriptions of this theory by others reveal such tendencies in a plain and conspicuous way.

The discussion has already lasted some 2500 years. The number of participants amounts to a thousand, and the number of articles and books devoted to the discussion is much greater. The number of standpoints felt as different or incompatible may be said to be 2, 100 or 1000 according to the criteria adopted. These estimates may be doubted — no one has tried to collect all the material relevant to the discussion. The author of this monograph has not managed to acquaint himself with more than 6 or 7 hundred papers devoted (more or less) to the "Truth-Problem". Small and partial classifications of the standpoints are worked out by philosophers, but they rarely take notice of more than some dozen. The principles of classification are various and unduly determined by the type of truth theory adhered to by the classifying philosopher.

Sect. 3. There are various types of theories which deal with the non-philosopher's opinion on the notion of truth. We find in writings by philosophers and philosophizing scientists statements of the following types: "The opinion of the man in the street on the truth-notion is — —", "To naive people truth means — —", "The usual criterion of error is — —", "Wenn man einen Bauer fragen wollte, warum er glaube, daß — —", "Die sinnliche Wahrheit ist die Wahrheit des Kindes", "Das Volk, als solches, oder der große Haufen, ist an seinen Vorstellungen an die Wahrheit der Sinne gebunden", "Der Character des Volkes und seiner Wahrheit ist

---

[1] *On the whole*, the discussion seems to us to have the character pointed out above. Philosophers writing papers on the notion of truth without criticising their colleagues severely are, for instance, decidedly *in the minority*. There is no cooperation between the workers in this field.

Realismus", "— — the definition of the truth and falsity of beliefs is not quite as simple as common-sense and MacTaggart suppose", "If common-sense had been asked to formulate what is meant by the truth of a belief, this is probably what it would have written — —", "— — Dies liegt in dem blossen Sinn der Worte wahr und falsch.", ""Wahr" (in der üblichen Bedeutung) ist — —", "Die Wahrheit ist, wie es scheint, von allen Menschen als etwas Festes, als etwas Unveränderliches und Ewiges, angesehen." In sect. 106 et seq. statements of this type are carefully discussed.

The common characteristic of the persons referred to in the statements quoted above is a negative: They are *not* philosophers. Their view of the notion of truth is by the philosophers expressed by sentences of the following type: "truth means correspondence with reality", "truth is an attribute of reality", "the truth of the masses is empirical truth". Some philosophical authors state that unreflecting people — i. e. all of us who are not philosophers — have no opinion on the truth-notion, others that we have. Some state that throughout all time, mankind has understood this or that by the word "truth", others that it has not.

How do the philosophers *know* these things? What is the source of their knowledge? What have they done to arrive at it? Much work with this treatise would have been saved (and — it may be added — many of our theses would in this circumstance turn out to be untenable) if the philosophers had indicated how they investigated the opinions of the non-philosopher ("the amateur") and how they arrived at the conclusion that there is a thorough-going difference between opinions (explicitly or implicitly) of philosophers and non-philosophers. But the fact remains: their writings contain almost nothing of this matter. Perhaps some of them have asked their wives or assistants for their opinions on the truth-notion, but there is very little to prove that they actually employed such a method. If they have worked out a method to determine the truth-theory of a man inspecting his general behaviour, why do they not mention this method? Considering the difficulties of our contemporary science of character to obtain highly prosaic correlations between opinions and general behaviour, the elegant and profound results of cs-theorists would, if empirically founded, mark out scientific victories of immense importance. Sometimes, however, the philosopher himself betrays that he thinks a contemplative and deductive method is adapted to the case: "If common-sense had been asked — — — this is probably what it *would have* written — —". Such things as truth-theories may be inferred by mere supposition!

Even very superficial questioning of non-philosophers would make it almost impossible for anyone to believe that the philosophers writing about the opinions of ordinary people actually ask others than themselves.[1] This being the case, one is forced to ask: (1) Have the philosophers any interest

---

[1] Cf. our argumentation in sect. 106 et seq.

in writing on a subject capable of empirical treatment[1] without knowing anything about it? What could the possible interest be? What is their intention when writing about it? (2) Why do the philosophers sometimes prefer to contradict each others' statements on the common-sense-notion of truth, sometimes prefer to agree with each other, when they probably all have the same material to build their opinions on, that is, when they all lack such a material?" These are difficult questions belonging to the psychology of philosophical culture. They will be but inadequately dealt with in the last chapter. Originally we intended to discuss general, "deep" problems of the *dynamics of philosophical culture* in the light of the material described in this monograph. It is our opinion, however, that such problems cannot be dealt with seriously without having collected a much more complete material than is described here. There is a sufficient number of superficial and sweeping psychological (and other) theories about philosophical thought and we do not wish to be responsible for any new one.

Sect. 4. Without having any clear idea of what the philosophers aim at when they construct theories of truth and polemize against each other, it is very difficult to take a view of what they call the non-philosophers' opinion on the truth-notion. How is it possible to try to find something without the slightest knowledge of how it looks? The statement "A (a person) means that — —" or "The opinion of A on the subject S is — —" refers generally to the explicitly (verbally) held meanings and opinions of A. This implies that it should be possible to indicate *a saying* of A which supports the statements or leads A to utter the opinion or meaning at issue. More seldom, one speaks of A meaning something or holding a certain opinion regardless of his own sayings. A may be said "implicitly" to favour this or that assumption, to believe in goblinry, sea-serpents, the law of causality or something else. It is in this case irrelevant whether A himself thinks he holds the opinion imputed to him. If a philosopher states "the non-

---

[1] In this connection we mean by "empirical" nothing more than "serious". Also in many other connections this substitution holds. We never by empirical mean anything connected with what is *defined* as "empiricism" by *philosophers*. — By "philosophy" we primarily mean "philosophy of the schools", "philosophic thought" as far as distinguishable from "scientific thought". We do not by "philosophic question" mean "all questions which cannot be adequately dealt with by any special science" because it is our opinion that the habits of thought and non-verbalized behaviour cultivated by scientific tradition ought to penetrate those who work with these questions. Stressing this method we emphasize the *unity of method* demanded of any earnest work whatsoever. There is no antagonism between faithfulness to scientific habits and the production of sweeping statements formed as solutions of the deepest problems one can imagine. But there is an antagonism between clear perception of inadequacy of the statements and the claim that they express any sort of knowledge, between the production of them as doctrines and as mere phantasies or pointed programmatical theses, between their pursuit as a profession and their pursuit as a recreation. As long as a spade is called a spade there is no antagonism.

philosopher means — — — by "truth"" it should accordingly be reasonable to expect that he (1) either means that non-philosophers have a certain *explicit* opinion or (2) that they have a certain *implicit* opinion. In some cases it is plain that the philosopher at issue means that there exist explicit opinions (for instance when he says: "If common-sense had been asked, *this* [reference to a fundamental formulation] is probably what it would have answered". In other cases it is probable that he does not take the existence of explicit opinions into account. One philosopher thinks, for instance, that the criterion used by the non-philosopher is "objective evidence". On account of the relative rareness of the *word* "objective" in such expressions, it should be improbable to hear a non-philosopher state: "I use the criterion objective evidence", or something closely similar.

It is hopeless to decide what just philosophers mean when they impute this or that opinion to the non-philosophers. Probably they do not all mean the same or perhaps they do not mean anything. *If* they generally (if more than, say, 50%) mean that non-philosophers implicitly and by their general, non-verbalized behaviour, presume a certain theory of truth, it is remarkable that they evade mentioning any procedure by which the alleged property of this non-verbalized behaviour can be established. It would, further, be remarkable that they directly compare definitions of truth held explicitly by colleagues or themselves with definitions imputed to the non-philosophers. They avoid mentioning the possible difference between explicitly and implicitly held opinions of philosophers. It seems to be taken for granted that there is harmony between the philosopher's explicitly held criteria of truth and his general behaviour, whereas non-philosophers — being less educated, less capable of abstract thinking or lacking the sufficient amount of scientific knowledge — cannot be admitted to be able to state any criteria with harmonious relations to their general behaviour. According to this view, a great difference should, for instance, be made between the two cases: (1) a sociologically "accepted" (successful) "philosopher" states "truth means agreement with reality" and (2) a non-philosopher, an "average" school-girl of 16 years or a householder states "truth means agreement with reality" — both being requested to state how they define "truth". In the first case, the statement should be a deep and genuine conception, perhaps arrived at by logical deductions and careful inferences from experience after years of genial meditation and dispassionate inquiry. That the schoolgirl definition is wordly identical with that of the philosopher, might be but an instance of the mockery of nature. In no case may it be taken in earnest — if it is to be decided what criterion of truth is used by the non-philosopher, a philosopher must be required: a man with accepted capability to solve, or at least to discuss, problems of the kind at issue.

How philosophers can decide that the person A (a philosopher) implicitly uses the general criterion c_1 and not c_2 and that B (a non-philosopher) implicitly uses c_2 and not c_1 we do not know. We have in vain tried to work out how sweeping theories of the philosophers about the non-philosophers' opinion on "truth" could possibly be controlled, assuming that the general non-verbalized and verbalized behaviour could be taken into account. We have in vain tried ro "reduce" — to use a concept of Carnap — the sentences of the philosophers to sentences about possible *observations* made or planned. The more we reflect on the theories, the more meaningless, ambiguous and superficial they seem to us. After some observations on discussions carried out by non-philosophers about truth, we decided to give up trying to control the theories conceived as theories about *implicitly* held opinions. We confined ourselves to thinking of possible means to control the theories conceived as theories on *explicitly* held opinions. As already pointed out, some theories are very probably meant as theories of the latter kind. To this come theories which can more likely be conceived as theories of the latter kind than of the former and theories which can be conceived as being both of the former and latter kind. Our question can accordingly be stated thus: *How may the theories of the philosophers on explicitly held opinions of the non-philosophers be controlled?* I have never heard a non-philosopher state something similar to a "definition of truth" without being urged. It is therefore necessary to collect material bearing on this subject by *constructing situations*, to which it is probable that persons react with statements analogous with "opinions on the truth-notion". Of such reactions, certain types are more valuable to purposes of comparison than others. The statement "man will never find the truth" is especially valuable if the person has also given a "definition" of truth. If he has not, we do not know, for instance, whether he by "truth" means "statements firmly believed by all persons", "agreement with reality" or "reality" or anything else. Utterances as "true means agreement with reality", "the common characteristic of what is true is that it serves life" etc., are therefore more valuable. These utterances are also more comparable than others about "truth". We shall call them *fundamental formulations*, and shall distinguish between several types of them. An analysis of these types is found in sect. 13. We may then say that our special aim in this monograph is to lead persons to react in a certain way and to find out in what situations and to what sort of stimulations these reactions — the fundamental formulations — are most likely to occur and to compare them with the fundamental formulations of philosophers.

Sect. 5. As our aim is to detect verbal reactions[1] of a special type, the problem arises, in what types of possible behaviour units ("Verhaltungs-

---

[1] An exact description of the use of the terms "verbal reaction" and "verbalized unity of behaviour" as termini technici cannot be given here. If a man in a burning house cries "fire" through the window the verbal reaction ("f — i — r — e") may be regarded in most cases as a constitutional element of a verbalized unity of behaviour (an act, a

weisen", "objectivpsychologische Urteile" according to the terminology in our work „Erkenntnis und wissenschaftliches Verhalten") we will find them hidden. Till now I have never witnessed that a definition of truth has been brought forward by a non-philosopher without direct or indirect verbal stimulation from another person. This being so, we have to give up constructing situations ("mazes") in which the ps are led to react with a fundamental formulation to the non-verbalized factors of the situation. The appearance of fundamental formulations seems to be very improbable without certain verbalized stimuli. The probability of a non-philosopher reacting with a fundamental formulation after an interval of hours is in every case so small that in would be practically impossible to collect any material relevant to the subject "the non-philosophers opinion of the truth-notion" on this ground. We are therefore forced to use some types of questionnaire-method trying to stimulate the ps by verbal utterances, for instance, by "questions about the notion of truth". Actually, our questionnaire method has, when the oral method is employed, the characteristic of *personal interviews, assisted by a standard list of questions.*

Experiments show that the p thus stimulated, probably answers with a fundamental formulation, and that his reactions generally have no specific non-verbal traits. He may run away, laugh, fall into stupor, look down on the floor, but these reactions also occur in situations when questions of the notion of truth are lacking as stimuli. If it is thus found that fundamental formulations do not occur embedded in any other units of behaviour than verbalized. They are, on the other hand, relevant factors of verbalized units of behaviour. These units will therefore form our first and most important subject in the following chapter.

Our first method was to put some direct questions like the following: "What is the common characteristic of what is true?" and then to examine carefully in which possible units of verbalized-behaviour the ps' answers occurred. This was done by letting the ps talk without trying to lead the conversation by further questions. They were allowed to associate freely. The subjects thus touched upon by the ps were adopted as subjects for further questions. All "Einfälle" of the ps were written down to get a picture of the verbalized behaviour-units thus connected with the reactions to the introductory question of the l and the eventual fundamental formulations produced by the p. Having used this method with about 50 ps we definitively gave it up, adopting a more rigid questionnaire-method. The main reason for the change of method was to get valuable statistical material bearing upon the differences of the fundamental formulations (and

---

habit, "spezifische Verhaltungsweise"). A man saying "fire, fire .." in state of ecolaly reacts verbally, but his reaction is no constituent element of a verbalized unit of behaviour. Only systematic observation justifies the inference that an observed verbal reaction is a constituent element of a behaviour-unit.

other formulations in reference to the notion of truth). The value of a statistical material is proportional to the stability of the conditions in which the different formulations occur. Accordingly, I tried to standardize the situations. This was done by standardizing the questions leaving less room for undirected explorations. During the collection and interpretation of the material, supplementary schedules were constantly worked out to meet the need for information not previously desired or obtained. To avoid suggestion due to preconceived opinions on the truth-discussion, we deferred the task of systematic interviews to a person without any knowledge about the questions involved. This person possessed written copies of the questionnaires and a list of instructions of the following type: "If a p is silent, do not give up questioning before 10 minutes have elapsed", "If a p defines truth by the word 'proof', ask him what he means by proof" etc. All questions and comments of the l were written down in the protocols. The influence of suggestion is therefore open to control.

All our conclusions are based on the method of sampling: in the field subjected to investigation no other method is possible. It is impossible to ask *all* people about "truth", impossible to inspect all produced truth-theories. *None of our conclusions we therefore think is in anyway secure* — we forecast that a considerable percentage of our statistically obtained correlations (say, 15 % of them) will prove deceptive if the number of ps is enlarged from 250 to 1000 or 5000. We further forecast that a certain percentage of those of our statements which are not introduced in close connection with realizable experimental conditions, must be classed as "meaningless" or "ambiguous to an extent which makes them worthy of rejection". There are people who think that the clear perception of this limited security must imply a very severe judgment of the scientific value of the work. We cannot agree with them: our daily-life-knowledge is a knowledge of correlations of the same type as those stated is this work, and so is much of our psychological and sociological knowledge: the difference is often only one of style: absolutistic formulations are very often predominant in fields where no earnest work is done and where careful statistical formulations are most needed. — If 70 % of sociological predictions based on correlations found in a sample of 100 individuals are confirmed taking into account 1000 individuals, we think the predictions are of a high standard.

On account of the lack of empirical investigations in the fields under discussion, adequate descriptions of procedures and observational data demand considerable space. There are no established (empirical) principles which can be unambiguously used and referred to — without complicated justification. Our inferences from the observational data have not always been as amply discussed and weighted as we would wish. It has often been necessary to abstain from minute descriptions of procedures (for instance, methods of classification) and to substitute brief references for them. In some extreme cases, we have but informed the reader that more adequate descriptions of procedures may be obtained from the author. Extensive parts of the manuscripts were omitted before printing. These parts may be consulted by any one who wishes to obtain a more complete picture of the observational material as well as of the statistical results. To avoid misunderstanding, we would point out that the so-called "programmatical" theses of sect. 105 are not affected by the omissions: they are not "inferences from observations" but from the main methodological standpoints of the author as much as from his empirical findings.

CHAPTER I

The Questionnaires.

Sect. 6. General Classification of Questionnaires. — As "non-philosophers" ("amateurs"), persons of different age, education and sex, functioned — but no person, who had published philosophic writings. In chapter 2 the types of ps are closely discussed. The following sections are devoted to a reproduction of the main questionnaires (qts). To obtain a lucid arrangement of the very numerous qts, we will class them as follows:

(A) and (B). Qts containing direct questions of definition of truth, rightness, correctness and analogous notions.

(C). Qts on knowing and believing in "things that are sure" and "facts".

(D). Qts containing an invitation to criticise the solutions of other testpersons to the questions put forward in the first two classes of qts or the solutions of the "truth-problem" advocated by philosophers.

A class "E" of Qts dealing with "meaning", "verification", "the semantic notion of truth", "antimony of the liar", "law of excluded middle", "unsolvable questions" and other subjects discussed among philosophers and logicians, must be left out of consideration. Lack of space does not permit a thorough-going justification of results as regards these complicated and somewhat special matters.

The qts were (1) either given to the ps together with an introduction how to give a written answer (Writing method) or (2) handed to the ps, so that they could look at them and answer by an oral examination. The ps were allowed to read the protocol of the l. Or (3) the qt was read before the p who answered orally. (Oral method.)

Of the first 75 ps, a great many were examined by the oral method, but the questions did follow preconceived qts. The aim of these examinations was mainly to find out the most effective types of questionnaires. The thoughts of the ps were to a certain degree followed without the l's intervention (Cf. sect. 5). We generally reject the material collected by this method for statistical purposes.

Sect. 7. Qts of Class A. — The prototype of cl. A is qt AA. We have tried to translate the Norwegian text as *correctly* as possible, leaving requirements of *style* wholly out of consideration. The translated text runs as follows:

(1) What is the common characteristic of that which is true? (The term "common characteristic" (c. c.) should be the nearest translation of the Norwegian term "felles kjennemerke". When the ps did not seem to understand (or did not believe they understood) the question, the terms "mark of identification", "common mark of identification", "common property" were successively substituted for the original term, or the question was given in this form "what distinguishes that which is true?" resp. "How do you use the word true?". The expression "that which" was under the same conditions occasionally dropped and "things that are" or "all things that are" was substituted.)

(2) Give me an example of something that is true.

(3) What is the c. c. of that which is wrong? (The same substitutions were used. The nearest verbal translation of the word "galt" occurring in the Norwegian text is "wrong", but "galt" has also the meaning of the English "false". The corresponding Norwegian term "falsk", however, means "insincere" and "deceptive". Generally, it cannot be substituted for "galt" so we therefore translate "galt" by "wrong". The word "falsk" never occurs in the Norwegian text. Misunderstandings are thus excluded.)

(4) Give me an example of something that is wrong.

(5) Is there something absolutely true? — (This is a direct translation of the Norwegian text. In certain cases both the terms "absolute" and "unconditional" were used.)

(6) (If the p examined answers q5 positively): Give me some examples.

(7) If the p answers q5 negatively: (a) l gives some examples of statements commonly believed and asks if they are absolutely true. (b) The following question is put: "Is it absolutely true that there is nothing absolutely true?"

(8) Have you considered the questions of the possible c. c. of true or wrong before you heard them (read them) on this occasion? (It has been explained that the questions may be formulated somewhat differently according to the context). Questions strictly analogous to q8 are all enclosed in the qts of cl. A and B. (They will therefore be left unmentioned below.)

These eight form the constantly recurring stock of questions. They were given to the ps who got qts by the oral method. Generally a great many questions were added to the "obligatory" ones. The contents of the additional qs are determined by the type of answers given to the obligatory questions.

All qts of cl. A (AB, AC, AD, AE, AF, AG) are closely similar to qt AA and cannot be represented in extenso. Differences can be classified as follows:

(1) Instead of q1 in AA "What is the c. c. of that which is true" we get the following: "What is the c. c. of that which is right". (It has to be observed that "right" ("riktig") in Norwegian now and then means the same as correct in "correct statements" etc.), "What is the c. c. of

right statements?" and "What is the c. c. of what you think is true". The q3 and the questions about absolute truth of AA are varied in accordance with the alterations of q1. (AG marks an exception) (2). The order of the qs 1, 2, 3, 4 in AA is changed so that the example-conditions come before the questions of c. c. (the "q. c. c."). (3) Qts AG and AH lack qs about absoluteness. (4) Some qts contain as the first sentence "*Is there any c. c. of — —*". If this q is answered positively, it is asked "*what* is the c. c. of" as in other qts. This difference gives rise to an "index of suggestibility" varying with the type of questionnaire. These differences of qts are all introduced to practise the *differential* method outlined in the next section.

Sect. 8. Qts of Class B. The Differential Method of qts-Construction. — The differences between the qts now to be described are impossible to indicate in a few words; they have consequently to be reproduced in extenso.

qt BA

(1) What is to be understood by the expression "something is true"? Define the expression.

(2) Give some examples of something that is true.

(3) Do you speak about differences in truth, so that you call something unconditional absolutely or quite true and other things only conditional, relatively or partially true? (a) (If the p answers positively:) Define the difference. (b) If the p answers negatively: State the reasons why you do not make any difference.

(4) (If the p has answered q3a positively:) Give some examples of something that you call absolutely true.

(5) How do you in a given case determine, whether a statement is true or erroneous ("feilaktig")? What methods do you employ?

(6) Do these methods always succeed or are there cases in which they do not succeed? (If second alternative:) Which cases?

qt BB

q1: Give some examples of correct statements.

q2: These examples are all different?

q3: (If the p. answers q2 negatively:) What is their c. c.?

q4: (If the p answers positively to q3:) But is there any c. c. of *all* correct statements?

q5: (If the p answers positively to q2:) There are therefore no c. c. of all correct statements?

q6: Are there absolutely correct statements?

q7: (If the p examined answers q5 positively). Give me (some) examples.

q8: If the p examined answers q5 negatively: (a) I gives some examples of statements commonly believed and asks if they are absolutely true. (b) the following question is put: Is it an absolutely true statement to say "There are no *absolutely* statements?"

qt BC

As qt BB if "erroneous" is substituted for "correct".

qt BD

q1: Are there any statements you call or have called "right"?

q2: (If positively answered:) Give some examples.

q3: (If q1 is negatively answered:) We usually discriminate between right and wrong. Why do you not use the discrimination?

q4: Are there any statements you call or have called "erroneous"?

q5: (If p answers q4 positively:) Give some examples.

q6: (If p answers q4 negatively: the same as q3).

q7: (If q2 or q4 have been answered positively:) What is the difference between what you call "right" and what you call "erroneous"?

q8: What is the c.c. of what you call "right" in opposition to "erroneous"?

q9: Is there anything you call absolutely "right"? (If p answers positively) Give some examples.

q10: What do you mean by adding the word "absolute"?

qt BE

q1: (As an introductory question:) What is to be understood by the expression that a statement is right? (Main question:) What characteristics ought the statement to have to be justly called right? (In case of misapprehension:) What ought we to expect from statements that may justly be called right?

q2: Are there actually any statements with characteristics that entitle them to be called right? If so, give some examples.

q3: How in a given case is it decided that a statement ought to be called "right" or ought to be called "erroneous"?

q4: May this be decided with complete certainty, or can one never be sure that statements in a given case show the characteristic that entitle them to be called right?

q5: Do you discriminate between relatively or conditionally right statements and absolutely or unconditionally right statements? (a) (If the question is positively answered:) What is the difference? (b) (If negatively:) Why do you not?

q6: (If q5 is answered positively:) Give some examples of absolutely right statements.

qt BF

q1: Give some examples of statements one calls right.

q2: Give some examples of statements one calls erroneous.

q3. What is the characteristic difference between what one calls a "right statement" and what one calls an "erroneous statement".

q4: What is the common characteristic of what one calls (is called) "right statements"?

q5: Do you discriminate between relatively or conditionally and absolutely or unconditionally right statements? (a) (If the question is positively answered:) What is the difference? (b) (If negatively:) Why do you not?

q6: (If q5 is answered positively:) Give some examples of absolute right statements.

qt BG

This qt is only put to ps who answered either qt BD, BE or BF.

q1: (The qts of the triplet DD, BE, BF, that have not been answered by the ps are placed before them) I have here two groups of questions. They resemble the group you already have made aquaintance with. I want to know if you would have answered the question of these groups in the same direction. (The qs of the two groups are read before the ps and the differences are pointed out. As relevant differences, the following are selected: "statements which *are* right" — "statements which *are called* right" — "statements which *ought to be called right*".

qt BH

q1. One speaks sometimes about the "truth", not only about a true thing or statement. What is meant by the expression "the truth"? What function does this expression have? What is the difference between the meaning of the expression "It is true" and "It is the truth"?

q2. What do you think is the meaning of the expression "I am the Truth and the Life"?

q3. Do you employ the expression "the truth"? (If answered positively:) On which occasions?

q4. Is it possible to find "the truth"?

q5. (If answered positively:) How are we to find "the truth"?

qt BI

q1. What is to be understood by the expression that something is "probable"? What is meant by the expression?

q2. Mention something probable.

q3. How may we show that these things are probable?

q4. Mention something not probable.

q5. What is the opposite of the probable called?

q6. What is the c. c. of the probable in opposition to the not probable?

q7. Is there any difference between what is probable and what is true?

q8. (If q7 is answered positively:) What is the difference?

q9. (If q7 is answered negatively:) How do you explain that it is often discriminated between true and probable?

The further questions vary in accordance with the answers of the ps.

qt BK

q1. Mention some expressions which have the same meaning as the expression "it is true".

q2. Mention some words or expressions which can be used instead of the word "true". (Mention some synonyms for the word "true".)

qt BL

q1. When is the expression "it is right (correct, true)" used about an opinion? What is intended by the expression, when you compare it with another expression:, "It is wrong (erroneous, not correct)".

q2. May what one intends by the expression "It is right (correct, true)" be obtained by other expressions? If so, give examples. (When the p does not find any, or any more examples:)

q3. Let us imagine a statement made by person P. A number of other persons view P's statement as follows. (The l hands the subjoined list to the p.) Does each of these judgments intend something different? Have they different meanings? Where is the (possible) difference? Which of these judgments do you use and on which occasions?

    A: The statement of P is erroneous.
    B: —»—   is untenable.
    C: —»—   is not correct.
    D: —»—   is wrong.
    E: P has a different opinion from mine.
    F: I cannot accept P's opinion.
    G: I call an opinion different from P's right.
    H: P's statement is not true to me.
    I: P's hypothesis is not helpful. I think that most people would prefer to work with other hypotheses as regards this case.
    L: With P's insight into the case, his hypothesis is the best founded. A deeper insight on the other hand shows that a different hypothesis is preferable.
    M: I do not find it possible to support P's opinion. (In case of misunderstanding, the questions are developed further and expressed in several ways.)

The considerable number of closely similar questionnaires made it possible to investigate the working of different factors by a comparison of the answers to groups of closely similar questions. This method (the "differential" method of questionnaire-construction) makes it sufficient to use one and the same questionnaire in a relatively small number of cases.

At this early stage of the description we cannot give any adequate picture of the motives which led us to work out just these qts and to vary them as indicated. Some suggestions: By arranging the first 4 questions so that the q. c. c. appears first, we have a good opportunity to test if the ps have any easily reproducible opinions on the q. c. c. If they have, they tend to answer the q. c. c. *spontaneously*. If they have not, they will, for instance, be bewildered, and no direct answer occur until (say) 5 minutes have elapsed. An initial request for examples favour new building of opinions on q. c. c. not yet entertained. — Asking "what is the c. c. of what is true" the l suggests that there exists a c.c. and that it may be expected that it can be formulated off hand. To investigate the eventual effect of such a suggestion on the part of the l, qts were worked out by which a less marked suggestion or a suggestion in opposite direction should operate. (Cfr. sect. 61). In philosophic discussion the question is ardently discussed if truth (o. so. s.) can be attributed to things or only to statements. It might be expected that answers to questions about true *statements* would favour other types of answers than analogous questions about truths or true *things*. Consequently, some questionnaires are concerned with statements others with things. It would hardly be of considerable interest to trace in detail which motives lead to exactly this or that form of the individual qts. Important it is to note that they were produced as the result of increased experience of the leader. If time were spent to include 250 new ps, we should *continue to remodel the qts*.

Sect. 9. Qts of Class C. — These qts deal mainly with the notions of "knowledge", "certainty", "fact".

qt CA

q1. Mention something you know with certainty.

q2. How do you explain that you know these things with certainty?

q3. What is the c. c. of things one knows with certainty?

q4. What differentiates it from something one only believes?

q5. Does it happen that something you have said to know with certainty afterwards proves to be an error?

q6. May you sometimes be sure that you have not been mistaken? That you would not arrive at another result?

q7. (If q6 is answered positively:) Show how you infer that you will not change your opinion and afterwards say that you erred.

q8. Do you think that we at the present time know more with certainty than in earlier days, e. g. 100 or 1000 years ago?

q9. Do you think that we shall know more and more with certainty or that we shall know less?

q10. Do you think that man at last will be able to solve all questions? Give the reason for your answer.

qt CB

q1. Mention something you know with certainty.

q2. Mention something you do not know with certainty but something you believe.

q3. Explain why you in the first group of examples used the expression "to know with certainty", while you in the last group of examples use the expression "to believe". Where is the difference?

q4—q11. As q3—q10 of qt CA.

qt CC

q1. Mention something you know with certainty.

q2. How do you explain that you know these things with certainty?

q3a. Are there any c. c. of things one knows with certainty?

q3. (If q3a is answered positively.) What is the c. c. of things one knows with certainty?

q4—q10. These questions are identical with q4—q10 of qt CA.

qt CD

q1. Mention something you know with certainty.

q2. Mention something you do not know with certainty but something you believe.

q3. Explain why you in the first group of examples used the expression "to know with certainty", while you in the last group of examples used the expression "to believe". Where is the difference?

q4. Are there any c. c. of things one knows with certainty?

qt CE

q5—q12. As q3—q10 of qt CA.

q1. Give some examples of something you know.

q2. What makes you state that you know these things.

q3. What is understood by the expression "to know something"? What distinguishes what one knows from what one does not know?

q4. May it happen that one is in error when sure of one's knowledge?

q5. Is there any difference between believing that one knows something and knowing that one knows it? Where should the possible difference be?

q6. Is there at the present time anything you believe to know with certainty which you cannot imagine that at some time in the future you will think of as an error?

q7. Possible examples.

q8. What sort of things is it possible to know with the greatest certainty?

qt CF

q1. What is a fact.

q2. Give some examples of facts.

q3. What is the opposite of a fact.

Sect. 10. Qts of Class D. — All qts of class D are of the same type.

qt DA

The l explains that some solutions of some problems will be brought before them and that all their statements of these solutions are of value. A list of formulations called the ABfrl is then given to the ps. This list contains all the answers of the ps. 1—150 on the q. c. c. that show certain characteristics (cf. sect. 13). The contents of the list are partially reproduced in sect. 14, in which the formulations are grouped in a special way. The l explains that the numbered statements are all answers to the question: "What is the c. c. of that which is true?" The ps are then asked to take up their standpoints to as many formulations as possible, the writing method being employed.

qt DB

DB is closely analogous to DA. The only difference is that instead of the l saying that the formulations are answers to the questions "what is the c. c." and "What is true in opposition to — —" the following is said: "These are definitions of what is true, proposed by different persons."

qt DC

The l explains to the ps., as in connection with DA, that various solutions of some problems will be brought before them and that their opinions on these solutions are of value. The ps are then confronted with a list of formulations containing 80 solutions of the questions "what is the c. c. of what is true?" and "Is there any c. c. of what is true?". They are all differently formulated and none are "identical" (cf. sect. 21) with the formulations of the ps or with those of professional philosophers known to me. They are simply written down by the author of this monograph as "Einfälle". The ps were asked to take a view of as many of them as possible.

qt DD

The ps are confronted with a list of formulations — mainly definitions — of the notion of truth. (It will be called "list of professional A-formulations": "PAfl"). The authors of these formulations are professional philosophers, philosophizing scientists and poets.

In addition to the qts reproduced in the foregoing sections, the ps answered a great deal of other questionnaires to be discussed in subsequent papers.

Sect. 11. Some Remarks on the Examination-Technique. — Using the writing method, only the questions of the questionnaires were answered. Using the mixed- and verbal methods, considerable further questions were given. The numbered questions in the qts functioned as starting points of a discussion with the ps. Occasionally the ps did not want to follow the terminology of the qts. The l then changed the formulation of the question according to the taste of the ps. The discussion was always written down in extenso by the l.

The number of ps tested (and only tested) by the writing method is only 30 or 12 % of ps 1—250. It was abandoned for the following reasons:

(1) The ps — especially of the lower-education classes — were not much inclined to sit down and write.

(2) The tendency to "misunderstand" the questions — owing to the very ambiguous character of the terms employed — had worse consequences when the writing method was employed.[1]

(3) The tendency to avoid writing remarks coloured by affections and feelings as regards the questions themselves.

(4) The poorness of material judged worthy of being written down, and more generally, the less amount of material produced per minute. The most sincere ps declared that they would have to spend weeks, months and years to get at a solution of the problems, which could stand their own criticism. Under such conditions it was very difficult to obtain direct answers, and when they answered, they were inclined to conceal their sceptical attitude towards the formulations. By the following "Instruction" we tried to eliminate the bad effects of this attitude:

1. Every thought about these questions that strikes you is of value to us — not only your (eventually) last and definite opinion regarding which solution of the question is correct.

2. If you have answered something you want to correct, or, if during the answering you change your opinion, then point this out and let all that you do not find satisfactory, stay. If you find that several solutions are possible, say so.

3. If you find a question ambiguous, obscure or meaningless, say so, and give the reasons for your opinion. A criticism of the formulation of the question is valuable to us.

4. If you react emotionally to a question, say so. E. g.: a question seems to you overwhelmingly idiotic, sublime, without contents, artificial, central, bloodless, trifling, — — —.

These introductory remarks did not have the desired effect, and this was a further argument for dropping the writing method. Exceptions were only made for special reasons.

In connection with the qts of cl. D a certain *group-technique* was employed. 2, 3, or 5 persons were asked to consider the formulations indicated in sect. 10. They were allowed successively to make their remarks and discuss the divergences.

---

[1] The reason why the questions had to be rather vague and ambiguous is easily seen if it is remembered that their aim is to work as catalysators for production of truth-theories among the ps. If the questions were stated as clearly and exactly as possible, it is an open problem whether the ps would tend to produce truth-theories as answers.

Sect. 12. A Selection of Typical Replies to Questionnaires. — It has not been found possible to reproduce the answers to the questionnaires, and lack of space prevents even the quoting of examples of every important type. As it is realized, however, that the reader must know something of the direct units of our material analysed in the following chapter, a few representative examples of the answers will be given.

Example 1. The following example is an exact reproduction of the l's protocol. The p examined is p 79, a student of medicine, 22 years old. The examination opens with questionnaire AA. The oral method is employed.

P 79 is a typical example of the ps who become confused by the unusual questions. At first, it seemed quite impossible to get any direct answer to the q. c. c. By means of some simple tricks, however, the p was made to answer. After an examination lasting about 20 minutes he began to answer more intelligibly without straying from the point. His A-formulation runs as follows "what I have been convinced of and what I have experienced."

L: What is the c. c. of that which is true? p: — (silence) — l: Have those things anything in common? p: That is not certain. — l: Is it quite incidental, when you in some situations use the word "true"? p: — It is probably founded on something or other — — (some talk) — — l: Think of some situations in which you use the word "true" and think of what is common to these situations. p: — — (thinks) — l: Quite simple things, nothing solemn is meant. p: — — (meditates) — — If one says a truth oneself or a truth is told — —? l: What is common to *all* that is true? p: Is it of importance who tells the truth? l: No. What is the c. c. of *all* that is true? p: — — (silence).

L: Give me an example of something that is true. p: — No, I do not think I understand anything of this — — l: Do you use the word "true" now and then? p: (the p looks rather unhappy) — — Why a thing is true? l: Concrete examples of something or other that is true. p: No. I believe I am a bad subject. l: Have you had your breakfast today? p: Yes. l: It is true? p: Yes. l: Are there some trees out there? p: Yes, that is true. l: Examples of this sort are true? p: Yes, but qualities — — I do not understand anything. I cannot understand what you are aiming at. l: Examples of what is true, as I have explained it. p: Miss Johnsen is engaged — in any case: she has been engaged. — — l: More. p: Is it true that there has been rat-typhoid here? — l: Not in the form of questions. p: It is true that there has been rat-typhoid here.

From now on the p becomes more willing to answer. The reproduced part of the examination lasted about 20 minutes.

Some comments: The l has in this case refrained from varying the formulation of the q. c. c., and repeated each time the expressions of the qt as issue, i. e. q1 and q2 of qt AA. While examining ps of that type, the l made it a rule to ask the subjects what they were thinking of in periods of silence. They were then invited to think aloud. The systematical variation of the formulation of the q. c. c. together with the question "What are you thinking of now?" tended to diminish periods of bewilderment like that of p 79.

Example 2. P 98. Schoolgirl 16 years old. An answer to the qt AE. The examination lasted 10 minutes and is reproduced in extenso. It is a typical "school-children-answer", obtained during a short examination. (10—20 minutes.)

l: Give me an example of something that is true. p: The door is closed, the blackboard is black. That that picture is hanging there. The window is closed. The wall is blue.

l: What is the c. c. of that which is true? p: I do not understand — l: Why do you use the word "true"? p: They are some notions — — It is something we have been taught to believe. l: Do you mean that you are taught to believe that the blackboard is black etc.? p: Yes. l: Is one never taught to believe that something is true which is not? p: No. l: Who decides what we learn? p: When we are growing up we learn from our father and mother. l: We may be quite sure of what we learn? p: Yes.

l: Give me an example of something that is wrong. p: That the blackboard is white.

l: What is the c. c. of that which is wrong? p: That is also something I have been taught to believe. l: Does that apply to what is true and what is false too? p: Yes. l: But are they not very different things? p: The same applies to them. We are taught to believe that the blackboard is black, that is the same as to say that it is not white.

Some comments: The answer to AE 4 seems at first to be nonsensical or away from the point, but it is as clear as any answer to the q might be. Some tacit assumptions are made, that is all. "True" is identified with "something I have been taught to believe is true" and "wrong" is identified with "something I have been taught to believe is wrong". Such formulations are called D-formulations (cf. sect. 13) and are sometimes found among professional philosophers.

Example 3. P 59. Schoolboy, 17 years old. Typical "philosophical" attitude towards the questions. The p tries to suit his formulations to his philosophy of life. They are found "relevant" as expressions of his philosophic ideology. He claims never to have thought of a possible definition of what is true, but he has read Schopenhauer and Epictetus and may therefore be classed as philosophically influenced. The protocol of the l is verbally reproduced. The duration of the oral examination was 15 minutes. Like several ps, p 59 later on gave written answers to the qts. In the written answer he deepened the relation between his answer to the q. c. c. and his philosophy of life. This answer, at first perhaps but an "Einfall", developed into an opinion, coherent and systematical.

l: What is the c. c. of that which is true? p: It serves life. l: What is the opposite of that which is true? p: What does not serve life. Truth is not relative. We ought always to be able to determine what serves life.

l: Give me some examples of what is true. p: Pure love. I doubt egoism — egoism may be truth — as individualism. Pure individualism. Finally everything serves life. l: Is then everything true? p: No. — (hesitates and returns to his starting-point) — What is not true, does not serve life. l: What do you mean by life. p: Display of spiritual and material energy. l: What does truth in science mean? p: True in science: all that can be documented — proof. Spiritual truth is more difficult, nearly impossible to prove. It may be proved by its realization in examples. However, spiritual truth is as true as scientific. — True is what is absolutely true.

l: Truth in physics. p: Also a form of display. It serves life. It is a display of faculties. l: This treatise serves my life. Are its contents true? p: If it serves life directly, it is true. l: The criterion of truth once more. p: To be in agreement with life. l: — (l gives an example, mentioning the distance to the railway station Myra.) — p: It takes about 3 to 6 minutes to Myra — that is an agreement with reality. (Hesitates.) A thing serves life if it is in agreement with the best in life, i. e., if it is true. l: Does that which is true agree with reality: p: Yes. l: Does the opposite hold? p: Yes. Anyhow, if we can speak of a deeper reality. Deep reality, truth and life are on the same level. l: May the physical realities be deep? p: They may be. l: What is superficial reality? p: What one sees. l: What is a deeper reality? p: When one infuses a meaning into what one sees. l: Is deeper reality a product of human mental faculties? p: I do not think that man himself creates the deeper reality. The deeper reality is independent of the views of man.

l: If a statement does not agree with reality, can it serve life? p: Yes — no — — no. Reality is truth and truth serves life. — (hesitates) —.

l: What is a fact? p: That which is in agreement with all kinds of realities. It is nothing positive. Something that stays still. Truth is something in growth. That the picture is standing there — is a fact. l: A stone is lying there — is it true? p: By lying there, it is, anyhow, a positive addition to life.

l: Have you considered the problem of the possible c. c. of what is true? p: No. — l: Is the problem of any importance? p: Terribly interesting.

Example 4. P 70. Schoolboy, 13 years old. QtAB.

l: What is the c. c. of what is right? p: It is reality. — That it is so. That it must be so. l: Examples of something that is true. p: The earth is round. That gravitation turns towards the earth. The door is made of wood. It is painted. l: Are these things certain? p: All that is real.

l: Examples of something that is wrong. p: If one does something that is wrong. The earth is flat, that is a wrong statement. Stones possess life. Books grow. That chair is made of iron. l: Once more: What is the c. c. of what is right? p: It is reality. It is something that must be acknowledged. l: if that which is right is reality, and statements are right, do you then call statements reality or parts of reality? p: No. If that which the statement expresses is reality, then the statement is right.

l: Is there anything absolutely right? p: If one drops a thing, it will fall to the earth. l: Is it possible to make unconditionally sure predictions? p: (withdraws his examples. They seem to him not to be unconditionally sure as expressions of predictions.) — I do not give credit to any prediction.

l: Are there any differences between what is right and what is real? p: True is something that is said, real that the door is white. l: What is a fact? p: What is both real and true. l: An example of what is a fact. p: That Hertzberg is Headmaster here. l: Is it not possible that he has been removed by the School Board to-day? p: It may be a fact that he has been removed. l: But that the door is white, is not that a fact? p: It is dificult to prove that the door is white. l: If a hundred people say that it is white? p: It has not been proved.

l: Have you ever considered problems such as that of the possible c. c. of what is right? p: No. Peculiar problems.

Some comments: The reproduced examination lasted 25 minutes. The p was asked to answer on a q. c. c. 9 months later. He took up his views already quoted.

Example 5. P 9. An "amateur-philosopher" with highly developed philosophic views. Age: 36. Formerly barrister, now a student of literature. The beginning of his *written* answer to some non-standardized qts is reproduced word for word and approximately in extenso.

l: (q131) Do you mean that there exists a c. c. of what you call "true" or "right"? (If you distinguish between the words "true" and "right" then take the difference into account in your answer.) What sort of investigation does this question require? Is it a "linguistic problem" or a "problem of fact" or is it neither this nor that?

p: I think that a c. c. exists: I do not differentiate between true and right. — The problem claims a logical and practical investigation. The question is both linguistic and founded on fact. — When I think of it, it may also be the question of a psychological, perhaps psychoanalytic investigation, if it is conceivable that an emotionally determined "choice" of what is to be looked upon as "true" is at issue. — Now, I am considering the problem of the truth-notion and the contents people give it — but I was perhaps asked to answer the question of c. c. *only*. So I have been talking nonsense, my answer was rash. — — I cannot write all that occurs to my mind in connection with this question. That would take the whole spring. The longer one thinks of these matters, the more doubtful the results. I prefer to consider the problems deeply, but for practical reasons I have to limit myself.

l: (q132). Presupposition: You answer "Yes" to q131. — Describe the c. c. of what you call "true" or "right". Give an example and show that the c. c. holds in connection with the exsample.

p: The c. c. is an agreement between something I have thought (beforehand or afterwards) and the result of observation. I suspect that 1000 pages could be written about this before a real start was made. — Verification = making true. Will, however, a statement be true only when compared with the observation? How can "agreement" between an image of thought and an observation be ascertained? And: other people must observe and hear the statements, and they must be able to speak about it. The test of truth by this means would in any case be exceedingly inaccurate.

Another test of truth comes into question when the statement is founded on memory, then it is not any longer possible to test the observation. — And: How severe must the claims to "congruence" be? It is the question about a cup — and it has lost its handle — does then the cup stand on the table?

As I am going to give an example, another possible source of error occurs to me — both the statement and the observation are to be expressed. (The word "true" is, however, also used when no practical means of observation are at hand, but when one takes into account the possibility of an observer.) The problem — or the sifting of it — seems to lead to the problem of the "Ding an sich". I am unable to create any new philosophy of the notion of truth — for lack of time (even if I had been able to do it as regards my qualifications). — I mean: these qualifications I do not possess. I must not be afraid that Ness will suppose that I am unable to go more deeply into the matter than is evident from what I have written — that I am not clever and skilful enough — that he will be disappointed in the answer.

The biological test is perhaps better than any other; let me take the example first. This is hydrocyanic acid. I drink it and die — the doctor declares: he died of hydrocyanic acid. — But sources of error may be imagined. Then I arrive at the conclusion that the word true is only to be used *practically*; then it indicates an agreement as accurate *as I need it*, not better.

l: (q134. As q131, if you substitute the expression "what *is* "true" or "right"" for the expression "what you *call* "true" or "right"".)
p: Practically no difference, if I have the social ethics: I do not say that anything *is* true without my "meaning", "knowing" etc., that it "is true" — that is, that it can be shown to others, in such a way that they also say, it is true — if they are also moral. — Phew: No, this was perhaps

terribly frivolously said. I now feel that pitfalls are concealed in the question. I suspect that the questioner (though scarcely with a bad intention — we are all human — *he* too) makes fun of those who are going to answer. — A pupil's feelings.

"*Is* true" — that is to say that one imagines something "absolute" — a world beyond our experience with phenomena, facts and laws, that we must acknowledge. It is easy to imagine, and I do it in practice. All things may, however, be resolved into discussions — and the "absolute" will at last become my personal conviction only, *my* faith. — I want this to be right, because otherwise my complete world picture would fall to pieces. I take for granted this or that in the surrounding world so as to be able to act with a chance of success.

Am I satisfied with what I have written here? No — that is to say, partly no — it has been written much too quickly. — However, I should like to be sincere, and not choose what may be said most shortly.

q135. (As q132 if one makes the above-mentioned substitution.)

p: It looks as if the question is answered by the previous one. The criterion is in practice the same. I *call* true what I mean "*is* true", that is, that the congruence I need "is there" — (that I *believe*) and that others are convinced.

l: (q137). Give some examples of something you hold to be perfectly undoubtful or certain. If you do not think anything perfectly undoubtful or certain, then say what you think least doubtful or uncertain.

p: I take it for granted that I have grown up in town. — Nor do I see any possibility of denying that I am married.

l: (q138). a. Do you mean that there exists something that is absolutely or unconditionally true? Give possible examples and c. c. b. Do you mean that there exists something that is absolutely or unconditionally wrong (false)? Give possible examples and c. c.

p: If I with "absolutely" true mean my own conviction, then it is absolutely true that I now sit here struggling. — But beyond human experience I do not reckon on anything being "true", even the statement "it is true" is a human product. — Much more could be said here, and I imagine the whole time that someone is contradicting and undermining my statement to the utmost of his power.

l: (q138b, cf. above) p: Answered by 138a. I am still alive — if anyone asserts the opposite, it is false (not-true in this connection) — because the word "true" to me covers my experience. (All the words in this sentence may be dissolved and turned into nothing.)

Now I have used at least an hour. Phew, there are still many questions left. My temper is getting worse, because I am thinking how everything resolves itself when we look critically at it.

A characteristic of the false: that there is no "agreement" between statement and observation (done or imagined).

l: (q139). Have you, before you read this questionnaire, entertained any opinion of or considered the questions you have answered?

p: Yes, but superficially and in passing, but more deeply at about the age of 15—16 and in connection with the "religious truths" — deeply — in proportion to the qualifications I had at that time — and now.

Lack of space makes it impossible to reproduce further material. What is produced gives a fair picture of the protocols as regards their main features. — We wish to point out the great variability of the ps' attitude towards the questions, the bewildering multiplicity of their answers, and the difficulties connected with the interpretations of the material. It is a delicate task to try to measure the depth of the answers. Some of them appear nonsensical and quite impersonal. They often prove to be very accurate and highly characteristic of the p. On the other hand, apparently clever, comprehensive and elaborate views sometimes upon further examination dissolve themselves into mere collections of words.

P 9 is one of the few ps, who gave a sincere intellectual expression of their emotional reaction to the qts, to the task of the p, and to the man who put the questionnaires to him. Thousands of delicate and obscure differences in this emotional reaction and a host of external circumstances influence the contents of the ps' answers. Such are the conditions under which we are to base our judgment of "the non-philosopher's views on truth". The majority of factors determining the choice of answer escapes the attention of the l. Of the factors that do *not* escape him, only a minority has any direct bearing on our subject. Most of them are too complex, too closely bound up with the total situation in which they operate to be adequately dealt with. In spite of this, we think it is possible to arrive at scientifically tenable statements in our field of research as in any other: the search for correlations by means of simple statistics does not meet obstacles of types other than those familiar to every scientist, nor does the interpretation of the correlations.

CHAPTER II

Fundamental Formulations among the Replies.

Sect. 13. In this chapter we shall deal with the fundamental formulations found mainly as answers — or at least as verbal reactions — following upon q. c. c. To facilitate statistical investigations we shall have to abstract from certain aspects of the formulations which are considered at length in chapter 4. It is especially important for the analysis of fundamental formulations to divide them into various types. In the list of abbreviations the names of these types are reproduced together with rough indications of their special characteristics. We shall in this section define the types more exactly.

(1 a) *A-formulations.* Consider the *"prototype"-formulation "the c. c. of what is absolutely true is* (agreement with the laws of nature)". Varying the expressions in the first part of the formulations one obtains closely related formulations identical or analogous to fundamental statements on the notion of truth as they are found in philosophic discussion. Leaving variations of what stands inside the parentheses out of consideration for a moment, we may define the necessary but insufficient criterion of an A- and B-formulation as follows:

A formulation is an A-formulation (only) if it is divisible in two parts as is the prototype-formulation and if the first part is identical with the first part of the prototype or diverges from it in a certain way: (a) Instead of "What is the c. c. of" as found in the prototype, the expressions found in the "list of expressions of defining" (sect. 65) or any other expression "similar" to these may appear. (b) Instead of the expression "what" of the prototype we may find any of the expressions found in the "list of types" (sect. 65) or no expression. (c) Instead of the expression "is" of the prototype any expression of the "list of tuv-expressions" or expressions similar to these — or no expression may occur. (d) Instead of the expression "absolutely" any expression of the "list of delimiting expressions" (wx-expressions) — or no expression — may occur. (e) Instead of the expression "true" of the prototype any expression of the "list of S-expressions" may be used, excepting the expressions 91—99.

(1 b) *B-formulations.* The necessary but insufficient criterion of a B-formulation may be easily defined comparing it with that of an A-formulation.

If, instead of one of the expressions 11 to 89 of the list of S-expressions, a formulation contains one of the expressions 91—99, it is a B-formulation.

These necessary criteria both refer to expressions contained in the first part of the prototype formulation. The following necessary and sufficient criterion refers to the complete prototype-formulation:

A formulation is

| an A-formulation if | a B-formulation if |
| it fulfils (1 a) | it fulfils (1 b) |

as well as the followings points:

(2) The formulations must not be "tautological". Verbal reactions are not called Af or Bf in spite of fulfilling point (1), if they are of the following type: "The c. c. of what is true is that it is true" "the c. c. of what is right is that it is right", "the c. c. of what is true is that it is right" and "the c. c. of what is right is that it is true".

The common characteristic of the "tautological formulations" of ps 1—250 is that they more or less clearly define "true" or any other positive S-expression numbered 11—35 by — and merely by — another of these notions. (We call "true", "correct", "certain" etc., positive notions as opposites of "false", "wrong", "not true" etc. Cf. the list of abbreviations.)

(3) The formulations must not imply a "dialelle" (according to the meaning of this expression in the manuals of logic): "True is what is proved to be true", "Erroneous is that which is considered by most people to be erroneous", "correct is what certain authorities call correct". To this class of formulation, "D-formulations", also those are counted, that substitute the word "true" for the word "right" or vice versa, and — to avoid certain complications in our "list of fundamental formulation roots" — in definitions of "facts" introduce the word "true" or "right", e. g., "A fact is what is true". (Definitions of "true" or "right" by means of "fact" is not considered a Df.)[1]

(4) The formulations must not be "definitions by opposite" of the following type (G-formulations): "The c. c. of what is true is that it is not wrong", "erroneous is what is not right". We class as G-formulations answers that contain the following opposite notions: (a) true-wrong, (b) right-wrong, (c) true-erroneous, (d) right-erroneous, (e) correct-wrong, (f) correct-erroneous.

Putting aside the first part of fundamental formulations we obtain what we shall call *fundamental formulation roots* (*Ffr*). Thus "agreement with reality" is the root of, for instance, "The c. c. of what is true is agreement with reality". The second part of fundamental formulations of type A is

---

[1] Some types of Df are found in philosophical writings. They are not universally rejected, either among professionals or among amateurs, as definitions or explanations. We exclude them from our list of Af and Bf for practical reasons only: the statistical investigations may be carried out in a more satisfactory way, when Df are kept apart from Af and Bf.

called "A-formulation roots", "Afr", that of the type B "B-formulation roots" (Bfr). A glance at the philosophic discussion on the notion of truth reveals how essential to the argumentation such formulation roots are. The whole discussion concentrates and culminates in acceptance or refutation of such roots occurring in various, heterogeneous fundamental formulations.

This chapter is wholly devoted to *roots* of fundamental formulations. Attempts will be made to interpret these roots in such a way as to make them relevant to the interpretation of whole fundamental formulations and to concrete *answers* or *reactions* which are schematicized as "formulations".

Treating answers to what is "true" and what is "right" (or what is "wrong" and what is "erroneous") as if they referred to the same subject-matter, we neglect many differences of meaning that the ps themselves have postulated. The qts used by the first dozens of ps, were based on the differences between "true" and "right" etc., found in dictionaries. It was soon found, however, that the p did not stick to the dictionaries, and this made the task of the l very difficult. However, the differences of the words "true" and "right" etc., were treated in the qts, the l was constantly interrupted by comments on linguistic problems: "You distinguish between words meaning exactly the same: x and y are synonyms." Trying to do justice to the opinion of the p, the qts were revised and altered in accordance with the ps' wishes. The result was only an interruption from the next ps: "But x and y cannot be identified at all with each other, x means t and y means u. I am unable to answer such ambiguous questions" or "No, you must distinguish between x and y, x means u and y means t." We decided at last to neglect the would-be important differences and identities between the words, leaving the question to be settled by philologists. The qts of cl. 1 were then worked out, in which no standpoint to the possible resemblances and differences in function of the words "true", "right" etc., is presupposed. No unsatisfactory effects were caused by that method.

Sect. 14 consists of a list that contains some of the 300 Afr and Bfr obtained from the 150 ps first examined. The list is called Abfrl below. We have carefully included all types of Af and Bf using the classification principle Gr1 (cf. sect. 34). At the end of the list we have placed some Af and Bf belonging to ps 151—250 which are *distinctly* different from the Af and Bf of ps 1—150 (using the Gr1-classification-principle as a standard). It does not reproduce the formulations exactly as they occurred, but in skeleton form as Afr and Bfr. If the answer reads "the c. c. of what is true is that it corresponds with reality", ABfrl has "that it corresponds with reality". A sentence like "I hold we might say that what is — phew, what is called — true is what is — alas — proved" is reduced to "what is proved". (Differences between "is true" and "is called true" etc. are treated in sect. 67 and onwards.) Some ABfr are linguistically defective, containing various common lapses of talk.

The intention of the p is, however, not more obscure in such cases than in others. For our purpose they are as valuable as stilistically brilliant formulations.

The formulations are arranged in accordance with a special principle of grouping, the Gr1-principle (cf. sect. 34). The aim of our statistical investigations demands several methods of grouping ABfr. One of the more essential and desirable objects — to compare amateur-formulations with professional answers — is effectuated by using the Grl-principle of grouping.

"Formulation root No." (cf. the list) refers to (1) the number of p, placed before the comma and to (2) the number of the formulations obtained from this p, placed behind the comma. If the p has produced only one Afr, no comma is found: "Formulation root No. 116" is *the* only A-formulation root of p 116, "Formulation root No. 129,8" is the 8. A-formulation root of p 129. — B-formulation roots are indicated by a B after the formulation-number.

Sect. 14. List of Some A- and B-formulation Roots Contained in the Replies of the Persons 1—150. (A Part of ABfr1.)

A. Gr1-groups represented by more than one formulation.

Group No.	Formulation root No.	
1	8,1 27,3 40,1	agreement with reality.
1	10	a statement (is true) if its contents agree with reality.
1	27,2	agreement with that particular reality one speaks about.
1	37,2	when I say something and this agrees with what is real (it is true).
1	60,3	agreement with the real things.
1	59 B	agreement with all sorts of reality.
2	2,2	agreement with the facts of the case.
2	24	agreement with facts.
2	40,2	agreement with the facts or the supposed facts.
2	55,2	agreement between statement and facts.
6	101,1	that it really exists.
6	61 B	real things that have happened or happen at the moment.
6	76 B	something that really is.
7	2,1	the fact of the case.
7	43	a fact.
7	71,4	it is a fact.
7	76,1	that it is pure fact.
7	96,3	what one may ascertain is a fact.
7	129,2	ne states lucid facts.
8	40,3	"it rains now" is true if it actually rains now etc. ("p" is true, if p).
8	37,3	"outside is warm" is a true statement, if it is warm outside etc. ("p" is true if p).
8	58,3	it is the case.
8	65	that it actually is so.
8	70,2	it is so.
8	101,2	what is as one says.
8	135	when I hold that it is like that and it appears to be like that.

Group No.	Formulation-root No.	
9	68,3	that it corresponds with what is decided beforehand.
9	108,4	that it is fixed by tradition.
10	49	that they can be proved.
10	81,1	it can be proved by people enjoying full recognition as authorities.
10	81,4	statements that depend on logically unassailable development.
10	84,1; 86,2; 89,1; 96,2; 100	what can be proved.
10	137,3	what I can prove by mathematical principles.
11	21,2	what cannot be attacked at any point.
11	36,1	what cannot be refuted by anyone, at any time.
11	41	that it is not refutable.
11	129,5	that it cannot be contradicted with reason.
11	129,6	that it in the future never will be refutable.
11	129,7	what no human being ever can contradict.
12	12,3	no one will be able to change it.
12	125,3	what cannot be otherwise.
12	126,1	we cannot think that it can be otherwise.
12	1,2 B	when nothing else is possible.
13	9,1	agreement between something I have imagined (beforehand or afterwards) and the result of observation.
13	9,3	agreement between statement and observation.
14	74,5	that it is impossible to err.
15	74,3	that one cannot doubt it.
15	74 B	things I have not yet found any reason to doubt.
15	111 B	what would never occur to me to doubt.
16	71,2	that they are said with a certain strength.
16	86,1	what is short and clear.
16	111	what we react to quite naturally and do not think about.
17	74,6	what I perceive directly by my senses.
17	114	what can be ascertained by one's senses.
18	23,2	what one has seen with one's own eyes.
19	137,1	it appears to us as immediately obvious.
19	137,4	what all people have found immediately obvious.
20	32,1	when it agrees with one's experience.
21	55,3	agreement between the impression of the statement and the impression of the facts.
21	61,1	what agrees with what one feels.
22	53	scientists' statements.
22	81,2	what people with authority say.
23	84,2	what resists a critic who surveys all possibilities.
24	35	what several can control.
24	63	several not having had any connection with each other have arrived at the same result.
24	97,3	agreement with a view that is the result of several people reacting in the same way to a certain situation (to a certain impression).
24	123,1	what the majority says.
25	97,2	agreement with a view that is common to all human individuals.
25	108,3	that all consider that it is so.
26	9,2	my own conviction.
27	94,2; 96,1	that it is my own opinion.
28	144,2	that it is certain.
29	25,1	that one knows it.
30	98	something that we have been taught to believe.
31	149	that the things have been impressed upon me.
32	59,1	it serves life.

Group No.	Formulation-root No:	
32	59,3	correspondence with life.
33	70,3	it must be so.
33	70,4	what must be accepted.
33	132,1 B	a thing that must and ought to be accepted by all.
34	69,1	it is as it ought to be.
34	108,1	I have been taught that it should be so.
35	62,1	it is absolutely trustworthy.
37	93,2	what to all times appears to hold.

Formulation roots each of which can be conceived as belonging to one of the groups Gr1. 1—Gr1. 37, if it is somewhat extended.

38	8,3	something that agrees with reality as I believe I have experienced it.
39	11	facts proved to be good for humanity.
41	32,3	that one accepts the statement.
42	36,2	what at the moment is expedient.
43	45	that it has prevailed as a fact.
44	48,2	one can bring the statement back to an experience.
47	59,2	what serves the display of spiritual and material power.
48	131,1	that the statement exactly answers to the situation.
49	91,1 B	a fact that does not run contrary to other facts.
51	143,1 B	a thing whose cause is determined with certainty.

Elementary (atomic) formulation roots not belonging to Gr1. 1—Gr1. 37.

88	6	the truth consists in concrete historical testimony.
89	71,1	what the instinct tells me.
90	87,1	that the things are logical.
91	87,2	that the things happen according to the laws of nature.
92	94,5	the certainty.
93	97,1	that it agrees with the objective view.
94	132,4	things contrary to some law or other.

Complex (molecular) formulation roots none of whose elements belongs to Gr1. 1—Gr1. 37.

97	21,1	what agrees with my way of thinking and my moral views or things whose validity I have tested by experience.
98	32,4	that one is ready to defend the statement, to direct one's behaviour according to it.

Sect. 15. Age of the ps. — In the following sections we always refer to the first 150 ps if nothing else is explicitly indicated.

The ps may be classed according to age as shown in table 15. 1. Most ps are young, 90% under 30. At first, I did not expect persons under 18—19 years to be able to answer consistently to the occasionally very complex questions of the qts. I soon found, however, that school children as young as 15 were fitted as ps and I consequently included their answers as being of high value to discussions concerning the genesis of philosophical theories in general and the genesis of truth-theories in particular. At a late stage of our inquiry we used 20 ps aged 7 and upwards to 13. These children were not picked out as prodigies.

Table 15,1. Age of ps 1—150.

Age	Cl. of age	Total number
13—15	1	17
16—19	2	56
20—29	3	62
30—	4	15

For statistical purposes the unequal number of ps in each class of age has the drawback that it complicates the *interpretation* of statistical correlations. It should be noted, however, that this complication does not necessarily diminish the worth of the material. One has to be careful, that is all.

Of the 150 ps, 83 or 55%, are males, 67 or 45%, females. The percentage of males and females in each class of age and education is roughly in proportion to the total number of ps in these classes.

Sect. 16. Social Groups Represented. — On the whole, the ps belong to the well-to-do classes, only 6 or 4% belonging to the poorer classes. Among the professions, undergraduates are especially well represented, with 32 or 21%.

Attention may here be drawn to some "selections" made by the ls working out the protocols. It was practically impossible to examine totally uninterested or hostile minded ps for periods as long as those of interested and benevolent ps. The class of "uninterested" and "hostile" is therefore much too small in relation to its absolute size. Far more important than this selection is the lack of material obtained from "silent" ps. Some ps belong to the type answering fluently and persistently whatever question they were asked, other ps belong to the type unwilling to give any definite answer in complete sentences. The majority of the formulations quoted in the ABfrl are products of ps who have a ready tongue. Our statistical material is influenced by these selections, some characteriological types thus being better represented than their absolute number of exponents should permit.

128 or 85,3% of the ps are Norwegian, 13 Austrian, 5 Swedish and 2 German and English. This material was of course found too scanty to allow of conclusions of influence of nationality.

Sect. 17. Education of the ps. — It turns out useful to arrange the ps according to school training and "degree of philosophical virginity". We consequently class non-philosophers as follows: In education cl. 1, all persons without as much as 9 years of ordinary school i. e. ps without having completed the Norwegian "lower grammar school" (middelskolen). In ed. cl. 2, ps with lower grammar school, but without baccalaureates are placed. Ed. cl. 3 contains ps with the Norwegian baccalaureates, which means that they are the best educated people having had no philosophical teaching whatever. Ed. cl. 4 contains persons with the Norwegian common examination in philosophy, psychology and logics (forberedende prøver). These ps have read the short text-books of H. Schjelderup and A. Aall. Ed. cl. 4 includes also ps with Austrian or German baccalaureates. In ed. cl. 5, masters of arts in psychology and philosophy, and students of philosophy with this subject as the main subject are placed. Persons with more philosophical education were excluded and so were persons with a doubtful philosophical amateurship. As the ed. cl. 5 only includes 3 or 2 % ps, we have to deal with non-philosophers of a very pure type.

Table 17,1. Education of the ps Nos. 1—150.

Ed. cl.	Number of ps
1	20
2	72
3	15
4	40
5	3

As the diagram shows, 71 % have had no teaching at all in philosophical matters. Occasionally a p of this group has read Schopenhayer, Nietzsche or some Norwegian philosophical essayist or has looked into a text-book of psychology, but no one was found to have cultivated any interest in subjects close to "theories of truth".

For statistical purposes it is generally convenient to leave the three ps of ed. cl. 5 out of consideration.

Sect. 18. Duration of Examination. — No p was questioned for less than 10 minutes. Other time limits did not exist, some ps were, for instance, examined for more than 10 hours. Table 18,1 shows the distribution of "duration of examination", *when only qts involving q. c. c. are considered*. At a late stage of investigation, the ps 1—150 were partly re-examined or received new qts to answer.

Table 18,1. Duration of examination on q. c. c. Ps 1—150.

Cl. of dur. of ex.	Dur. in minutes	Number of ps	Per cent of 150
1	10—20	43	29
2	20—29	38	25
3	30—49	38	25
4	50—79	24	16
5	80—119	4	3
6	120—	3	2

a = 36 min.

Including all qts and the partial re-examinations, the average duration of examination amounts to c. 1 hour. This quantity refers to the *oral* examination. Including the time spent by the ps writing answers to the qts, $1^1/_2 - 2^1/_2$ hours is a fair estimate of the average time spent by the ps to solve the "problem of truth".

Sect. 19. Persons Having Considered the q. c. c. before Being Examined about Them. — A small group of ps declare that they have "considered the question (or the questions) concerning the c. c. of what is true" (o. s. n.). They are ps who answer question 8 of qt AA or any analogous question positively. The group contains 18 ps or 12 %.

It is found that easy interpretative correlations hold between age, education and "considerateness" in the very special meaning of the term adopted. Ps grow considerate with age and more marked with education.

Table 19. 1. Correlations between age, education and considerateness Ps 1—150.

Relative frequency of considerate ps....	Age cl.	1 0,06	2 0,11	3 0,13	4 0,20	
Relative frequency of considerate ps	Ed. cl.	1 0,05	2 0,08	3 0,00	4 0.22	5 0,67

The cl. 3 of ed. involves only 15, i. e. 21 % and 38 % respectively of the number of ps in the classes 2 and 4 of ed. It is therefore plausible that the irregularity of cl. 3 is due to the small number of ps included in it. This assumption is supported, taking the material of ps 151—250 into account.

The rapid increase of the percentage of considerate ps during the years of puberty and post-puberty is probably not due to selections in the material. It is remarkable that some ps of the cl. 4 and 3 of age, mention explicitly puberty as the time when they thought about the q. c. c. Most of them seem to have done it in connection with problems relating to religious faith.

Ps who apprehend the q. c. c. as questions of the difference between truth and falsehood, or moral and immoral behaviour, and consequently state they have considered the q. c. c., are left out of consideration.

Sect. 20. Number of Formulations in the ABfrl. — The total number of Afr in the ABfrl is 269, the total number of Bfr, 31. This makes 300 ABfr or 2 formulations each. Taking into account the prevailing close resemblance between certain types of these amateur formulations and corresponding professional formulations, it may be said that *the amateurs turn out to be of considerable philosophic fertility*. We arrive also at this conclusion after an inspection of table 23.2 that shows how many minutes of mediation and discussion are necessary for the ps to arrive at the possible solution of the truth-problem.

Sect. 21. Mean Variability of the ABfr. — Not all 300 ABfr of the ABfrl are different. To get an idea of the degree of the variability, we adopt the following criteria for 'identical formulations':
Two formulations are identical
(1) if they contain the same words in the same order. (The Norwegian text is here used).
(2) if they, translated into Norwegian, satisfy the condition (1). This criterion has to be used in connection with foreign ps.
(3) if the one is an abbreviation of the other.
(4) If their differences in contents are due to a different formulation of the q.c.c. posed "they correspond to reality" and "when they correspond to reality", for instance are classified as identical because the diversity is caused by the difference between the following questions: "What is the c. c. of true statements?" and "Under what conditions are statements true?" In several cases, the p did not exactly answer the verbal form of the question. This brings in a variety of irrelevant differences in the answers.
Whenever none of the previous four conditions was satisfied, the formulations are classified as "different from each other".

When interpretating the following statistics on identical formulations, it must be borne in mind that the ABf occurred as answers to different questions. These differences are wholly neglected when fundamental formulation *roots* are concerned (ABfr). In the ABfr they are consequently concealed. If, e. g., the whole answers of two ps are "the c. c. of what is true is correspondence with reality" and "the c. c. of correct statements is correspondence with reality", both answers appear in the ABfrl as "correspondence with reality". The justification of this argument is given in chapter 4, where the individual differences are discussed.

"What can be proved" (belonging to Grl. 10 in the ABfrl) is the most prevalent formulation, forming a subsection with 5 members. Next to this come "It can be proved" from the same group, "that one can see it" of Grl. 18 and "agreement with reality" from group 1 each being stated 3 times. 11 formulations occur twice. Of the 300 formulations, 278 or 93% thus turn out to be different, if the above-stated — somewhat rigid — definition of identity is used.

Of the 36 formulations falling into 15 groups of identicals, only 6 fall into groups (3 pairs) of identical answers to *identical questions*. One may therefore state that only 6 ps (p 17—84—100—133—134) have answered with an ABfr already stated by another p in relation to the same question. p1 and p7 answered the same to q1 of qt AE, p84 and p100 answered the same to q1 of qt AA, p133 answered the same to q2 of qt AF.

If two ps produce verbally the same Afs, this does not guarantee that they will explain them in the same or closely similar way. In the ABfs of a relatively great number of ps, the notion of "proof" occupies a predominant place. Some identicals are conditioned by this circumstance. As in the case of philosophers, one cannot with any reasonable degree of certainty forecast whether ps identify two formulations A and B as regards meaning. Two closely similar formulations from a verbal point of view may be judged diametrically opposite from the point of view of meaning. Apparently conflicting or wholly different formulations may, on the other hand, be conceived as having the same meaning. Such identifications among the ps as well as among the philosophers are carried out implicitly. Suddenly B is substituted for A, then A re-occurs without comments and so on. The inquiry how ps react towards the formulations of their colleagues reveals that much the greater part of the ABfr is conceived as having different meanings (Cf. sect. 88 et seq.).

Sect. 22. Tendency of Some ps to Produce Several ABfr. — 75 or exactly 50 % of the ps have suggested more than one ABfr as an answer to q. c. c. We will call the groups of formulations belonging to the same p, "multiple formulations". Complex formulations of the type "that it is provable or that it has been seen" or "what I have seen and what is proved" are always reckoned as single formulations. Generally, it is not obvious if the p holds that his multiple formulations are logically coherent. Often it is not clear if the p holds that "a or b" is a solution of the problem of issue, or if he holds that "a" or "b" is satisfactory. Similarly, it is difficult to distinguish complex formulations of the type "a" and "b" and single formulations of the type "a and b". Some of the cases of multiple formulation are clearly suggested by the p to mean the same, others seem to betray an attempt to view the problem from several points. On the whole, however, the following three types of multiple formulations are practically indistinguishable:

(1) different formulations intended to mean the same.

(2) different formulations intended to form a complete solution of the problem, when held together.

(3) different formulations intended to represent different independent solutions of the problem.

(4) different formulations, among which at least one is meant to represent a solution of the problem.

In the following sections no attempt is made to discover the intention of the ps in any individual cases.

The tendency to multiple formulation is approximately the same by ps of all classes of age and education. Statistical computation based on the material of ps 1 to 150 (300 ABfr) does not indicate any marked correlation between age, education and tendency to multiple formulation.

There is no evidence of diminished capacity among persons under 15 or with less school training than 9 years to react with a multiplicity of ABfr. (The tendency to multiple formulation is here contrasted with the tendency to single formulation — not with the tendency to react with no ABfr *or* one ABfr.)

Sect 23. **Number of ABf in Relation to the Duration of Examination.** — If we find that the number of ABf increases steadily in correspondence with the increase of examination time, this would indicate that there is no constant relation between the contents of the formulation and the structure of the reaction-system of the test person. It must also be regarded as a symptom of some indefiniteness inherent to the q. c. c. The opposite case, a steady decrease in the number of ABf with increasing examination time, would tend to favour analogous conclusions. It is easy to see that both possibilities, steady increase and steady decrease according to the lenghts of the examination, are of importance to the interpretation of ABf. To get a picture of what the ABf by p 1—150 indicate, we have to seek for several factors now to be discussed.

As the first factor, the relation between the number of ABf and the average time per examination will be investigated. We use the time values referred to in table 23.1. Examination on questions loosely connected with the q. c. c. is included. Below, however, we take only such ps into account as have been examined for less than 1 hour. Ps examined for a longer time, were to a rather large extent asked to answer questions that were only indirectly (or sometimes not at all) connected with the q. c. c.

Table 23, 1. Duration of examination and number of ABf.

Number of ABf	0	1	2	3	4	5	6	7	8
Average time per examination (in minutes)	24,4	21,6	21,9	26,7	29,1	23,3	30,0	35,0	20,0

$a = 25,7.$ $r = 15.$ $\sigma = 4,5.$ $V = 17,5.$

The table indicates that, if ABf occur at all, they occur — regardless of number — as a rule during the first 35 minutes of the examination. Taking the statistical properties of our material into account, we may conclude that table 23. 1 neither supports the view that steady increase nor steady decrease, but a fairly constant relation, holds between examination time and the number of ABf. Ps with several ABf produce more each minute, and the more formulations a p is able to state the quicker he produces them:

Number of ABf	1	2	3	4	5	6	7	8
Production of ABf per min. .	21,6	11	8,9	7,3	4,7	5	5	2,5

If a p had already produced an ABf, the examination-time was not prolonged in order to make the ps produce further ABf. On the other hand, a lack of ABf was in the leader's view judged as a defect and the q. c. c. at issue was more often repeated and restated before *such* ps as were unable to make a statement, than before others. The relatively high average time per examination in connection with "o" ABf is therefore real.

It would have been of use for us now, if the exact time of the occurrence of each ABf had been noted. This, however, required two leaders present at each examination — an arrangement practically impossible for us. But the average number of words employed by the l and the p before a certain ABf appears, may be of the same use. This number can be determined with great precision by means of the protocols. We pick out the p 75—124 as especially fitted for our purpose. Most of them are examined under very much the same external conditions.

In contrast to the method previously adopted in this section, we leave the examination on questions with loose connection with the q. c. c., wholly out of consideration. Words occurring in the discussions of the q. c. c. and these only are counted. Also discussions of examples and of absoluteness of truth are dropped. We will, however, make one exception. Some ps, whose qts opened with q. c. c. were either not willing to or not able to answer with an ABf until examples of something true were stated — either by the l or by the p. The discussions until an ABf was set forth in such cases are included in the statistics.[1]

Table 23.2 shows the average number of words employed in the discussion between the l and the p before the production of the n'th ABf.

Table 23,2. *Average number of words before the occurrence of the n'th ABf.*

Values of n	1	2	3	4	5
Number of words	67,2	138,1	151,1	203,6	203,0
Number of ps included in the statistics	43	24	11	8	3

[1] The initial q. c. c. that opens the discussions is not counted. If a p stated an ABf immediately after this question, the discussion is said to consist of o words.

The individual differences in speed are very marked: 19 ps out of 50 answer immediately with an ABf, p 79 answers after 363, p 96 after 396 and a p after as many as 502 words have been employed in the discussion.

If we take the numbers of ps with 0, 1, 2, 3, 4, and 5 ABf, and relate them to the corresponding average number of words before the occurrence of the n'th ABf, table 23. 3 shows the expectations that n ABf occur after m words have been employed in discussion.

Table 23, 3. Expectation of the occurrence of n ABf before m words have been employed in discussion.

Number n of ABf	$m=1$	$m=10$	$m=100$	$m=200$	$m=300$
0	0,81	0,73	0,46	0,32	0,27
1	0,17	0,20	0,30	0,34	0,36
2	0,02	0,07	0,13	0,21	0,22
3	0,00	0,00	0,04	0,04	0.05
4	0,00	0,00	0,04	0,05	0,06
5	0,00	0,00	0,04	0,04	0,04
Total...	0,19	0,27	0,54	0,68	0,73

The values in table 23. 3 indicate expectations based on material from p 75—124 as follows: The expectation that of 100 test persons each will produce an ABf before m words are spent in discussion is indicated by the number 1, that none of them will do this by 0, that $x (0 < x < 100)$ of them will produce an ABf by 0,x. Partial control by means of material from a greater number of ps supports the tabulated values.

If the curves that may be constructed according to the values in table 23. 3 are plotted, and values beyond $m=300$ extrapolated, we find that the justifiable expectations increase very rapidly when the number of of words increases from 0 to 100. The rate of increase, however, diminishes continuously. ABf are started more and more seldom. The expectations converge (not mathematically, but practically) towards values lying between 0,78 and 0,82. *This means that the value of a continuance of the discussion after 100 words decreases rapidly.* When the amount of words employed in the discussion reaches 300, we cannot expect more than one p out of ten to produce an ABf (his first or his n'th) however much the the discussion may be prolonged. In spite of the somewhat scanty material, some important consequences may be inferred with reasonable safety from these statistical results.

The whole questionnaire method adopted in this book is based thereon that certain opinions, or more generally, certain reactions of a specific type, may be provoked by an examination *within some 20 minutes*. We tentatively experimented with shorter examinations, but finally fixed 10 minutes as the lower limit. 29 % of ps were examined between 10 and 20 minutes, the average duration of the examination was approximately half an hour. We never doubted that an examination of one hour or two hours on the average would give us more valuable material. In spite of this *we claim that the material collected gives an approximately adequate picture of the subject being discussed, that our conclusions to a certain degree are reliable.* We claim, e. g., that the ABf collected within half an hour's questioning are representative of the persons examined. This is, however, only the case if it is to be expected that relatively few ABf occur after an examination of 10 minutes. It might be that the first ABf occurring to the test-persons mind are more representative of the person than the later, but this would be very difficult to prove — unless very abstract and vague psychological maxims were used as arguments. We are therefore forced to control in some way or other our assumption that 10 minutes may do as a lower limit for an examination. A rather indirect but very convincing control may be effectuated by using the statistical results of this section.

It is found that the ps 75—124 who have not been examined more than 10 minutes, i. e., 9 ps on the whole, have been protocolled with 220,4 words on an average. P 101 with 303, has the greatest number of words, the smallest, p 104 with 176. The average number of words employed in discussions of q. c. c. is 152,3, that is, 69,10 % of the entire protocol. P 101 was involved in the greatest discussions with 240 words, p 122 in the shortest, with 85 words. Comparing the average values with the values of table 23. 3, it is clearly perceived that *comparatively few new ABf can be expected after the first 10 minutes of the examination.* When the examination lasted less than 30 minutes, the relative length of the discussions of q. c. c. was approximately the same as when the examination lasted for 10 minutes only. Our conclusion may therefore be repeated in connection with this group of ps. When the examination lasted longer than half an hour, the relative duration of the q. c. c. discussion decreased, but the absolute duration remained sufficiently high to justify our conclusion in these cases too. *Our adopted examination time is sufficiently long to obtain the ABf representative of the p examined, if any ABf may be said to be representative of the p.* (The question as to what may be said to be 'represented' by the ABf, what may be said to connect a certain p, will be dealt with in sect. 62).

In this connection we shall also deal with a second method of justifying our assumption. It is more direct, but less intersubjectively controllable. During the oral examination of about 200 ps, the ls noted down some impressions with direct bearing upon the subject discussed. These impressions may be partially reproduced by reading the protocols.

(1) Restatements of the q. c. c. did not stimulate the production of new ABf if the p had already produced a formulation. The p tended to repeat his ABf or to neglect the repeated requests.

(2) On his own initiative the p almost never gave a restatement of the ABf he had already stated. When the test-person had given the ABf he would comment on it, more or less, pointing out defects, giving examples etc., but, on the whole, he was unwilling to experiment with other ABf.

(3) Repeated requests for explanation and justification of the extension and intention of the stated ABf, tended to embarrars the ps when the successive questions were more than two or three. The p showed a marked tendency either to drop his ABf without trying to find a new formulation or to defend what he had already proposed with embittered or desperate energy. No further ABF were offered such a malicious inquisitor.

(4) An "exploratory-method" by which the test-person was confronted with his own examples and asked if he found them compatible with the proposed c. c. could, not be used indefinitely. When all the p's examples were controlled, nothing more could be done by means of this method. This point was reached relatively soon.

(5) Prolonged general discussion of the q. c. c. — sometimes undertaken after intervals of various length — did not create conditions favourable to the multiplying of ABf. Some ps had already spent more than 5 hours, writing answers to qts of the q. c. c. They grew "professional", and were, already, for this reason, unfit for further examination. As they were not ambitious of stating their "own theories of truth" — they did not aim at any career as philosophers — they tend to get increasingly sceptical as regards whatever ABf stated. These changes of attitude after prolonged consideration, however, do not concern us here: we have asked for the conditions favouring the multiplicity of ABf — irrespective of the possibility that they do not stand their authors' criticism when emphasized intensively. One such condition is prolonged examination, but it is not the only one and cannot be relied upon indefinitely.

Sect. 24. Spontaneity of Formulations. — It is for several reasons important to see how spontaneous the ABf occur as reactions to q. c. c. Especially important is the problem if the ps can be said to 'entertain opinions', explicitly or implicitly, on the q. c. c. This problem brings us to investigate the degree of spontaneity. Great spontaneity speaks in favour of the existence of — if not actual — at least implicit opinions — opinions, that may be inferred from other opinions entertained but never 'actualized' by direct questions.

Some qts open with the c. c. questions of what is true (qt AA) or what is right (qt AB) or of true statements (qt AG). Of the 29 ps answering these q. c. c. 9, or 32 % answer spontaneously with an Af, 12 or 41 % answer with an Af after some discussion (but before the next question of the respective qts is put), 2 or 7 %, do not react with an Af until inquired of as to examples of something that is true (or right or is a true statement). The rest of the ps, 6 or 21 %, belong to the ps who are not represented by any Af.

Some qts open with a question for examples, not for c. c., e. g. AF, AD, AG, EF, and then bring the q. c. c. forward. Of the 25 ps who answered these qts, 13 or 52 % react spontaneously with an Af. The increase of the spontaneous answers Af is very marked and indicates that it 'helps' the p very much to get the question for examples first. (The percentage of spontaneous answers to this question is very great, indicating that the ps are familiar with this type of questions).

Of the 114 ps, who answered the AE, CA, CB, AG, AF, CC, CD, AD, BB, BA, AG, AG, BF or CE 60 or 42 % replied spontaneously to some q. c. c. or other with an Af.

One may say, that the 32 % reacting with an Af spontaneously and to a q. c. c. not given in any connection with questions for examples have a disposition ready-made for entertaining an 'opinion of q. c. c.', or a 'solution of q. c. c.'. We do not think, however, that the spontaneity may be regarded as sufficient criterion. An opinion is a reaction that shows some *steadiness*. The p must show tendencies to react with the same formulations during an interval of time, and be willing to defend them. The Af classed as non-representative in the next section do not satisfy this condition. Corrected, the percentage of spontaneous answers turns out to be 24 %.

About 40 % of the ps who answered qts AA, AB or AC had to struggle with the q some time before giving an Af. Their disposition for opinion of q. c. c. does not seem to be ready-made. They have to make a basis for their opinions. For this purpose they spend from 10 seconds up to several minutes. The fact that as much as 52 % of the ps when first getting the question for examples, react spontaneously to the q. c. c. following it, indicates that manipulations with example-questions tend to create a disposition for entertaining opinions of q. c. c.

The notion of 'opinion' is so vague that we do not consider it worth while to describe any further the reactions of the ps in terms relative to that notion. Vague notions do not, however, exclude the possibility of forming vague statements of some worth. Such a vague statement is the following: Very few non-philosophers have ready-made opinions of q. c. c. when invited to answer our qts. (Cf. sect. 19). Less than the half of our ps form opinions expressed by ABf during the examination. *Prolonged examination tends to strengthen the character of opinions of the ps' answers to q. c. c.* This is of great importance to the understanding of professional truth-theories. If a p does not reject his definition of truth hit upon almost immediately, *he shows a tendency to stick to that definition whatever arguments are put forth against it.* It is "rationalized", incorporated in the more stable opinions of the p and constantly interpreted in a way that makes it compatible with views apparently conflicting with the definition. We infer these tendencies after a partial reproduction of whole truth-discussions involving a great number of debaters each defending his definition, and attacking more or less severally other standpoints. The amount of arguments is continuously increasing and so is the tendency to over-simplify the standpoints of others.[1] The behaviour of the ps tends thus to cover that of the philosophers, and one may with great confidence state that the ps have got *opinions* on the subject.

Sect. 25. ABfr Not Being Representative of the ps, Who Propose Them. — Whenever a p uttered a sentence with some definite characteristics, it is classed as AB-formulation and put into the ABfrl. The problem has until now been: How are we to obtain formulations with close resemblance to certain types of formulations to be found in philosophic papers? This question made it inconvenient and irrelevant to take the standpoint of the ps towards their own ABf into account. Some ps utter their ABf as convictions, others as conjectures. It is now necessary to put the question: How often do the ABf represent opinions held by its author?

We have in the last section discussed the question how many ps may be said to entertain opinions of the q. c. c. at the moment when invited to answer them. In this section we will take into account the standpoint of the ps towards their own ABf and ask of what sort it is. — Some ps comment on their ABfr, saying that they have no settled opinions of a possible c. c., or that they ultimately doubt the existence of any c. c., or that, strictly speaking, nothing is true or wrong. These ps (85, 88, 136, 138) entertain opinions badly represented by their 4 ABfr occurring in the ABfrl.

Some of the ABf that are non-representative of their authors are dropped explicitly as 'bad', or withdrawn to the advantage of some other ABfr. They are 6 in number, or 6,7 % of the ABfr in ABfrl.

Persons with somewhat complicated and differentiated views on the c. c.-subject were not able to condense their opinions into one formulation or one sentence. The ls did not try to move the ps to compress their answers more than it was natural for them. It was clearly seen that some ps did not feel any need of short expressions for their standpoints towards the q. c. c. Consequently, when they gave a formulation of the ABf-type, it was never representative of the p's opinions. It may be valuable as a symptom of the general views, general inclinations and tendencies of the author, but cannot be taken as adequate expressions of opinions. (The following ps belong to this group: Nos. 9, 10, 32, representing 7 ABfr.)

Collecting all the ps who in some way or other entertain opinions badly represented, we find their number to be 11 or 7,3 % of all the ps represented in the ABfrl. The corresponding number of ABfr is 18 or 12 %.

---

[1] Experiments with such discussions are going on. Cf. "Common Sense and Truth", Theoria 1938.

One may ask if the others, *89,8 %* of the *ABfrl-ps*, actually may be said to entertain their *ABf* as opinions. Our answer coincides with that of section 24.

Sect. 26. The D-formulations. — The definition of a "Df" is found in sect. 13. It is of considerable length and we cannot reproduce it here. Instances of Dfr:

Gr1. m No.	Dfr No.	
22	81	what people with authority say is true.
33	96,1	that it fulfils the requirements we ourselves make of that which we think is right.

If a test person according to the protocol has answered a q. c. c. with the words 'what is proved is true' or 'what one can prove is true' he *may* have meant something quite different from what is expressed by the statements 'what is proved, is true' or 'what one can prove, is true'. The former answers are Af, the latter Df. In some cases the difference in the p's intention are clear: If he says that 'what one can prove is wrong' is the c. c. of what is wrong, he almost certainly does not mean to say that 'what one can prove, is wrong'.

To what degree do the ps actually distinguish between Df concerning positive values and corresponding Af? The question is not unimportant when it is realized that one may expect one Df to occur for every third ABf. To solve our problem we had to write some new qts, by which the ps are directly and indirectly invited to take a view of the existence of possible differences between Df and corresponding Af.

On an average, a p produces 0,6 Df. We found that of the 150 ps taken into account in ABfrl, 136 or 91 % were represented by formulations. Under conditions similar to those of our ps, ABf may be expected to occur nearly 3 times as frequently as Df. On an average, a p produces 2 ABf, i. e. approximately 3 times as many ABf as Df. In spite of this, one may say that the Df are very frequent among non-philosophers. — There is an interesting tendency to prefer Df as answers to q. c. c. of what is wrong (a. s.÷n.). 36 % of the Df are definitions of negative values, whereas only 3 % of the Af deal with them.

We have mentioned the Dfs partly because they reveal a great field of possible divergencies of opinions among non-philosophers. An apparently unlimited number of similar fields may be detected and mapped out. Some of these opinions are refound in philosophical literature, for instance, "a Df is no good definition: it involves a circle". It may be due to chance (to an exceedingly complex constellation of approximately equally active conditioning factors) that just these opinions are incorporated in the philosophic culture and that others are left out. But once an opinion is incorporated, it gets a surplus value compared with those which are not. Such considerations may lead to a partial explanation why the diversity, as well as the reasonableness, of opinions found among amateur-philosophers are underestimated. Centuries of tradition elevates the traditional fields of discussion and the published "solutions" to a lofty plane and secures the sociological position of the "philosophers".

This is not here the place to discuss the more general questions and pseudo-questions of the value of philosophic culture. As we, however, fear that the reader might take the above-stated opinion as a symptom of a wholesale rejection of philosophic culture as far as it claims to increase human knowledge, we think it justifiable to try to correct the impression. The discussion on the notion of truth is but one achievement of the philosophers: *if* it be that this discussion exhibits very different traits from those going on within the fields of scientific specialists — and even closely resembles a wholly worthless play with more or less profoundly-sounding nouns, this does not, according to us, annihilate the worth of philosophical discussions. Only if such discussions as those similar to the truth-discussion — and especially those, which centre around "the definition of truth" — are put forward as an argument in favour of the value of philosophic achievement, we protest: this value must be found elsewhere — and can be found elsewhere, according to us. What we aim at in this connection is to support the view that many "problems" which by tradition are localized outside fields demanding earnest research (of the sort demanded, for instance, of a scientist) and are made a privileged playground for those occupying the positions called "philosophic", are reminiscences of types of thinking and feeling fundamentally foreign to the most valuable tendencies of our epoch. Once they are touched upon by inquirers unburdened by respect of ancient modes of thought, they partly evaporate and partly present themselves as misleading expressions of underlying, real, problems.

Sect. 27. Questionnaires Concerning the Ambiguous Df. — A list of ambiguous Df is placed before the p and he is asked to take a view of some of them (3—5). Having done this he gets another list, containing the corresponding Af (derived by converting the Df). Nothing is said about the connection between the formulations of the different lists. As a rule, the p ask at once if he has not got the *same* formulations twice. 'That is what you shall decide' is answered in such cases. — The experiment is varied by giving the converted Dfr first and then the Dfr.

4 out of 12 ps answered that no difference existed between the Dfr and Afr or simply referred in their answers to the formulations they at first had treated. P 132 replied that a formal difference existed, but that, in reality, both types have the same aim. 3 ps made a difference between them and added that the Df were 'better'. P 207 stated that the different types of formulations concerned different subjects but he did not consider

any one 'better'. We might probably have obtained further interesting views by multiplying the number of ps. The only thing of importance to us, however, is to establish that *there are several different opinions of the relation* between ambiguous Dfr and their corresponding Afr, which seem to be about equally frequent among non-philosophers. The dialelle is not universally rejected in everyday language. Here as elsewhere the types of answers of the ps were impossible to forecast. Only profound ignorance of the diversity of opinions among non-philosophers and a strong tendency to take the opinions of professional philosophers more seriously than those of amateurs, can account for the belief that non-"philosophers" use this or that definite linguistic rule.

Sect. 28. The T-formulations. — We call the tautological formulations referred to in sect. 13 "T-formulations". They are relatively rare and insignificant. Some of them are not more than a play on words — and are uttered by the ps in such a way that it is clear that they "do not mean anything with it". Others are stressed as real opinions. The p. wishes to point out, that the only possible way of defining what is true (o. s. n.) is to say that what is true — is true: p 76 "The c. c. is that is is true — but that is no answer", p 77: "The c. c. is that it is wrong, but by saying this we only turn round and round." Some philosophers seem occasionally to adhere to analogous opinions. (Spinoza, B. Russell, Pratt.) We therefore quote some examples of this sort of formulation: (Some T-formulation-roots contained in the replies of p 75—150):

76,1 T, 87T, 130T,	that is true.
88T, 138T	that it is right.
115T	I know it.
122T	they are true.
144T	that it is certain.

One should expect about 7 Tf for every 100 ABf. The tendency to produce Tf is relatively strong among young ps, and very strong among the less-educated — so far as we may judge from the scanty material.

One may say that 4 out of the 5 ps stating their Tf without making any remarks on their possible defects as answers to q. c. c. entertain the Tf as opinions. One non-philosopher out of 19 may be expected to put forward a Tf as his opinion on q. c. c.

Sect. 29. The M-formulations. — Some ps conceived the q. c. c. as questions of morality. Their formulations, the M-formulations, will be treated in this and the following section. The truth-theories of the philosophers are not as a rule stated as concerning moral questions; we therefore cannot discuss them as lengthily as the ABf.

It is necessary to distinguish between several types of moral view on the q. c. c. The boundaries are difficult to trace, and not a few of the ps are grouped in a somewhat arbitrary way. On the whole, however, the groupings are important to understand the reaction of the non-philosophers to the q. c. c. as a whole.

Some ps answer with a formulation analogous to ABf, but are concerned with moral standards. We will call them Mf. They fall into two groups: (1) identifications of what is true (o. s. n.) with what is truthful of identifications of the opposite values with a lie. (2) identifications of what is true (o. s. n.) with some other types of moral relations, occasionally including the truth-lie relation. A list of Mf including some of the Mf produced by p 46—250 is reproduced in the next section. The notions referred to in the individual Mf are indicated in a special column of the Mfr-list. We find that of the notions commonly referred to as 'true' (a. s. n.) 'right' and 'wrong' were particularily apt to be conceived as moral notions.

Some ps answer with statements ('Mg') resembling the Mf in general, but lacking the character of definitions. They are only 6 in number. Examples: "truth' is moral, ethical', 'in 'true' and 'truth' lies a moral judgment, a valuation, that is not imminent in 'right', 'unright".

Other ps reply 'morally' when requested to give examples of something true (o. so. s.) They derive their examples from moral life, as illustrated by the following: 'to be an honest man', 'not to tell a lie', 'not to steal', 'to act on one's conviction'. This does not prevent them from stating an amoral ABf 'that it is so', 'agreement with reality' and so on.

In this connection may also be mentioned some examples that are derived from moral life only in its broadest sense. Perhaps the name 'normative examples' cover the whole range. 'It is right to eat when hungry', 'It is right to operate on a man when ill', 'That I did not close the door', 'A peasant sows when the weather is so and so' are specimens. One might say that what is true (o. so. s.) is here identified with what is expedient, what is well adapted to some purpose. — Finally, the examples of p 88 have to be noted: 'If I meet a man, I may say that he is not right', 'An idiot must be wrong enough'. 'Wrong' is here a synonym for 'insane', 'right' for sane.

All moral or normative views on what is true (a. so. s.), expressed by choice of general formulations or by examples, may be divided in two: those proposed explicitly as moral and whose authors add that other views are possible, and others. In the Mfrl the difference is indicated, d means "differentiating". Instances: See table p. 61.

Sect. 30. Statistics Relating to the MFrl. — On the average one p out of 8 produces a Mf. We found that among the 150 ps taken into account in ABfrl, 127 or 84,7 % were represented in the list. ABf seems to be approximately 16 times as frequent as Mf. These figures do not, however, give any adequate picture of the relative distribution, if it is not remembered that 'ambiguous formulations' — statements that equally well

Mf No.	Subject of qts	d or non-d	
53	right		That conscience does not protest against it.
54	true		That it is not mischievous to the conscience.
55	true		What conscience says.
58	true		The opposite of a lie.
82	wrong	d	That is that an action which is being executed is partly not in agreement with established rules and partly harmful to oneself or society.
83,3	the opposite of true		A lie.
217	truth	d	Truth is a notion man has adopted to get a platform, a fixed point during his whole life — a moral, scientific and religious stand.

could be classed as moral and equally well as amoral — are contained in the ABfl. E. g.: 'it sounds natural as a rule', 'it is said with a certain strength', 'what is short and clear', 'it is as it ought to be', 'that I have been taught that it should be so', it is absolutely trustworthy', 'what agrees with my way of thinking and my moral views or things whose validity I by experience have tested', — all these ABf *may* be classed as exclusively moral. Doing this, we find that ABf occur only 12 times as frequently as as Mf. — The original figures may be further corrected if the examples that, according to the p should illustrate his ABf, are taken into account. The following formulations that until now have been classed as unambiguous ABf are by their authors illustrated with moral and only moral examples: 'it serves life', 'what serves the display of material and spiritual power', 'agreement with life' by p 59, 'what is in accordance with the experiences we at the moment have and what can be controlled and verified' by p 82 and 'that it is my own opinion', 'what can be proved', 'what one may ascertain that is a fact' by p 96. Adding these ABf to our class of moral formulations we find that on the average one p out of 5 produces a formulation of this type. This means that they are about 10 times less frequent than ABf.

It would be misleading to take the moral examples of something that is true (o. so. s.) as symptoms of a moral view of the c. c. of what is true (o. so. s.), if the p propounding the moral examples also puts forward amoral. But he may be said to show a tendency to explain the functions of the word true (a. s. w.) stressing moral situations. We thus obtain the following figures as expressions of the intensity of a moralizing influence: Of the ps 46—250, 47 or 22,7 %, refer to situations in moral life, 87 or 19,0 % of all 157 Abf (of ps 46—250) are produced by ps with moral views of some sort.

Sect. 31. *Moral Views and Age-education.* — Table 31,1 shows the relation between the tendency to produce Mf, Mg or Ms with age and education. Of the ps 46—250 who have been asked q. c. c., 60 ps or 30,3 %, have produced moral views of some sort. Only such ps are studied who do not explicitly propose their moral views as moral or add that other views than the moral are possible.

Table 31,1. Relation between age, education and moral views on q. c. c. or q. s.

Cl. of age	1	2	3	4	Cl. of ed.	1	2	3	4
Number of p with moral views	9	25	18	10		10	28	10	14
Per cent ps with moral views	47	29	24	50		44	29	33	28

The table 31,1 indicates a *big drop in number of moral points of view with increasing education*. On the other hand, the correlation between age and number of moralizing attitudes is less conspicuous. It seems that a relative amoral view is a quality of the ps of age cl. 2 and 3, ps of other classes developing only half as frequently by such views. We wish to point out the uncertain character of these interpretations, the number of ps in age cl. 1 and 4 developing moral views being only 9 and 10.

Sect. 32. Mf and Type of Questionnaires. — It is to be expected that some of the notions "truth" etc. more than others, should call forth ethical formulations. Ps often stated that between two such notions there is a difference of ethical relevancy, but the notion claimed as "ethical" varied with the ps. Some ps find that "true" is intellectual and "right", moral, others vice versa. Comparing the expressions "true", "right", "wrong", "call true", "opposite of true", "true statements", we find that none of them suggests exclusively moral or exclusively intellectual views. Mf are most frequently held in connection with the expression "wrong", but "opposite of true" and "right" are also frequently defined as ethical standards.

CHAPTER III

Typology of Fundamental Formulations.

Sect. 33. How to Group the ABfr. Introductory Remarks. — Any group of phenomena may be grouped according to any principle. If the purpose of classification is exactly known and is a common type in every day life, one may expect that it would be easy to carry out the grouping, and that the results on the whole would be judged satisfactory to different investigators. Wholly different and fundamentally distressing are, on the other hand, the prospects of classification, if purposes are nowhere explicitly mentioned, are vaguely formulated or are of a kind foreign to every-day classifications. Both circumstances are realized as dealing with principles of classification applied to truth-theories. Such principles are developed in the philosophic discussion, but are very hard to apply — especially if consideration is given to views on the truth-notion that do not belong to the more well-known types. In this connection, we shall only take standpoint to the question: "May interesting, statistically supportable results be expected if ABfr are classed in agreement with philosophic classifications?" Without excluding the *possibility* that interesting and controllable results should emerge, we find it highly improbable, and for the following reasons:

(1) traditionally recognized groups of truth-theories are very few in number compared with the *types of ABfr* and are constructed only to fit a number of truth-theories that is very small compared with the *number of ABfr*. Most ABfr may therefore be expected to fall outside all traditional groups of truth-theories or to belong to one of them as much as to any other.

(2) Philosophers who carry out the classification, generally adhere to a certain ABfr or type of ABfr. Other formulations tend to be classified solely according to their divergences from this ABfr or type of ABfr. We do not aim at any classifications favouring a single type of object in this way.

(3) To use the philosophic principles of classification, one has to take standpoint to philosophic questions, because the border-lines between the groups are generally traced by the application of philosophic distinctions such as "realism-idealism, "(epistemological) subject — (epistemological) object" etc. We deem the use of philosophic distinctions unneccessary and cumbersome and it is quite contrary to the methodology of the present treatise.

(4) The definitions of the main traditional groups, "correspondence theory", "coherence theory" etc., vary among the philosophers carrying out classifications.

There are also other reasons to avoid the philosophic principles of classifications, but the four mentioned should suffice to justify an attempt to use new principles.

Much tiresome work is associated with the grouping of several hundred ABfr, however simple the principle may be. To test the fruitfulness of such a principle is even more laborious. We admit that this "fact" was the only reason why we did not carry out any great number of groupings. Our aim has been to adapt our principles of grouping to as many purposes as possible without seriously offending against the logic of clear and consequent grouping.

We have especially had in mind the following purposes in this work:

(1) To find such groups of ABfr that are "intuitively felt as unities". In other words: Reading through the list of ABfr without concentrating attention on any particular feature of the ABfr, those in connection with which we get the "Einfall" that they are similar, should be grouped together. This criterion is in a large number of cases deceptive as repeated reading of the list sometimes leads to other groupings than the first. Very often an ABfr a is found similar to another b, and b similar to c, a is not found similar to c. In all such cases conscious application of some principle of grouping must be carried out to avoid inconsequence. In spite of these defects the classification in accordance with the first "Einfälle" and without conscious use of "principles" cannot be dispensed with. It is probable that the method leads to groups of ABfr closely connected from a superficial and preliminary point of view. As it is perhaps the most common and constant, the value of the grouping may be detected when correlation between type of ABF's and age, education and sex is sought for. Leaving this "preliminary" point of view, the overwhelmingly large number of "aspects" of the ABfr strikes one and makes the choice of grouping principles much more arbitrary and liable to be rejected as "unnatural", "sophisticated" or "irrelevant" by other investigators.

(2) The individual groups ought to be comparable in size, excluding the possibility that extremely numerous and extremely poor groups emerge out of one and the same grouping principle. The standard deviations from an average number of ABfr per group ought not be very great.

(3) Border-lines between each pair of groups should be fixed in such a way that the rules involved neither become too complicated nor too difficult to use. This implies that "tiefsinnige" psychological, as well as logical, distinctions cannot be applied. We have refrained from attempts to look at the ABf as products of asthenics or pycnics or any other characteriological types. Our comments with each grouping of an individual ABfr would probably on an average amount to a page and is thus impracticable,

however interesting such an attempt might be. Similar things may be said about current logical principles of classification. Without innumerable comments and explanations it seems to us improbable that any two investigators would carry out the classification (i. e. would apply the principles) in the same way.

(4) The ABfr ought to be classified according to principles worked out to suit them and not according to professional formulations of the traditional grouping of formulutions worked out by philosophers. No fruitful comparison between amateurs and professionals seems to be possible without having at first classified amateur-formulations according to principles elaborated to satisfy their own structural peculiarities.

We shall at first introduce a grouping-principle (Gr1) with great applicability. The ABfr quoted in sect. 14 are grouped according to this principle.

Sect. 34. The Gr1. — If the ABfr of p Nos. 1—150 are arranged according to Gr1, they fall into 37 groups with more than one, and 61 groups with one, individual. The ABfr falling outside the groups with more than one individual may be divided into two types, the molecular and the atomic. Molecular formulations are aggregates of the atomic held together by a logical constant, "and", "or" etc., or by a sort of infusion into each other. Example of a formulation of the latter type: "That I am sure that it is the case". Atomic formulations are: "That I am sure" and "that it is the case". Another example: "what is proved to have happened". Atomic are "what is proved" and "what has happened".

No *short* formula is at hand to describe the principles of grouping used to arrange the ABfr into the 98 groups of the ABfrl. This is the case because it was found important to get groups of about equal richness and with easy traceable characteristics. Using short formulated grouping principles, the groups have a tendency to grow very unequal in size or to be felt more or less "unnatural".

In the following description the ABfr are treated *as if* they were parts of the definiens of proposed definitions of (or statements on) "the common characteristic of what is true". As seen from the qts, other expressions were also used. These differences are taken into consideration in sect. 64 et seq.

In the description below, the expression "identification of what is true with what is A" is frequently used. It does not mean an identification in the strict sense of the word. If a p says that A is the c. c. of what is true, he is not compelled to "identify" truths with "something having the quality A". As a matter of fact, he may often be inclined to claim an "identification" in the stricter sense of the word, but he may also reject it. By "identification", therefore, we mean in the following "identification of some sort or other".

The grouping-principle Gr1 as described below is not adapted to classifications of unlimited material. Primarily, it is adapted to the very limited material of p Nos. 1—150, secondarily, to the material of p Nos. 1—300. By suitable and easily performable changes it may be turned into a grouping-principle adapted to unlimited material.

According to Gr1, an ABf belongs to

group 1 (i. e. to Gr1. 1) if what is true is identified with a *relation of agreement* (Übereinstimmung) or accordance between something and a *r-factor*. We call "reality", "real", "the real things" and "things", r-factors. By saying that "something" is identified with "something else" we do not mean that the expressions "something" and "something else" must be found in the ABfr being grouped. Instead of "something", the expression "statements", "contents of statements" etc. may occur. We also include the possibility that the p speaks of an *agreement with* a r-factor and not of an agreement between two items. In this case only one relatum is mentioned.

group 2 if what is true is identified with a *relation of agreement* between something and fact(s), the fact(s) or "actual things". The latter expressions we call f-factors.

group 3 if what is true is identified with a *relation of correspondence* (Zuordnung) between something and a *r-factor*. Formulations showing this characteristic, but containing an expression that diminishes the extent of the r-notions (reality, the real things etc.) are looked upon as a sub-section. "A statement is true if it corresponds to the real things described by the statement", for instance.

group 4 if what is true is identified with a relation of correspondence between something and a f-factor.

group 5 if what is true is identified with something that happened or *happens* — undetermined or at a certain time (in the past, in the future, or just now).

group 6 if what is true is identified with an *e-factor* or a *r-factor*. E-factors are expressed by the words (1) existence, (2) exist, (3) the objective, (4) is. What is true is according to these formulations that exist, what is objective, what really is etc.

group 7 if what is true is identified with a f-factor. "True is what is pure facts, truth means that one states lucid facts", for instance.

group 8 if what is true is identified with what is the case, what is so, what is as one says or with similar factors. Common to these factors may be their aim in conversation: They function in ordinary conversations as special means of affirming what other people state. Sometimes they are clearly expressions uttered in order to save the repetition of what some person has said. This function is indicated in the following examples:

    I. A: Mr. A, you are wanted on the telephone.
        B: (1) Mr. C, you are wanted on the telephone.
           (2) it is so.
           (3) it is the case.
           (4) it is as Mr. A says.

II. A: It is raining.
   B: (1) it is raining.
   (2) it is so.
   (3) it appears to hold.
   (4) it appears to be so.
   (5) yes, Sir.

In connection with these examples, the formulations may be said to state that "it is true" occurs as a sixth alternative of what B may say. Most q. c. c. did not favour answers belonging to group 6. Questions formulated as follows: "How do you use expressions as "it is true", "true" or "it is a truth"? "Describe the function of the expression "it is true" in a conversation. "Why do you use the expression? Can you equally well use some other expression?" probably would favour ABfr of the group at issue. Comparing the ABfr of group 6 with types of philosophers' truth-theories, we note, however, that only a very few of them show any similarity with the formulations of group 6. This is the reason why we have not worked with questions as the above quoted, which would probably only have favoured the production of ABfr analogous to one or a few types of truth-theories. Two answers to the q. c. c., 40,3 and 37,3 do not show similarity with any professional formulation except that of the formal logician *Tarski* in his works devoted to the "truth problem". The answers are not easily reproduced unless formulated as *Tarski* does: "p" is true, if and only if p.

group 9 if what is true is identified with something that is fixed and determined by man himself. This fixation must have been done beforehand.

group 10 if what is true is identified with that which can be proved or which (actually) is proved. In other words, truth and actuality or possibility of proof is identified.

group 11 if what is true is identified with what cannot be challenged, disproved, contradicted, discussed or with what is undisputable.

group 12 if what is true is identified with what is unchangeable or what cannot be otherwise. Central notion: changelessness.

group 13 if what is true is identified with the relation of agreement or correspondence between something and *observation*.

group 14 if what is true is identified with something unmistakeable, with something that cannot be *mistaken*.

group 15 if what is true is identified with that which cannot be *doubted* or with what is not actually doubted by anyone.

group 16 if what is true is identified with something that appears or is stated in a certain way: what sounds natural or probable, what is a matter of course, what is stated with certain strength or in a short and clear way etc.

group 17 if what is true is identified with what is arrived at by using one's *senses*.

group 18 if what is true is identified with something someone *can see* somewhere or with something someone actually *has seen.*

group 19 if what is true is identified with what someone has found *obvious* or *evident.*

group 20 if what is true is identified with what is *experienced* or with what agrees with someone's experience.

group 21 if what is true is identified with what is connected with human *feelings* or *impressions* in a certain way.

group 22 if what is true is identified with what some *authority* or other says. The formulations do not, directly or indirectly, assume beforehand that these authorities are infallible.

group 23 if what is true is identified with what the authorities say is presupposed, directly or indirectly, to be "infallible" or "competent".

group 24 if what is true is identified with what is determined by counting noses in a certain way, with what is said by several or the majority. These persons may be witnesses, "people with connections with each other", "people arriving at the same result", "the majority of sane people", "people reacting in the same way to a certain situation" or only the simple, numerical majority.

group 25 if what is true is identified with that with which all people *agree.*

group 26 if what is true is identified with someone's *conviction.*

group 27 if what is true is identified with someone's *opinions* or with what someone *thinks.*

group 28 if what is true is identified with what is *certain* (or sure).

group 29 if what is true is identified with what someone *knows.*

group 30 if what is true is identified with what someone *believes.*

group 31 if what is true is identified with what someone has *learnt* or what has been impressed upon him.

group 32 if what is true is identified with what in some way or other serves life or corresponds to it, what is good to mankind, what is expedient to man.

group 33 it what is true is identified with something that *must be* thus or thus. E.g. "what is as it must be", "what all expect that must be so".

group 34 if what is true is identified with something that *ought or should* be so, that ought or should have a certain quality. In groups 33 and 34 also complex formulations are arranged. E. g. "I have been taught that it should be so", analysable into the factors "I have been taught it" and "it should be so".

group 35 if what is true is identified with what is trustworthy or with what one may trust.

group 36 if what is true is identified with what is the result or conclusion of some activity, (e. g. of computations).

group 37 if what is true is identified with what *holds* (or appears to hold).

The rest of the 300 ABfr are, according to the Gr1, arranged in groups containing only one formulation each. It was difficult to arrange them in a satisfactory way in the above-described 37 groups or to arrange further groups to which more than one formulation could be referred.

Sect. 35. The Relative Homogeneity and Consistency of the Different Gr1-groups. — The aim of the Gr1-principle of grouping is wholly practical. The arrangement is carried out without philosophical or logical arrière-pensées. Consequently, no stress is laid on forming more homogeneous groups than are implied by practical categories of every-day life. The degree of homogeneity and logical consistency is different in different groups and so is its kind. Some groups contain formulations in which almost the same words occur in the same order, e. g. groups 10 and 21. The formulations of group 10 may be said to show high "verbal coherence", but also, presumably, high "coherence of function". Group 21 may be said to show some verbal coherence, but less coherence of function. Some groups contain formulations with closely analogous function in ordinary conversation, e. g. group 8. Their verbal coherence may be very small. The intention is that conspicuous similarities at the first glance should be common to the groupings of Gr1.

Sect. 36. Gr1-groups Containing a Multiplicity of Formulations. — It is of great importance when testing the philosophers' idea of a specific 'common-sense view' on truth to investigate groups containing the greatest number of formulations. They may be said to have the greatest 'frequency' — the most important factor when trying to decide if a view may be maintained as "the non-philosophers' view" or not. Table 36,1 shows the relative strength of the 15 more assured candidates to the title, when the frequency of occurrence is chosen as the supreme criterion. (Other criteria are taken into account elsewhere). The items of the last column are named 'frequency points' and show the relative strength of the ps' tendency to choose a certain group of Af. When a p produces and maintains only one Af, his choice may be said to be 'whole-hearted' and we give his group elect one point. If he produces n ABf of the same group (and only these), his group gets n points. If the p states r Af from s different groups, his choice may be said to be 'r/s hearted', and we give each group 1/s point for every Af it obtains. The total sum of points which each group obtains is indicated in the column "frequency points". Bf are left out of consideration.

Table 36,1 reveals how contrary to sound principles it would be to choose or crown any special kind of formulation to express "*the* non-philosopher's view of truth" or "*the* non-philosopher's theory of truth" when

Table 36,1. *Relative size of the Gr1-groups.*

(1) Frequency candidate	(2) Gr1-No.	(3) Number of ABfr	(4) Percentage of 300	(5) Frequency points
1	10	33	11,0	15,9
2	5	11	3,7	7,3
3	18	13	4,3	7,0
4	11	20	6,7	6,6
5	1	12	4,0	6,5
6	2	9	3,0	5,5
7	8	9	3,0	4,6
8	24	8	2,7	4,0
9	12	8	2,7	3,6
10	6	9	3,0	3,0
11	26	6	2,0	2,9
12	7	6	2,0	2,7
13	23	6	2,0	2,6
14	16	6	2,0	2,2
15	29	7	2,3	2,1

frequency of occurrence is taken as criterion. No group comprises as much as 15 % of the Af. The 10 greatest groups according to frequency of occurrence contain, on an average, only 3,4 % of the ABf.

Very conclusive arguments against the postulation of "the non-philosopher's view of truth" may be based on the great variety of formulations proposed by one and the same p. The list of formulations reproduced in sect. 39 may convince the reader.

It may here be anticipated that among non-philosophers the non-philosopher's view on truth is most often identified with a special sort of formulation including the words "agreement" and "reality" or "fact". Let us first consider the group with "agreement" and "reality" as central notions. This group consists of 10 or 7 % of the ps, 10 or 3 % of the ABfr. These values — if included among the Gr1-groups — give it the place No. 7 in the "frequency candidate" column, place No. 6 in the "number of ABfr" column and place No. 8 in the "frequency points" column. The group in which "fact" occurs in the place of "reality" consists of 7 ps or 5 %, 7 or 2 % of the ABfr.

It is very difficult to see why one of these groups or both taken together should be called "the common-sense theory" of truth. There is no evidence in support of the hypothesis that anyone has made any attempt to investigate "common sense" in the sense required. Philosophic "truth-theories" seem wholly to be the fruits of "contemplation" and "intuition".

9 groups contain as much as 10 ABf or more, but they contain together not more than 109, i. e. 36,33 % of the total sum of ABf. The expectation that a test person answers a q. c. c. with a formulation of a group containing more than 3 % of all ABf — *if* he answers with an ABf at all — is about $^{1}/_{3}$. The expectation that of the ABfs of a certain test person at least one belongs to a group with more than 3 % of all ABf, is about $^{1}/_{2}$.

By the characterization "a non-philosopher's view of truth" we understand a verbalized view of this notion, i. e. *actually propounded statements* on the notion of truth. When we say that the amateur N entertains the view V on truth, we put forward the hypothesis that N has propounded V or that he is apt to do so if requested to state his opinion on the subject. There are many instances in philosophic literature showing that " a non-philosopher's view of truth" denotes such opinions actually entertained. There is, however, also evidence of other conceptions. Godeckemeyer speaks about the "truth of the the transcendent truth-notion", "der seinen Namen daher hat, daß er die Wahrheit bestimmt als die in der ganzen bisherigen Philosophie der vorherrschende gewesen ist, und daß er auch das ausdrückt, was der *sogenannte philosophisch Ungebildete* wenn auch meistens ohne klares Bewußtsein, unter Wahrheit versteht."[1] From these words it is clear that the behaviour of the "philosophic uneducated" is looked upon as symptomatic of his view of the truth-notion. He may say this or that or exhibit this or that verbal and non-verbal behaviour pattern and is on behalf of the type of his behaviour judged to adhere to a certain notion of truth. As already indicated, clear prescriptions — so far as I know — are totally lacking in philosophic literature as to what should be understood by "a non-philospher's view of the truth-notion" in such cases. There is nothing to indicate by which methods the behaviour should be investigated. Without such indications the results they arrive at are worthless and can only cause futile disputes. The following might be some of the possible methods:

1. The I asks for examples of something true. These examples are compared with those put forward by philosophers. The possible, systematical differences are finally formulated and used to construct a definition as follows: "the non-philosopher's notion of truth can be defined thus: — —". But if the only systematic controllable difference turns out to be, for instance, caused by the length of the examples of the philosophers? Should in this case the definition be formulated thus: "True is that which is expressed on an average by w words"? We have gathered more than 1000 examples from non-philosophers and a great many from philosophic literature, but it is by no means plain how we from this collection should be able to infer any *general* statement resembling definitions. How should we manage to arrive at statements having the character of definitions? We fear that this doubt must arise in whatever manner the interconnection between example-production and view of the truth-notion is conceived. We do not deny the possibility of someone being able — intuitively or by means of statistics — to find very deep-rooted characteristics of what "non-philosophers" declare to be true, but we seriously doubt that the results should be stateable in the form of a definition or in the form of any other expressions similar to what philosophers call "criteria of truth", "meaning of the word 'true'", "nature of truth" etc. Our investigations leave us no hope.

---

[1] Zeitschr. f. Philos. u. philos. Kritik. Bd. 120, p. 186 et seq.

2. The l observes systematically the verbal and non-verbal behaviour of non-philosophers. If this behaviour, on the whole, satisfies the conditions $c_1, c_2 \ldots c_n$, he expresses this by saying that A and not B is the criterion of truth to a non-philosopher. The l then systematically observes philosophers' doings and sayings. If their behaviour on the whole shows the characteristics $C_1, C_2 \ldots C_m$, he expresses this by saying that C and not D is the criterion of truth to a philosopher. The characteristics of A which C lacks, will in this case define the difference at issue.

Such a programme is preposterous at every point. How are we to determine $c_1, c_2 \ldots c_n$ and how are we in practice to judge if they are realized or not? How many trends of behaviour are to be observed? The more we contemplate the implications of such a programme or any similar one, the more incomprehensible the whole "Fragestellung" appears.

If we take the sayings of the philosophers literally, they can very often be interpreted only as propounded results of carrying out a programme similar to that outlined above. It is plain that the relative frequency of types of ABfr does not have any bearing on results (claimed to be) obtained in that way. We therefore do not pretend that our frequency-distributions *directly* invalidate sayings of the philosophers. What we maintain is this: If we were in a position to direct an institute for the observation of non-philosophers and had a dictator's power over the test-persons, we should perhaps arrive at a very general conclusion on what non-philosophers may be said, directly or indirectly, to judge as true. We do not see, however, how we ever could arrive at as general (and sweeping) a conclusion as the philosophers. Consequently, we are cut off from the possibility of either validating or invalidating these conclusions. On the other hand, one may find possible interpretations of the expression "a non-philosopher's view of truth" which lead to readily controllable statements. Such are the statements expressing frequency-distributions of ABfr. If the programmes outlined under 1) and 2) were realizable, the importance of the statements with respect to opinions on "a non-philosopher's view of the truth-notion" would be very small. The utopian if not meaningless character of the programmes, increases the importance of the frequency-distributions. We shall especially mention the following quantities:

Relative frequency of types of ABfr
(1) measured by the total number of ABfr
(2) measured in frequency points.
(3), (4) among ps of education class 1.
(5), (6) among ps of the education classes 1, 2 and 3.

Each of these 6 quantities expresses *something* — but not *all* — we have to say about "a non-philosopher's view on the truth-notion". (1) and (2) are investigated in this and the following sections, (3)—(6) in sections 49—55.

The Gr1-principle is only one possible grouping-principle applicable to ABfr. We will now describe some other principles. Two of them, Gr2 and Gr3, are not independent. They are means of grouping the Gr1-groups.

Sect. 37. The Gr2-principle of Grouping. — The Gr2-groups may be derived from the Gr1-groups by combining some of them as follows:

Gr2. 1 contains Gr1. 1 — Gr1. 2 — Gr1. 3 and Gr1. 4.
Gr2. 2 » Gr1. 6 and Gr1. 7.
Gr2. 3 » Gr1. 16 and Gr1. 19.
Gr2. 4 » Gr1. 15 and Gr1. 30.
Gr2. 5 » Gr1. 17 and Gr1. 18.
Gr2. 6 » Gr1. 20 and Gr1. 21.
Gr2. 7 » Gr1. 22 — Gr1. 23 — Gr1. 24 — Gr1. 25 — Gr1. 26 and Gr1. 27.

The justification of these combinations is clear: By dividing the Gr1-groups in this way, they give us 7 relatively homogeneous and logical consistent groups containing 116 or 38,7 % of the ABf. Table 37,1 shows the relative size of each group.

Table 37,1. Relative size of the Gr2-groups.

(1) Frequency candidate	(2) Gr2-No.	(3) Number of ABfr.	(4) Percentage of 300	(5) Frequency points
1	1	25	8,3	14,0
2	7	29	9,7	11,6
3	5	16	5,3	9,1
4	2	15	5,01	7,5
5	4	12	4,00	5,3
6	3	8	2,7	4,4
7	6	11	3,7	3,0

Comparing the Gr2 groups with the major Gr1 groups (not contained in any Gr2 groups), we find that Gr1. 10 holds its leadership also under the new conditions with 15,9 frequency points against 14,0 of Gr2,1. How is it to be explained that the notion of "proof" only plays a very modest rôle in the professional truth-theories? One of the factors worth considering seems to us to be the tendency of classical logic and of mathematics to have monopolized the notion of proof. The broad, primitive sense of the expression "it is proved" intimately connected with the expression "it is shown (to be so)" is scarcely found in philosophic literature. A truth-theory with some, but rather superficial similarity with those of Gr1. 10 has been put forward by Dürr in Erkenntnis 5, p. 217 et seq. We call the similarity superficial because of the technical sense of "begründen" used by Dürr. More closely related to Gr1. 10 is the definition of Newmann: " . . . the active recognition of propositions as true must be exercised at the bidding of reason, and reason never bids us be certain except on absolute proof". (Grammar of assent, p. 345.) Of 500 professional definitions only this definition of Cardinal Newmann was found to be classifiable under the heading "Gr1. 10".

The explanations of what is to be understood by "proof" and "it is proved" vary to a degree comparable with that of fundamental formulations. Of 36 explanations, 29 may be said to belong to different groups, if they are grouped according to Gr1. Very few — 4 — explain proof as a mathematical or logical notion. P 81 (age class 3, ed class 4) says: "A proof is a perfectly logically unassailable development from a condition to a proposition", p 165 (age class 2, ed. class 3) identifies proof with mathematical proof. There is therefore much in favour of the hypothesis that students of philosophy change their attitude towards the notion of proof in such a manner that it grows less suitable in A-formulations.

Inspecting a list containing 313 definitions of truth, put forward by 164 professionals, we find that 114 can be classed as "complex" and 199 as atomic according to the classification-principle Gr1.[1] The half (97) of the atomic PAfr belongs clearly to Gr1. 1 — Gr1. 37. Of these 97 PAfr, three are identical with amateur-Af. — Example: Professional Afr of Kroman: "agreement with reality", amateur Afr of ps Nos. 8, 27 and 40: "agreement with reality". — Very close resemblance is found between 16 of the 97 PAfr and amateur-Afr. Example: PAfr of Bolzano "propositions which predicates something as it is". Afr of p No. 70: "that it is so". A resemblance close enough to justify the statement "this type of PAf is represented among our ps" can be found in 41 of the 97 cases. Example: PAfr of Feder "Übereinstimmung der Vorstellungen mit dem was an den Dingen wirklich ist". Afr of p No. 60: "agreement with the real things", Afr of p No. 37: "when I say something and this agrees with what is real". — Consequently, we may say that of 97 atomic PAfr, 94 or *95,9 % are refound among the Afr of 250 ps*. The PAfr classed as "unrepresented among amateurs" are: (1) The formula of le Roy according to which truth means "la certitude légitime". (Nearest amateur-Afr: "what one is certain of", "the certainty"), (2) F. C. S. Schiller's identification of truth and "the *best* (i. e. most valuable) alternative its asserter could think of" and (3) his formula "the 'true' way of conceiving an object or judging a situation is simply the way most valuable for our purpose". (Nearest Afr: "what is expedient".)

We shall not tire the reader with further detailed comparison between Gr1-distribution of PAfr and Afr. Among the 102 atomic PAfr not belonging to Gr1. 1 — Gr1. 37 we find 8 which are not represented among our 250 amateurs. As many as 56 are, however, doubtful, due to the occurrence

---

[1] Explicitly "formal" truth-definitions are not included among the 313 PAf.

of technical words or for other reasons. Complex formulations are more difficult to compare. Of 114 complex PAf, only 4 (or 3,5 %) are certainly not represented among our 250 ps, but as many as 35 are doubtful, 31 are clearly and completely represented, 40 but partially represented.

Without detailed description of our principles of comparison, quantitative statements on the relative variability of PAfr and PAf are out of place. The statistical results of detailed comparison (adopting Gr1) indicate that the variability of amateur Afr is as great or (more probable) greater than the variability of professional Afr. Thus, there are more Afr among 400 amateur Afr lacking among 400 professional Afr, than there are professional Afr lacking among the amateur Afr.

Of the first 37 Gr1-groups, 23 are represented among professionals. Gr1. 1 is much the greatest group. Then come Gr1. 8, Gr1. 6 and Gr1. 4. Of the 7 Gr2-groups, 4 are represented among PAf. Group Gr2. 1 is nearly 10 times as frequent as all other groups taken together.

Sect. 38. The Gr3-principle of Grouping. — Gr3. 1: The "thing-group". What is true is identified with[1] something in some sort of agreement with something existent, permanent and on the whole non-human. Examples: "reality", "the objectively real", "what happens", "the objective", "what is so", "what really is so". The thing-group covers the Gr1-groups 1, 2, 3, 4, 5, 6, 7 and 8.

Gr3. 2. The conversational group. What is true is identified with what has some important quality or other in conversation, with capability of being proved, with what is unchallengeable, permanent (as opinion), unquestionable, etc. The Gr3. 2-formulation may be conceived as answers to the questions: "What is a truth as it is uttered in a discussion?", "How to discern a truth in a discussion?". Similarly, the Gr3. 1-formulations seem more likely to be answers to the questions: "What distinguishes true things from imaginary?", "What sort of a being is a truth?". The conversational group covers the Gr1-groups 10, 11, 12 and 14.

Gr3. 3. The thinking group. We collect in this group the formulations that point to a human disposition as the criterion of truth. The dispositions referred to are such that are important when we think, meditate and make up our minds: the states of doubt, conviction, thinking, assurance (feeling of certainty) and belief are identifications of what is true with "own opinions", with "what someone feels to be so", and with "what someone knows" is also included in this group. Comparing the Gr1-groups with the Gr3-groups we find that Gr3. 3 covers the Gr1-groups 15, 19, 21, 26, 27, 28, 29 and 30.

Gr3. 4. The observational group. What is true is identified with that which has certain connections with observation and experience, e. g. what

---

[1] We use in this section the same expressions as in connection with the Gr1-groups. Cf. our remarks on the terminology in sect. 36.

one can see, what one has experienced oneself, agreement between statement and observation. This group covers the Gr1-groups 13, 17, 18, 20.

Gr3. 5. The authoritative group. According to the formulations of this group, some authority or other, or more generally, some assemblies of people or some human institution guarantee what is true. We may also represent the standpoint by the following words: "true is what certain assemblies of people say or what some human institution has postulated". Human tradition is reckoned among the institutions, cf. the formulation "that it is fixed by tradition", as well as human conventions, cf. the formulation "that it corresponds with what is determined beforehand". As authorities are mentioned: scientists, witnesses to an event, the majority, sane human beings, several, everybody. This group covers the Gr1-groups 9, 22, 23, 24, 25.

The strength of the Gr3-principle is that it arranges 223 or 74,6 % of all ABf in as few groups as 5 without leaving the territory of easily manageable criteria. Table 38,1 shows the relative frequency of the 5 Gr3-groups.

Table 38,1. Relative size of the Gr3-groups.

(1) Frequency candidate	(2) Gr3-No.	(3) Number of ABf.	(4) Percentage of 300	(5) Frequency points
1	1	60	20,0	30,7
2	2	64	21,3	16,3
3	3	47	15,7	13,0
4	4	22	7,3	9,7
5	5	22	7,3	9,1

It is interesting to note the large number of frequency points obtained by Gr3. 1. This reflects the tendency to choose one definite formulation of Gr. 1, if any.

Grouping 450 professional Afr according to Gr3, we find that Gr5. 1 is much the most frequent with 17,5 %. Next comes Gr5. 3 with 3,6 %. Thus, the thing-group prevails among professionals, leaving little room for other Gr3-groups.

Sect. 39. Tendency of the ps to Adhere to One and Only One Group. — If a p produces several ABf, is he then apt to produce formulations that resemble each other? If he is, the grouping principles may be tested. A grouping principle would be suitable when ps with several formulations only tend to be represented in one group. We could try to arrange the formulations so that all or a considerable fraction of ps with several ABf are represented in their respective groups. This is, however, found to be impossible. A short glance at the list of ABfr from the 2 ps with 6 ABfr each may convince the reader:

(1) ABfr of p 97, 20 years old, cl. of ed. 4, dur. of ex. 20 min.

97,1 agreement with the objective view.
97,2 agreement with a view that is common to all human beings.
97,3 agreement with a view that is a result of several people reacting in the same way to a certain situation (to a certain impression).
97,4 a fact of which one has palpable proofs.
97,5 a fact that cannot be disputed.
97,6 the opposite of a hypothesis.

(2) ABfr of p No. 119, 19 years old, cl. of ed. 3, dur. of ex. 25 min.

119,1 it happens.
119,2 I feel it as a fact.
119,3 it is my own experience.
119,4 it is my own or others' experience.
119,5 what I myself attend and see.
119,6 something that happens without man's interference.

The above-quoted formulations show what we have already suggested: that the tendency to multiple formulations is borne by various needs of the ps. Among these, some are of such a kind that a grouping-principle intending to bring the ABfr of a certain p under *one* heading, would be totally misleading: the ps want to see the q. c. c. from various points of view and produce, therefore, as different ABfr as possible.

Table 39,1 shows to what degree ps with more than one Af tend to adhere to one and only one Gr3-group. We choose Gr3, as we think Gr1 consists of too many groups to show the possible tendency.

Table 39,1. Tendency to produce ABfr of one and only one Gr3-group.

(1) Gr3-No.	(2) Total number of Af	(3) Number (n_1) of p with more than 1 Af	(4) Number of n_1 adhering to one and only one Gr3-group	(5) Per cent of n_1 adhering to one and only one group Gr3
1	58	26	10	38,5
2	54	33	8	24,2
3	46	28	3	10,7
4	20	13	1	7,7
5	20	13	2	15,4

Classifying 400 professional definitions of truth according to Gr3, we find that the tendency to produce ABfr of one and only one Gr3-group is comparable in weakness to the corresponding tendency of amateur Af.

Sect. 40. ABf on Positive and ABf on Negative Values. The Principle of Excluded Middle. — Of the 300 ABf, only 9 or 3% concern negative values as wrong, incorrect, false etc., in spite of these values being asked for almost as frequently as their opposites. Undoubtedly the order of questions posed is responsible for much of this inequality. The question on positive values was constantly put before the corresponding questions on negative ones, and the ps were thus invited to define the negative values in terms of corresponding positives already defined.

Some qts which cannot be dealt with in this volume were used to obtain information about the ps' view on the principle of excluded middle and the relation between positive and negative values in general. The ps' opinions appear to be various and complex. Most ps can be said to "adhere to the principle of excluded middle". Quantitative estimates have no sense without complicated discussions of the material and without distinguishing between different formulations of the principle. There are many rather different formulations in philosophic literature and it was consequently necessary for us to use several qts. The variability of answers to these qts is great, indicating the existence of a considerable number of embryonic, mutually exclusive, standpoints towards the principle of excluded middle.

Sect. 41. The Gr4-principle of Grouping. — This principle is founded on the difference between ABfr with reference to "something human" and ABfr without reference to "something human". The first group of ABfr tends to place man in the centre of attention, the second evades mentioning anything connected with man and his activities. Accordingly we call the formulations of the first group 'homopetal' and the formulations of the latter 'homofugal'. Examples of marked and obvious homopetal Afr are 'what I perceive directly by my senses', 'as a rule it sounds natural' and 'no one is able to change it'. Examples of homofugal Afr are: 'that it agrees with reality', 'the facts' and 'what has happened'. Less obviously homopetal is, e. g. 'what may be proved', 'what appears never to change'. They contain nevertheless references to intellectual activities. On the other hand, 'what never changes' should be classed as homofugal. Similarly, 'when nothing else seems possible' (unobserved Afr) should be reckoned as a homopetal Afr, 'when nothing else is possible' as a homofugal Afr.

'Statements' are classified as something human. Consequently, the Afr 'agreement between statement and reality' is homopetal, 'correspondence to reality' homofugal. If 'propositions' had occurred, we would have considered the formulations containing this word 'homofugal' (if the rest of the formulation were homofugal).

It is somewhat difficult to group an Afr containing the word 'absolute', e. g. 'what absolutely has occurred'. A p expressing himself in this way, might — it seems — equally well express himself by the formulation 'what unquestionably has occurred'. When 'what seems to have occurred' is classed as homopetal, one might also call formulations with 'absolutely', homopetal. We think, however, it is more adapted to philosophically 'neutral' principles to let the formulation pass as homofugal. Something similar may be said about Af with the word 'possible': 'what possibly has occurred' (unobserved), 'what is possible' (unobserved).

If we consider the context in which we find the ABf, i. e. the whole conversation between l and p, it is, of course, to be expected that the decision what is homopetal and what is homofugal would be more significant psychologically considered and therefore also more justifiable. The operations with ABf are, however, to be carried out consistently and this implies that we abstract from every context. We do this as an experiment and do not claim that the results necessarily or probably will, give the insight we mostly need and wish. Such an experiment is, nevertheless, necessary for us so far as we put the question: How are we to bring non-philosophers to produce *formulations* that resemble the truth-theories of philosophers and which qualities do these have as *formulations*? If we mix contextual qualities into the definition of groups of ABfr, we have ceased to treat them as formulations. This we will ultimately do, but not in connection with the question mentioned above. Here, a non-contextual treatment is demanded.

Some ABfr contain the auxiliaries 'should', 'ought' etc. in a certain way: 'what we ought to believe', 'that it must be so'. We group them as homopetal. — 'It is lucid facts' is classed as homopetal, 'it is mere facts' or 'it is facts' as homofugal. We admit that a grouping according to the Gr4-principle must in these and analogous cases be arbitrary.

According to Gr4 'that it agrees with reality' ('it' relating to 'a statement') and 'that it agrees with reality' ('it' relating to 'something' or 'a thing') are both homofugal. Similarly, 'what' and 'that' may either relate to 'statement' or to 'something' or to 'thing', but are in both cases grouped as homofugal. The difference cannot be defined without taking the context into account and this we are not as yet allowed to do. In chapters 4 and 5 the immediate and mediate context will be carefully discussed.

Sect. 42. **The Size of the Gr4-groups.** — Table 42, 1 shows the size of the homopetal and homofugal group.

Table 42,1. Relative size of the Gr4-groups.

(1) Frequency candidate	(2) Gr4 No.	(3) Number of ABf	(4) Per cent of 300	(5) Number of ps	(6) Per cent of 150
1	3	253	84,3	99	66,0
2	1	47	15,7	37	24,6

The table supports the view that the non-philosopher is not inclined to choose 'realistic' and 'ontological' opinions of the notion of truth as often supposed by the philosophers. The so-called 'naive realism' is naive, but philosophic, not prephilosophic. Grouping 200 professional Af, we find 63 (31,5 %) belonging to Gr4.1 and 137 (68,5 %) belonging to Gr4.3.

Sect. 43. The Gr5-principle of Grouping. — According to this principle the ABfr are grouped in the same groups that contain the same notions. Some notions as "reality" and "proof" occupy a significant place in many formulations. They are *"central notions"* in formulations as the following: "what agrees with reality", and "of what one has a proof" respectively. Comparing these formulations with the two next: "what agrees with facts" and "what one has experienced", it is found, however, that also "agreement" and "one" may be called central. Formulations containing the word "agreement" identify truth (a.s.n) with a relation of a particular type, formulations containing the word "one" with something that stands in a certain relation to human subjects. This makes it natural to group the quoted formulations in such a way that all formulations containing "reality" are put into one group, all containing "agreement" in another, and so on. Contrary to the foregoing principles of grouping, Gr5 will therefore allow one and the same formulation to occur in several groups.

Sect. 44. Relative Size of the Gr5-groups. — We shall select 27 notions that seem to play an important rôle in the ABf of the non-philosopher. They all occur in more than 5 formulations of the 300 under discussion. Group divisions were originally based on the Norwegian text.

Table 44,1 shows the relative size of the 16 largest Gr5-groups. To save space we have omitted the data of Bf from the table. Mainly for two reasons it is interesting to compare the groups of Gr5 with similar ones of Gr1:

Gr1 was constructed so as to exclude the possibility of one and the same formulation being attributed to more than one group. This had primarily the effect that formulations which certainly had closer relation to group a and group b than to any other groups, but did not belong to any of them, were classified in neither a nor b. Example: "a fact of which one has palpable proofs" has both the main characteristic peculiar to Gr1.7 and Gr1.10 and is classed as a special group, Gr1.52. According to Gr5, this ABf is classed in both Gr5.4 (facts, actual) and Gr5.1 (proof, prove) (corresponding to Gr1.7 and Gr1.10). The frequency distributions of the groups are thus effected and in such a way that groups with more ABfr, half belonging to them and half to some other, get a higher value of frequency than those with less. The other reason to compare the frequency distributions of Gr1 and Gr5, is that a great deal of the 61 ABfr forming groups of Gr1 with only one member, are absorbed into Gr5 groups with a greater number of individuals. The groups are thus rendered more homogeneous in size.

It is notorious that according to Gr5, ABfr based on the notion of proof or something provable or proved are the most frequent ones.

Of the specific Gr5-groups, the group of ABfr including the word "I" range at the top of the list. As much as 18,7% of the ps put forward ABf with important references to their ego's.

Table 44,1. Relative size of the Gr5-groups.

(1) Frequency candidate (%)	(2) Central notions	(3) Percentage of 300 ABfr	(4) Frequency points
1	proof prove provable	14,7	22,4
2	agree agreeably accordance	13,3	20,6
3	I	12,0	15,4
4	facts actual	8,7	13,1
5	real reality	8,3	11,3
6	can be attacked, contested, proved, etc.	7,3	11,0
7	experience	4,3	6,0
8	seen	3,7	5,2
9	feeling feel	3,3	5,6
	my, me	3,3	3,2
	conviction convinced	3,3	5,2
	see	3,3	5,7
	things	3,3	3,6
	exist	3,3	4,6
15	doubt doubted doubtful	3,0	1,6
	know	3,0	2,9

The distribution of the Gr5-groups is, on the whole, analogous to that of the Gr1-groups. The notion of "proof" turns out to be the most frequent of the central ideas. One p in 4 produced at least as much as one formula with reference to this idea, whereas 1 in 5 tried to characterize truth (o. s. n.) as a sort of agreement or correspondence. References to "I" and "my" are remarkably frequent. Summing up the number of ABfr with references to "I", "me", "my", "all", "several" or "nobody", we find that as much as every fifth ABfr shows such references.

Sect. 45. The Gr6-principle of Grouping. — One may ask how ps, by using their formulations in discussions, should be able to discern truths

(o. so. s.). How many factors have to be taken into account to identify them? If e. g. an ABfr reads 'what can be proved', one has to search for something that can be proved. If the p after a careful inspection states 'x can be proved' x may be called true according to his ABfr. Another p finds that the c.c. of what is true (o. so. s.) is 'that he holds that it is like that and it appears to be like that'. If this p finds that something — x — is held by himself 'to be like that' and he also finds that 'it appears to be like that' we are justified in stating 'x is true' according to his 'theory of truth'. We may call the contents of ABfr 'criteria of truth' and ask how many are found in given cases. In philosophical discussions, however, "statements" of the "nature (essence)" or of the "definition" of "truth" and "statements" of the "criteria" of truth are sometimes sharply distinguished. We will therefore be careful, and make no apparent presuppositions as to what the ps have intended: if they propose their ABfr mainly as criteria or as definitions or if they ignore the difference alleged. Instead of using the expression 'criterion of truth' we will therefore speak about 'factors' by which a truth (o. so. s.) is determined according to a certain ABfr, or about 'determinants'. We may then say that 'what can be proved' and 'that I hold that it is like that and it appears to be like that' involve one and four determinants respectively. The latter are 'I (and not anyone else) hold, that it is like that (and not e. g. like an elephant)', 'and it appears', 'to be like that'. The ABfr 'that it agrees with reality' may be said to involve two determinants — if we, as we always do in these groupings, retain the *expressions* or formulations used by the p. If r claims to be true, one has to decide whether r is connected with 'reality', and whether this connection may be called 'agreement'. One might find that r stands in a certain relation e. g. disagreement. to reality or that it agrees with something, e. g. human opinions, but not with reality. Two factors are to be taken into consideration — according to the p's ABf. This does not mean, of course, that *we* take any definite view of what actually had to be taken into account, if the ABf should be used. We only state that if a p calls "what is x" true, we are justified in expecting that if he — the p — in a discussion holds that y is an x, that he will also be apt to hold that y is true. What we maintain is a group of prognoses concerned with the behaviour of our ps in certain situations. The ABfr 'what agrees with that particular part of reality of which one speaks' involves another determinant: one has to decide if the possible agreement between r and reality exists as regards this particular part referred to in the discussion at issue. The ABf may therefore be said to involve three determinants.

It might be possible to set up rules so rigid that by them we might decide with practically perfect stringency the 'number of determinants' of a certain ABf. The value of a logical consistency will, however, be counter-balanced by practical inconveniences. We choose, therefore, to make a compromise. As determinants we will class factors relatively independent of each other in practice and relatively easy to distinguish for an outsider (an investigator with no special knowledge of the test persons' way of speaking); other factors will be left unconsidered. Examples of factors not considered: (1) The difference between 'know' and 'really know' in ABfr of the type 'what one (really) knows' (2) The difference between 'immediately obvious' and 'obvious' in ABfr of the type 'what is (immediately) obvious' (3) The difference between 'what one can see' and 'what can be seen'. All ABfr with the indefinitive pronoun 'one' are classed in the same way as ABfr with verbs in passive. 'Something', 'that', 'it' are similarly rejected as determinants. As the last example, we take 'what is in accordance with what people say who know the common laws of nature'. We arrive at the result 4 determinants by the following argumentation: "A specific relation is demanded (1 det.). The first relatum is unspecified (no det.). The second relatum is 'people's sayings' (1 det.). Not all of these utterances are truths (o. so. s.): 'the people' must know the laws of nature (1 det.). Which? All of them? Some of them? — They must know the *common* laws (1 det.)."

In many cases the decision as regards how many determinants a given ABf involves, is rather arbitrary. It is only of importance to us to be able to arrange the ABf so that the *decidedly* richer as to factors, are separated from the *decidedly* poorer, and the very complex from the very simple. According to our opinion, our computation of the number of determinants permits us to obtain this moderate degree of accuracy.

Some search for simplicity seems always to be a motive when choosing ABf. Very complex ABf are rejected because of their mere intricacy. If the ABfr involved 100 determinants on the average, every analogy with professional theories would disappear: Professionals also seem to be seeking for simplicity. (We do not in this connection think of simplicity in words chosen, but of structure of theory of number of determinants etc.)

Sect. 46. Size of Gr6-groups. — Table 46,1 shows the frequency of the different numbers of the determinants, and their mean values. Gr6.n means "the group of ABfr, which contains all ABfr with n determinants."

Table 46,1. Frequency of the different numbers of determinants.

Gr6.n	1	2	3	4	5	6	7	8
Number of ABfr ...	91	130	49	22	5	1	1	1
Per cent of 300 ...	30,3	43,3	16,3	7,3	1,7	0,3	0,3	0,3

$a = 1,43$ $r = 7$ $\sigma = 1,1$ $V = 52,9$

69,7 per cent of the ABfr involve 2 or more determinants "Truth" (a. s. n.) is, therefore, according to approximately two out of three definitions a complex value, a relation or a simple combination of characteristics. If the context of the ABf is taken into account, the mean number of determinants increases considerably. The ps generally comment on their ABf in such a way that these would grow very intricate if the comments were expressed by *one* statement and related to the ABfr. — Grouping 200 professional Afr we find that they contain on an average 3.0 determinants.

Sect. 47. We have grouped ABfr according to 6 principles representing 147 group-divisions. Further types of classifications would no doubt bring interesting results. The possible points of view are innumerable, and each implies its own grouping-principle. On the other hand, as ABfr are rather arbitrarily dissected parts of comprehensive units of verbal and non-verbal behaviour, it is not likely that something like a "natural classification" of these behaviour-units could be worked out. Linné may, by his famous system, be said to have classified the stamens "naturally", the plants "artificially". So we have tried to classify the ABfr naturally, but this classification breaks down as "artificial" if the ABfr are viewed as symptoms of types of "the ps' answers" or as symptoms of types of ps". Artificial classifications have a limited value, and we shall show that our ABf-groups are noe xceptions. The answers (of the ps) will be grouped according to more "natural" principles in sect. 65, when more comprehensive units of verbal behaviour are taken into account. This is the reason why we stopped the production of ABf-grouping-principles after having used only 6 of them.

Little care has been taken to ensure a high degree of homogeneity and uniformity of the ABfr-groups. This would be possible only by dangerously elaborate psychological and philosophical means. We could show how a successive elaboration and amplification of the definition of "homopetal" and "homofugal" groups is of no importance from a practical point of view: the statistically observable effects of slight rearrangements implied by the elaboration are too minute. We forecast that 9 out of 10 of other elaborations carried out in order to ensure a high degree of homogeneity, uniformity, and psychological significance, will prove equally deceptive in practice — unless the number of ps is at least ten-fold.

Sect. 48. **Concluding Remarks on the Size of the Groups.** — If it is admitted that the question "what is the common sense view of the idea of truth" has a meaning, the simplest answer would be to propound an ABf and add, "*this* is the view". This simple type of answer is given by most philosophers. Having recognized that hardly any of our ps give the same answers to questions concerning the notion of truth, no such simple answer is possible for us. One could state that "most or all ps really mean the same, intend the same etc.", but how is this gratuitous statement to be controlled? We think that only further questioning and detailed comparison can supply material for control. (And this control would be a very indirect one because of the extreme vagueness of the statements.)

The inference that most ps mean the same with their apparently conflicting definitions has an interesting consequence, however: if it is accepted, one has to accept the view that most philosophers mean the same.

Our material does not support the statement that everybody, or the majority, means the same or approximately the same. It is therefore nonsensical to speak of *the* common sense view of the truth-notion. Equally nonsensical it is to speak of *the* view of the man in the street, of the uneducated, of the prephilosophic mind etc. No philosopher speaks of *the* philosophic view of the truth-notion and regards a certain ABf as expression thereof. This would not, however, be any more ridiculous than to speak of *the* common sense view. As it is impossible for us to point out any single ABf as particularily representative, some sort of grouping is unavoidable. If it were possible to work out a principle of grouping that was felt as "to the highest degree natural" and if this principle would lead to the conclusion: "the view v is much the most frequent", there might be some reason to label "the common sense view". In reality, we do think that many grouping-principles can be constructed, leading to frequency distributions of the type required. Our Gr4 represents an example.

If someone finds that the grouping principle Grx is "to the highest degree natural", it is to be expected that others will — if they are interested in such matters — put forward a considerable number of principles considered "equally or more natural". The possibility of finding satisfactory and conclusive frequency distributions is consequently minimal. The indetermination is the greater, the more subtle and complex interpretations of the formulations are tolerated. As soon as one allows arguments as "x and y cannot be meant to signify something different". "x and y certainly has a different meaning". "The sense of x is the same of y, the difference being but one of expression and of taste" etc., the possibilities grow unlimited. The more hypotheses of this sort we actually try to control, for instance, by questioning the ps themselves, the less confidence we have in the meaning of such interpretations, especially when they are as subtle as most philosophic classificatory criteria. Considerations of this kind lead us to conclude that there is no reason to call any type of view produced by ps, "*the* most frequent type". The size of our 147 groups does not indicate anything of this kind. What it indicates is: "employing the grouping-principle Gix, the group No. y is the most frequent", and this is to us by far the most important. If, on the other hand, a fairly well-determined principle of grouping is adapted and carried out in practice, it is found that the relative size of the groups *remain fairly constant* even among rather different collections of ps.

Sect. 49. Correlations between Age, Education and Groups of Afr. — Is there any inclination of the younger ps to adhere to ABfr of certain groups and avoid others? What types of ABfr do the more philosophical educated prefer? May the choice of ABfr tell something about the age and education of a person? Does the standpoint of amateurs to q. c. c. undergo a traceable development? Which are the most, and which are the least, "professional" ABfr, if the most educated ps are considered as the most professional, and the least educated the least professional? — These and other questions present themselves as soon as the astonishing variety of ABfr is clearly perceived. We will try to solve some of them in the following sections.

To get a statistical material as homogeneous as possible and at the same time to obtain groups with sufficient individuals, we reject the Bfr and confine ourselves to the 269 Afr.

The ps do not fall into equally numerous classes of age and education. To form a true picture of the relative strength of possible connections between certain groups and certain classes of age or education, one has to give the obtained per cent different weight. This will be done when discussing the tables.

Sect. 50. Correlation between Gr1, Gr2, Gr3 and Age, Education. — There is no correlation between types of ABfr and age, education, the existence of which could be shown without taking all interconnections into account. Correlations have to be pointed out by careful statistical analysis. The place for "intuition" and deduction from general principles is minimal. Complete analysis of our statistical data is impossible for lack of space and we are consequently forced to abstain from a scientifically justifiable exposition of our material. In the case of Gr1 we shall permit ourselves, however, to reproduce *some* of the relations at issue. They give no unfair picture of the general properties of all relations in this field. We limit ourselves to the material put forward by ps 1—150. The values of columns (3)—(6) are percentages of total number of Afr in each class of age or education.

Table 50,1. Relation between age and choice of Gr1-group.

(1) Gr1 No.	(2) Total number of Afr	(3) Age cl. 1	(4) 2	(5) 3	(6) 4
1	11	11,8	3,5	6,4	13,3
2	9	0,0	5,4	4,8	20,0
5	10	17,6	5,4	6,4	0,0
7	6	0,0	1,8	6,4	6,7
8	10	11,8	8,9	3,2	6,7
10	33	23,5	28,6	12,9	6,7
11	16	5,9	5,4	9,7	6,7
12	7	0,0	7,1	4,8	0,0
15	6	5,9	1,8	4,8	0,0
16	6	5,9	3,6	3,2	6,7
18	13	0,0	12,5	8,1	3,3
21	6	5,9	7,1	1,6	0,0
23	6	0,0	5,3	3,2	0,0
24	8	0,0	7,1	6,4	0,0
29	7	0,0	7,1	4,8	0,0

Table 50,2. Relation between education and choice of Gr1-group.

(1) Gr1 No.	(2) Total number of Afr	(3) Ed. cl. 1	(4) 2	(5) 3	(6) 4
1	11	10,0	2,7	0,0	12,8
2	9	0,0	4,2	0,0	15,4
5	10	5,0	9,7	13,0	0,0
6	8	5,0	4,2	6,7	2,6
7	6	5,0	1,4	20,0	2,6
8	10	10,0	6,9	0,0	7,8
10	33	20,0	24,7	20,0	10,3
11	16	5,0	5,6	6,7	12,8
12	7	0,0	6,9	0,0	5,1
15	6	0,0	2,8	6,7	5,1
16	6	5,0	4,2	6,7	2,6
18	13	20,0	9,7	13,3	0,0
21	6	10,0	4,2	6,7	0,0
23	6	5,0	4,1	0,0	2,6
24	8	0,0	5,6	0,0	10,3
29	7	10,0	4,2	6,7	2,6

It is no easy task to interpret the tabulated values. A very important feature of the distributions is their lack of simple, marked regularities. There are no obvious correlations dominating great groups of Af. The many more or less elaborate statistical formulas available do not make our task — to pick out "real" correlations — in any way easier. One of the reasons for this is the smallness of the ABfr-groups. This does not make the formulas inapplicable, but makes the interpretation of the results very intricate. Considerations of this kind do not in any way indicate that the data above tabulated are worthless: they but indicate that the subject under discussion is complicated. In such cases the worth of a material based on 300 Afr is of considerably greater value than a material based on only 100 formulations — and of decidedly less value than a material based on 1000 Afr.

Without going into detail, we think it justifiable to make the following statements:

(1) *It is highly improbable that most types of Afr are intimately correlated with age or education or both factors.* By this we mean: it may be forecast with a fairly high degree of certainty that there is no marked, real correlation between most groups of Afr and age, education.

By "real" we mean to say "capable of confirmation by increasing the statistical population considerably (say, 10 times)."

By "marked correlation" we mean to say here: a correlation of 80 or more per cent found to hold good for more than half of the groups of ABfr."

(2) It may be stated with a fairly high degree of certainty that there are marked real correlations between *some* groups of ABfr and age or education or both.

Among the groups which show correlation, we shall pick out the most marked. As a criterion for marked correlation we adopt:

Let g denote the obtained percentage ABf of any group as regards a certain class of age or education. Let g_1, g_2, g_3, g_4 denote the individual values for each class of age and education. If one of the two inequalities

(1) $\qquad 2\, g_1 + g_2 > (g_3 + 2\, g_4) \cdot 2$
(2) $\qquad 2\, (2\, g_1 + g_2) < g_3 + 2\, g_4$

holds good for a group, the tabulated values show marked correlation with age or education. Using the percentage frequency-points and denoting by g the percentage frequency-points of any single group as regards a certain class of age or education, one arrives at the same equations. In the following section we shall discuss those groups for which equations (1) or (2) hold good interpreting g as percentage ABf as well as percentage frequency-points. They will be called groups showing *"marked"* correlation with age or education. The groups arrived at may conveniently be divided into 4 categories: Low-age and low-education groups in connection with which unequality (1) is valid and high-age and high-education groups by which unequality (2) is realized.

Sect. 51. Low Age- and Low Education-groups According to the Grouping Principles Gr1, Gr2 and Gr3. — Of the 15 Gr1-groups represented in table 50,1, only 4 show marked correlation with age. This is, however, a much greater number than would have been probable if the values were distributed at random. Of these 4 groups, one is low age- as well as low education-group: Gr1. 21. Of the 15 Gr1-groups, as many as 8 show marked correlation with education, of which Gr1. 18, Gr1. 21 and Gr1. 29 are low education-groups. To these groups Gr1. 10 may be added in spite of the fact that it does not fulfil the above-mentioned criterion of a marked correlation. It is the most frequent group of all.

Low age groups but not low education groups are Gr1. 5, and Gr1. 10. Of the 7 Gr2-groups, Gr2. 2 and Gr2. 3 are low-age groups, and Gr2. 5 low-education group. Of the Gr3-groups, Gr3. 5 is a low-age group.

In sect. 48 we have rejected the possibility of finding any single group of ABf that might justly be given the title "the most frequent view of the truth-notion among non-philosophers". There are many Gr1-groups which are about equally frequent, but not one which contains as much as 25 % of all ABf. It may here be added that the splitting up of the ps — the non-philosophers — into classes of age and education support our rejection. If, by a non-philosopher, one means a p of education class 1, 2 or 3 or, perhaps, of only classes 1 and 2, there is no group which is especially well represented in these classes in comparison with other classes and which at the same time contains more than 20% of the ABf of any of the low-education classes. The most extreme low-education class is Gr1. 18. 20% of all ABf of education class 1 belong to this group and no ABf of education class 4. This group is the one, however, which is represented in a rather different way among the ps 151 to 250. Taking all 250 ps into account, one obtains the values 9,5% in education class 1, 2,9% in class 2, 2,7% in class 3 and 0% in class 4. This means that the group is not so frequently represented as table 50,2 would indicate. Another factor is important when discussing eventual "typical non-philosophic groups". If a typical non-philosopher is viewed as a p of education class 1 or 2, one must face the fact that as much as 66 Gr1-groups of ABf are represented by ps of these classes. If the number of ps were increased, one may expect this number to increase. Our conclusion is, therefore, that there is no reason to pick out any group as one of typical non-philosophers. We arrive at the same result defining "typical" in other ways.

Someone might possibly argue that the typical non-philosopher must be defined in terms of the science of character. One may, for inst., distinguish between reflecting and unreflecting types of persons, and these may be insufficiently characterized by age and education. Some philosophers find that it is naive to assume that truth means agreement with reality whereas the acceptance of their own Af is supposed not to be naive. One must consequently assume that these authors would have classed the ps according to degree of naiveté or to a similar complex characteristic. Nothing would interest us more than correlations between experimentally (operationally) defined traits of character and type of ABf. There is, however, strong reason to suppose that such correlations, if they existed and could be arrived at in a scientifically sound manner, would also hold among philosophers. By this we mean to indicate that the position of the problem is based on the misconception that amateur philosophers are different in character from professional philosophers — and in such a way that one may speak about the first group of people as "naive", "unreflected", and about the latter group as "reflected" etc. The great variability of standpoints towards all main problems of the so-called truth-theories speaks in favour of the assumption that all types of professional philosophers may be re-found among the amateurs — among philosophers on occasion.

The problem could be put otherwise: Instead of a comparison between professional and amateur philosophers as regards character, one might plan out a comparison between types of amateurs. The reason why we have not carried out any such comparison along the lines of the experimental science of character is solely the tremendous complexity of tests and the large number of test-persons which would be required to arrive at any results. We have carried out one test only (cf. sect. 75) and this convinced us of the complexity of the problems involved. The observation of the behaviour of 150 persons did not lead to any belief in easily traceable correlations between type of ABf — or any other trait of truth-theories — with character. If a highly developed science of character were available as an existing instrument, things would have been otherwise.

Sect. 52. **High Age and High Education Groups According to Gr1, Gr2 and Gr3.** — Of the Gr1-groups, Nos. 2 and 7 are both high-age and high-education groups. The first group is of special interest as it includes the ABf often called "the non-philosophers' view of truth". These Af occur very often among ps of 13 and 15 years, become continuously rarer until the ps receive a University education, taking philosophy, or reach the age of 30 or more. Suddenly the frequency of Af of Gr1. 2 rises to a height not attained by any other group than Gr1. 11.

Of the Gr1-groups, Nos. 6, 11, 15 and 24 are high-education groups. In connection with divergencies between correlation with age and such with education, the insufficient number of ps with high age and low education should be remembered. In spite of the scanty material, there is some evidence supporting the view that Gr1-groups are more closely related to education than to age.

Of the Gr2-groups, Gr2. 1 is a high age and high education group. Of the Gr3-groups, No. 4 is a high age, and No. 1, a high education group.

Sect. 53. **Gr4- and Gr5-groups. Relation to Age, Education.** — Omitted tables computed as those of sect. 50, indicate no marked correlation between Gr4-groups and increasing age or education. The distributions are to a conspicuous degree more "at random". Corresponding tables for Gr5-groups offer, on the other hand, much the same picture as those of sect. 50 (dealing with the relation between Gr1-groups and age, education.) The correlations stated in sect. 51 and 52 are supported by them. — Af referring to "I" (the self of the test-person) are approximately equally frequent in all classes of age. The frequency of definitions of truth (a. s. n.) as a relation of agreement (accordance etc.) increases markedly with age and education.

Sect. 54. **Relation between Gr6-groups and Age, Education.** — If the sum of the determinants of the ABfs belonging to ps of a certain class of age is divided by the number of ABfs in any such class, very conclusive evidence of rapid increase of complication with increasing age until the twenties is obtained: the average number of det. is 1,56; 1,95; 2,28; 2,27, resp. The analogous increase with increasing education is even more marked, the average number of det. for each class being 1,79; 1,94; 1,95; 2,51.

Here as elsewhere, we speak of correlation between some function and age, without trying to analyse the great number of factors determined by the age of a person. Education, as here defined, is, for instance, to some degree a function of age: There are close correlations between age and education of ps. In spite of leaving these questions untouched, the data just given have considerable bearing on questions central to our subject-matter: "How complicated may one expect the ABf of persons of a given age or education to be?" The ABf of professional philosophers have on an average a complication clearly higher than those of ps of education class 4, namely about 3,0. The increase of complication with increasing education is much more marked and widespread than the changes in contents: The nucleus of the ABf is generally retained whereas the ABf are expressed more amply and carefully.

Sect. 55. **Variability of ABf and the Factor's Age, Education.** — It may be asked whether the ABf of ps with low age or education are scattered over a number of different types — for instance, Gr1-groups — comparable with the corresponding number of types represented by ABf of ps with high age or education. *Do ps with low education put forward more, or less, distinct kinds of solutions than ps of high education?* Is the range of possible solutions narrowed down with increasing education? This might be expected if one believed in a *development towards definite types of truth-definitions as "adequate"*. Believing this, it would be natural to expect highly educated persons — persons with great knowledge and experience — to eliminate less adequate types from earnest consideration.

Our material permits us to indicate something with a bearing on these questions. We shall make choice of two quantities: (1) the percentage of all 98 Gr1-groups of ABf which contain ABf of a certain class of age or education, and (2) the number of great Gr1-groups represented among 20 ABf belonging to persons of a certain class of age or education. — The first quantity may be said to measure the variability of types as it occurs in the ABfrl. It is a quantity which depends on the number of ps in each class class of age and education. A class with many ps must be expected to represent more distinct Gr1-groups than a very poor class: The ps of the latter class have not got the same chance to make their wealth of ideas felt. The second quantity measures the variability of ABf, if allowance is made for the different number of ps in each class of age and education. On account of the small number of ps of age class 1, the standard sample of ABf cannot include more than 20. As "great" Gr1-groups we class all groups containing 5 or more members.

According to table 55,1 the variability is so great that more than half of the greater groups are represented by ABf of each and every class of age and education. Selecting 20 ABf of ps of age cl. 1 at random, it is found that 6 of the great Gr1-groups are represented among them.

Table 55,1. *Variability of ABf and age, education.*

	Age cl.				Ed cl.			
	1	2	3	4	1	2	3	4
Percentage represented of the great groups......	58	100	100	53	79	100	63	90
Percentage of the small groups	15	38	59	6	15	51	14	42
	6	8	11	10	9	10	8	9
Number of great groups repr. among 20 ABf...	·	7	10	8	10	6	5	7
	·	7	7	·	·	6	·	5
Average variability	0,3	0,4	0,5	0,5	0,5	0,4	0,3	0,4

Dividing 6 by 20 we obtain the measure of variability given in the fourth main row. The value 0,3 indicates that 3 out of 10 ABf put forward by ps of age cl. 1 belong to different great Gr1-groups. The numbers 8, 7 and 7 found in the second column and the third row, are obtained by picking out 20 different ABf three times. Table 55,1 supports the view that the *variability of ABf increases with age.* Taking into account the statistical properties of the material, it is scarcely justifiable to put much reliance on this view. On the other hand, we think it justifiable to state that *great changes* in variability with increasing age are improbable. — The decrease of variability with increasing education is too small to be of any interest. A high or even moderate, real correlation of variability with increasing education is even more improbable than in connection with age.

Our main conclusion cannot but be the following: *There is inconspicuous evidence in favour of the hypothesis that the number of types of ABf found adequate by the ps decreases with increasing education,* and strong evidence against the view that the eventual decrease is considerable.

Sect. 56. Age, Education and Truth-theory. Conclusions. — The statistical results show convincingly that younger and less educated ps are inclined to prefer other types of ABfr than those most frequently used by older or more educated persons. *The preference is one of degree, however.* No type of ABfr appears to be exclusively adhered to by one class of ps. This holds good of the more frequent types of ABfr. Lack of material forbids us to draw any conclusion regarding 70 to 80 of the groups on account of their rarity.

Our material is great enough to give evidence of the complexity of the phenomena under discussion. There is no short-cut method to investigate correlations between conceptions of the notion of truth and age, education. The subject demands extensive and detailed observations and *the results must be of a kind very different from the elegant formulas found by those who trust the power of "reason"*. If somebody wishes to obtain short, general and "interesting" results — results throwing light on general psychological and philosophic problems viewed as "fundamental" — he should give up observation at once and limit himself to the examination of the smallest possible number of cases: the smaller the observational data, the greater the force of intuitions and "freedom" of thought.

There is no evidence to support the view that philosophic education considerably changes a p's attitude towards ABfr. This is seen when comparing the types of ABfr chosen by ps of ed. class 3 (without any philosophic school training) with those chosen by ps of ed. classes 4 and 5.

The ABfr are, on the whole, poor as symptoms of the age and education of their authors. Exceptions are ABfr containing "difficult" or technical words, or crude lapsi linguae.

To be able to investigate the possible development of ABfr of the same ps as age and education increase, tests would have to be made during several years. It is to be feared, however, that the disturbing influence of a periodical examination — for instance every other year — would cause the possible development to take a very different course from that arrived at without any such interference. We may safely assume that the average difference between the ABfr of persons of different ages and education depict to some extent a difference due to the persons' individual development, and that the difference constitutes features of the development. In this sense, it may, for instance, be said that the ABfr undergo a development towards what is often called "relativism" and grow more complicated with the increasing education of the ps. (Cf. the sections in which the individual grouping-principles and effect of age and education are discussed). To obtain scientifically sound conclusions on these matters, very careful discussions had to be carried out. What we have done here is but "preliminary inquiry". Under no conditions can we attribute any value to statements on these matters deduced from general philosophical views or from "intuition". If one wishes to *know* something about the matter, the traditional methods of attack must be radically and definitely abandoned.

Sect. 57. **"Elementary" and "Discerning" Classifications.** — One may separate classifications into two groups: "elementary" and "discerning". Our ps have been classified, for instance, according to their school education. Instead of this, they might have been classed according to, let us say, "environmental stimuli furthering interest in and occupation with philosophic problems". The second classification might be expected to afford material for a large number of psychological problems on genesis of truth-theories, which the first classification cannot be expected to do.

The second classification is complex and discerning and creates interest. We shall call the first one "elementary" and the second "discerning".

Trying to accord with classifications other than crude, one finds in most cases that it is safe to *begin* with a crude one. Our classification according to school education facilitates a general classification of all ps as regards their education and can be easily carried out and easily transferred to new groups of ps. But the causal connection between school-education and the typological traits of their answers as ps may be a very indirect one.

Let us, on the other hand, consider the following classification: Ed. cl. 1: (a) ps not having read books or articles commonly labelled "philosophic", and (b) stating that they have not considered any problem dealing with the definition of truth. Ed. cl. 2: Ps having read a small amount of philosophic writings, let us say, between one and ten articles or books or between 5 and 1000 pages, but "having considered" according to the definition of sect. 19. Ed. cl. 3: Ps having read but a small amount of philosophic writings and "having considered". Ed. cl. 4: Ps having read more philosophic literature than those of ed. cl. 2 and 3 but not "having considered". Ed. cl. 5: Ps both "having considered" and having read as much of philosophic literature as ps of ed. cl. 4. Carrying out this classification (let us call it "E 2") we find correlations between that and the classification according to school training (E1). Ps of E1.5 (ed. cl. 5 according to the "school training" criteria) belong to E2.5 and vice versa, no p belongs to E2.4, nearly all ps of E1.4 belong to E2.2 and nearly all ps of E2.2 belong to E1.4. (The last is, however, something peculiar to countries (Norway, for inst.) in which lessons in philosophy are only given at the universities). Some people without university education read philosophy, but they are comparatively few. We have tried to get the age classes 2 and 3 particularly well represented. Readers of philosophy, who have no university education, belong mostly to age class 4. This class is not very numerous, however. Consequently, the ps of E2.2 not belonging to E1.4 are far too few to allow any statistical analysis. The ps of groups E2.3 are found in E1.2, E1.3 and E1.4, ps of E2.1 are scattered over the total classes of E1 except E1.5. If one has already computed the distribution of ps over the E1-groups there is no reason to deal with E2 as a classification into 5 groups: two groups will suffice, E2.1 and E2.3. Writing E3.1 for E2.1 and E3.2 for E2.3 we arrive at the following conclusion: Adopting the *semi-elementary* principle of classification, E2, 3 of 5 groups become either too poor to be utilized statistically or then coincide with groups of the *elementary* classification E1.

Sect. 58. Concluding Remarks. — The method of this chapter has been one of extreme simplification. We have picked out so-called fundamental formulations from the ps' answers and discussed parts of them — the "roots",

Considering it possible, if not probable, that these "roots" are to some degree symptomatic of the character and whole reaction system of their exponents, we have investigated the relation of such "roots" to various very simple qualities of the ps. The distribution of types is found to be far from "random" and consequently permits us to assume that there actually are correlations between the items at issue. The important thing about these correlation is, in our eyes, that they are found by relatively simple statistical investigations and by analysis of a very restricted number of answers (150).

CHAPTER IV

The Main Features of Amateur-Theories of Truth.

Sect. 59. Introduction. Ps Who Are Not Represented by Any Af. — In this chapter we shall deal successively with the main features of amateur-theories of truth. In sect. 59 to 66 fundamental formulations are discussed, in sect. 67 to 79, standpoints towards absolute and correlations with "confidence", in sect. 80 to 87, examples of something true (o. so. v.) and, finally, in sect. 88 to 102, the ps' standpoints towards the fundamental formulation of other ps.

Of the 150 ps whose opinions on truth are collected and abbreviated in the ABfrl, 23 or 15% do not answer the questions of the l with any ABf. Of the ps 151—250, 14% behave in the same manner. The reasons why these ps are unrepresented are various and deserve some analysis. Among philosophers, it is not uncommon to abstain from any Af discussing the notion of truth.

Group 1. If a p consistently denies or doubts the existence of any c. c. of what is true (o. so. s.) he will be unrepresented by any ABf. The same will be the case if he states that he does not know if there are any c. c. Ps of this type form a first group. It should be noted that some ps at a certain moment reject the existence of any c. c. and shortly afterwards produce ABf. They are not always *consistent*. The groups of ps either denying, doubting or ignoring any c. c., consequently contain our first group of non-represented ps as a sub-group.

Group 2. Some ps seem to try to find formulations satisfying the definition of ABfr but they *do not arrive at* any. Some of them content themselves with D, F, G or H-formulations, with formulations unintelligible to the l. or with definitions of a certain group of truths (o. so. s.), ("moral truths", "mathematical truths" etc.). They may also put forward definitions supposed to cover the field intended by the l, but which to the l seem altogether too narrow or too wide.

Not all 37 non-represented ps can be easily classified as either belonging to group 1 or 2. Of 33 easily classifiable, 6 belong to group 1, and 27 to group 2.

One may try to discover possible characteristics of ps who accept tacitly or explicitly the q. c. c. as a question that deserves direct answer, who seem to search for ABf, but who do not find any. In some of these cases the question whether the p may be said to have understood the q. c. c. or not, remains open. It is quite a natural thing for a p to simulate understanding, behaving as if he "thinks the question over" or searches for the most suitable verbal form for his thoughts. If no conclusive symptom of the lack of understanding appeared, the ps of the doubtful group were gathered under the heading "ps who do not arrive at any ABf".

Some cases of non-representedness were undecidable. Computing the "percentage of all non-represented", these were subtracted from the total sum 37.

From very plausible arguments of general psychological character, it seems natural to expect that the more educated ps are more able to find ABf than less educated — if the latter wish to find any. Such an argument is only convincing if one also supposes that the more educated ps do not demand more or something different of their ABf than less educated. Suppose, for instance, that low educated ps have a strong tendency to utter whatever ABf that occurs to their mind without scrupulously examining possible criticisms, whereas high educated ps are endowed with a highly developed critical sense: under such conditions it should be reasonable to expect that a greater percentage of high educated ps "does not arrive at any ABfr". Other influences are readily imagined supporting the expectation of the frequency-distribution. Is one of these influences much the strongest, or are they of comparable strength? As everywhere in psychological and social sciences, such questions can hardly be answered without very careful statistical analysis. Different possible interpretations of the actually found distributions should be compared with each other. They are readily conceived as supporting one individual interpretation more than any other, whereas the distributions are always interpretable in various ways with the same order of certainty (with the same value to purposes of forecasting).

The actual computed (but non-reproduced) frequency distributions give some support to the following view: There is no marked correlation between age, education and ability to arrive at ABfr. A sample consisting of 27 ps is too small, however, to support any statements on less marked correlations. If such less marked correlations exist, it is more reasonable to expect increasing ability to find ABf with increasing education than decreasing ability: The percentage of non-represented ps of ed. cl. 1 is as much as 18,5 that of ps of ed. cl. 2, 10,5, whereas but 8,3 and 8,9 per cent of ps of ed. cl. 3 and 4 are not represented by any ABf.

Sect. 60. Ps Who Deny, Doubt or Ignore the Existence of c. c. — In this section consistent as well as inconsistent ps (cf. sect. 59) will be emphasized.

The question "Is there any c. c. of what is true (o. so. s.)" does not seem to allow great diversity of answer. A small group seems to represent the more natural of them. Theories of truth depend entirely on its author's standpoint towards the existence of c. c.; we will therefore map out this group as it appears to us.

Questions "Is there any c. c. of what is true (o. so. s.)?"
Answer I: Yes.

a) There is a c. c. of what is true and it is the following — —
b) There is a c. c., but it is practically impossible to find.
c) There is a c. c., but it is theoretically and practically impossible to find.
d) There may be a c. c.

Answer II: No.

a) If one distinguishes between different kinds of truths, each has a c. c. (If that which is true is divided into groups, each group has a c. c.).
b) There is no c. c.
c) It is impossible that there are any c. c. "The material relevant to the decision is continually increasing." "The word 'true' (a. s. w.) is used in contradictory ways by different people or by the same person at different times", "The attempt to find a c. c. involves a circle", etc.

Answer III: Commenting answers: "Neither yes nor no".

The q. c. c. "Is there a c. c. of what is *called* true (o. so. s')" permits similar differences of answers. This is also the case as regards all q. c. c. obtained by varying the wx-expressions explained in sect. 65.

Other q. c. c. as e. g. "How is the word "true" to be defined?" "Is it possible to define the word 'true'?, seem at first sight to facilitate other kinds of answers than the first-mentioned. These, however, are easy to coordinate to those already tabulated. If the q. c. c. reads "Is there any adequate definition of what is true?", the answer corresponding to the above mentioned I a is: "There is an adequate definition and it runs as follows — —".

The word "definition" may be interpreted thus: "If d is a definition of what is true (o. so. s.), then d contains a reference to a c. c. of what is true". It is, however, to be expected that some ps do not demand so much of a definition as a description of common characteristics.

Every general remark elucidating the function of the word "true" (o. s. w.) may seem adequate to them as a definition. This holds also in the case of q. c. c. like the following: "What is the meaning of the word "true"? The subject-matter of the professional truth-theories is, on the whole, closer related to formulations obtained as answers to questions about common-characteristics, than to formulations obtained as answers to questions about "definition", "meaning" and similar subjects. We accordingly adopted the term "common characteristic" in most of our qts.

Group 1 and 2, but not group 3 of our list of "natural" answers, are represented. Answer I a is much the most frequent. It is, however, very difficult to decide exactly which answers can be identified with I a. Here as elsewhere the classifications are not intended to be more than approximately rigid: If 4 out of 5 workers in experimental psychology agree with 9 out of 10 of our classifications, we are satisfied. By saying that they eventually "agree" we mean in this case the following: They agree with us, if we and they find — adopting the same principle of classification — that the answer A of the p P may be said to be of the type T (e. g. I a) of our list.

Only 19 of 150 ps answer explicitly that they think there is a c. c. Other ps answer for instance, "agreement with reality" or with any other ABf. We allow ourselves to interpret these answers as I a-answers. "Agreement with reality" we interpret as "Yes, and the c. c. is agreement with reality". If a p at first states that there are no c. c., but after some discussion changes opinion and explicitly sets forth a supposed c. c., we similarly class his answer as a I a-answer. This we also do if he states a Df, or Ef and utters nothing against the assumption that there is a c. c.

The following statistics are based on the assumption that the ps do not entertain seriously different opinions of what constitutes a c. c. There are, however, probably some such differences and they will be discussed later on. Answers of type III are lacking.

Table 60,1. *Frequency of the different standpoints towards the existence of a c. c. of what is true (o. so. s.). Ps 1—250.*

Name of stp.	Per cent ps	Name of stp.	Per cent of s
I a............	94,0	II a.........	0,8
I b...........	0,4	II b.........	3,6
I c	0,4	II c	0,4
I d...........	0,0	Undecided ..	0,4

The argumentation of the ps, who do not follow the majority is sometimes too instructive not to be quoted. The following is a supposed fair sample of the arguments:

P. 15 distinguishes between the existence of a c. c. from an "objective view" and from other points of view. "They (statements I call true) have the common property that I accept them as true from my individual point of view. From an objective point of view certainly no c. c."

P. 32 rejects the possibility of a c. c., but states that "one cannot at all say: Something *is* true".

P. 162 states: "I cannot exactly find any well-defined conception that can be common to them all (the correct statements)". To the question of the l: "Do you think that it is impossible to find anyone, or do you think that there is none (such conception)" the p answers: "I cannot believe that it is possible to trace a limit (between all correct statements and not-correct statements)".

P. 179 denies consistently that there is a c. c. to that which is wrong, she seems on the other hand to believe in a c. c. of what is true. This standpoint cannot be said to indicate lack of consistency. It is very common that non-philosophers do not judge true and false (or wrong) to be ("contradictory") opposites.

P. 214: Every definition of truth must be more or less subtile. One can define mathematical truth. That is one thing. From the point of view of natural science another thing, and then come *facts* as: I am sitting here. There is a series of kinds of true things. But to find a word that covers all things is, I think, quite impossible — and if a man so ingenious as to discover such a word should exist I should view his whole thinking as perfectly aimless."

Sect. 61. A Possible Source of Suggestion. — The questionnaire-method is particularly open to the influence of suggestion. During the examination we sometimes had the impression that the ps might be suggested to believe in the existence of a c. c. of what is true because the first question very often reads "*what is the* c. c. of that which is true?" We therefore decided to use three versions:

(1) what is the c. c. — —?
(2) is there any c. c. — —? (if positively answered): what is the c. c. — —?
(3) q. 1. give some examples of correct statements.
    q. 2. These examples are all different?
    q. 3. (If the p answers q. 2 negatively): What is their c. c.?
    q. 4. (If the p answers positively to q. 3): But is there any c. c. of *all* correct statements?
    q. 5. (If the p answers positively to q. 2): There are therefore no c. c. of all correct statements?

Following well-established psychological principles we may state that version (1) supplies strong positive suggestion to acknowledge the existence of a c. c., version (2) a weak positive suggestion in the same direction and version (3) a strong negative suggestion.

The following statistics refer to a fair sample of 119 ps, of which 76 were under strong positive, 29 under weak positive, and 14 under strong negative, suggestion. Of these 119 ps, 89% directly acknowledged the existence of a c. c. or indirectly acknowledged it by giving an Af. 88,2% of the ps under strong positive, 89,7% of the ps under weak positive and 92,9% of the ps under strong negative suggestion acknowledged a c. c. We may therefore safely conclude that suggestion does not play any important rôle at this point of our qts.

Of the 119 ps, 10 or 8,4 % did not arrive at any c. c., 9,21% of the ps under strong positive, 6,90 under weak positive and 7,14 under strong negative suggestion. 2,52% or 3 ps of the 119 ps denied or persistently doubted the existence of any c. c., of these, 2 were under strong positive, one under weak positive, and no one under strong negative suggestion. Taking the number of ps involved into account, the test of suggestibility must therefore be said to show wholly negative results: There is strong evidence against the assumption that ps are easily suggested to acknowledge or deny the existence of c. c.

Sect. 62. Ps Whose ABf Do Not Picture Adequately Their Opinions. —

In this section we are concerned only with one type of ps whose opinions are badly represented by their ABf. It is largely a speculative question to ask if ABf's fulfil the characteristics — psychological and sociological — of "opinions". Some ABf are clearly inadequate, however, and the inadequateness may be shown by a simple confrontation with the context in which they occur. We have in sect. 25 analyzed such cases. Here we will make some additions to our previous conclusions, taking ps 1—250 into consideration.

The ABf referred to in this section may be classed as follows:

a) ABf which are explicitly given up by the p. The p declares that he has made a mistake or that the ABf is bad or inadequate.

b) ABf which are indirectly or implicitly given up (withdrawn) by the p. During the examination, ps often stated things which invalidated their ABf as expressions of opinions.

c) Weakened ABf. Some ABf's cannot be said to be directly or indirectly *invalidated* as opinions by the comments of the ps, but they seem at least *weakened*. If, for instance, a p states A — a statement not concerned with ABf — and one awaits that the acceptance of A excludes the acceptance of *any* ABf, the ABf of the p are said to be "weakened" — not wholly "invalidated". It is a common experience that ps may entertain opinions that from the point of view of a somewhat trained student of philosophy would seem to contradict each other. As examples of "weakening comments" the following is typical: "One cannot, strictly speaking, arrive at any c. c. without turning round in circles" (p88). It is open to doubt whether the statements "The c. c. of what is true is B" and "Strictly speaking, I have to turn round in circles to arrive at the stated c. c." are both held as opinions by p88. We therefore group it under c).

In the groups c we also put ABf which the ps try to improve, restating them in new terms. In the most easily interpreted case, the p replaces the ABf (A) by a new (B) saying "A, or better (rather) B".

The relative frequency of these three groups of non-adequateness is shown in table 62,1.

Table 62,1. Relative frequency of groups of ABf, which are inadequate as pictures of opinions of the ps.

	Group a	Group b	Group c	Total
Number of inadequate ABf	12	7	30	49
Per cent of the ABf	4	2,3	10	16,3

The table shows that in the case of 251 or 83,7 per cent of the total number of ABf, we have no direct evidence thereof that they do *not* picture opinions adequately. This does not mean that they necessarily *are* opinions. Some of them may be mere "Einfälle". It is to be expected that an analogous analysis of professional truth-definitions would lead to the classification of a great percentage Af into group c. Among the comments of their own, are often found statements which weaken them.

Sect. 63. Do the ps Understand the q. c. c.? — The question "Do the q. c. c. have a meaning" is too vague and abstruse to answer. If I am asked in a restaurant in Oslo what is meant by the word "eplekake" and the inquirer is a stranger, I should defend the thesis that both the question and the word "eplekake" has a "meaning". From this very concrete case of a question of meaning down to the question about "the meaning of q. c. c." — the situation in which the expression functions left unmentioned —, a continuous scale of graduation may be constructed according to how complicated and badly-working the answers have to be, if *direct* answers are sought for. Before reaching the groups of questions as vague and abstruse as the discussed, the situation is already of the sort, where we do best to drop the "Fragestellung" and adopt others that allow less complicated and more handy answers. The endless philosophic discussion based on the habit not to allow other points of view than those favouring statements as abstract and general as possible, simply makes it a duty to avoid the *non-specified* question of "meaning". To this must be added that the whole monograph and, therefore, our whole questionnaire-technique is based on principles which exclude that we take up any position to the questions (1) if the q. c. c. have meanings and (2) what the (supposed) meanings are.

This being the situation, it is clear that we do not conceive the question about the understanding of the p as a question about the meaning they are able to give the q. c. c. We cannot allow ourselves to say that this or that is the meaning of a particular q. c. c. and that answers showing symptoms of apprehension of this meaning are brought by p "understanding" the q. c. c., others "misunderstanding" it or "lacking the understanding of it". Our "Fragestellung" has been: how are we to produce verbal reactions of the kind called opinions about the nature of truth or sometimes "theories of truth" in unsophisticated subjects? The q. c. c. is shown to be powerful — perhaps the most powerful and well working — stimuli drawing out such verbal reactions. Their form is suggested by the philosophical discussions themselves, what strengthens their relevancy for our purposes. Our criterion about "meaning of q. c. c." cannot, according to this situation, be any other than *the observable function (Leistung) of the q. c. c. in philosophic discussion.*

The problem is: How is the relation between the function of q. c. c. in philosophic literature and the function of these questions in the discussions of the amateurs? Are the ps e. g. able to assimulate the q. c. c. into behaviour-wholes of the sort observable in philosophic discussions? Such problems arise if the question "Do the ps understand the q. c. c.?" is more precisely formulated. We certainly cannot state that the professionals do not understand the q. c. c, but how may the statement that they do understand them be controlled? Only by describing how the philosophers "manipulate" these questions, what they write and say about them, how they try to make others believe that they have found the "solution" of them and so on. Now, if the ps are able to manipulate the q. c. c. in a way very similar to that of the philosophers, they may be said to have understood them.

This criterion is difficult to apply if stated as completly as possible, but it may be formulated so that we can easily arrive at some interesting conclusions of relatively high probability. This formulation is chosen with close attention to the purpose of our treatise and to the definitions already being used:

(1) A p has understood the q. c. c. if a formulation of the sort called "definition" or "criterion" of truth in philosophic literature is given as answer. If he reacts with an A-, B-, D-, F-, G-, or H-formulation, this condition is fulfilled. Some philosophers entertain opinions closely analogous to D- or F-formulations. Specimens of this sort may, for inst., be found in B. Russell's "Introduction to Mathematical Philosophy" and in the polemic of Pratt against pragmatism. It would therefore be misleading to include A and B, but not D- and F-formulations.

(2) A p has understood the q. c. c. if he does not react with an A-, B-, D-, F-, G- or H-formulation, but with comments on the q. c. c., for instance, on the position of the question, and if these comments are of a kind observable in philosophic literature. (By being "observable" in philosophy we mean that this kind of comment occurs so often that it must be referred to in moderately extensive descriptions of the truth-discussion.) "There is no c. c. of what is true", "Do you mean morally true things or rather mathematical truths. *Mathematically* true is — — —" are examples of such comments. Formulations aiming at a division of truths in compartments and followed by a characterization of truth in one of them, may be regarded as "comments" of philosophic bearing.[1]

---

[1] A person holding consistently the opinion that q. c. c. have no sense, no meaning, is classed under the "understanding" ones.

(3) A p has not understood a q. c. c. if he consistently states that he has not, or if his answers are unintelligible, or if his answers seem wholly out of place. (Answers of a type found among philosophers are used as a standard of evaluation.) The most common misapprehension of the q. c. c. consists therein, that "what is true (o. s. $+$ n)" is defined so as to include also "what is false (o. s. $\div$ n)", or conceived so narrow that only selected examples can be put forward as "examples of something true". If the p does not corrigate his formulations of this kind, i. e. when he holds them consistently, I think a lack of apprehension of the term c. c. is present. The p does not, in this case, "manipulate" the c. c.-term as do the philosophers, and the difference is systematical, not sporadical.

(4) The question if the p has understood q. c. c. is undecideable if the p consistently reacts with formulations belonging partly to group (1) or (2) and partly to group (3). By saying that he "consistently" reacts in this way, we mean to exclude the cases in which the conversation between l and p opens with grave symptoms of disorientedness, but ends with brilliant philosophic disquisitions on the part of the p.

A superficial glance in the protocols suffices to weaken the statement "No persons without any philosophic training (i. e. belonging to the ed. class 1, 2 or 3) are capable of understanding questions on the nature of truths". Closer inspection weakens it further. The same holds of the statement "All persons without any philosophic training, but showing no mental defects and being more than — say — 15 years understand the q. c. c." Trying to verify more differentiated statements on this matter, we meet great difficulties. It is e. g. very hard to distinguish grave disorientedness of the ps caused by the strangeness of the q. c. c. to the non-philosopher and incapacity to understand the q. c. c. Questionnaires opening with the question "What is the c. c. of that which is true" are, for inst., apt to throw the p into confusion. He will perhaps for a long time only react with statements very difficult to interpret and being "semi-nonsensical". P No. 79 whose status of confusion is illustrated in sect. 12 is a type that may cause the l to class ps understanding the q. c. c. — but only after a long conversation — among the clearly incapable ones. Perhaps some of the ps being classed as "incapable of understanding the q. c. c." would have shown the same behaviour as ps No. 79 if they were examined twice or three times as long. It should therefore be noted that the statistics of "not-understanding" ps, refer to ps examined for half an hour on an average. This does not make the statistics less interesting: Ps being examined for several hours are no more philosophically virgin and one could maintain that they are not representative of the typical non-philosopher.

14 or 9% of the ps do not understand the q. c. c. — according to the definition of this section. Other definitions of the understanding would imply other relative frequencies, but this does not weaken the results *when carefully interpreted.*

It should not be necessary to point out that the criterion of "understanding" adopted here is very superficial. The use of more satisfactory criteria would imply very extensive studies. To us it is enough to be able to state the following:

Normally, ps manipulate the q.c.c. very much in the same fashion as the philosophers, in so far as they arrive at formulations closely analogous to the central formulations of truth-theories and they can therefore be said to understand the questions. Exceptions are few in number if the ps are aged 13 or more. If someone holds that "real" understanding of the q.c.c. is lacking among the ps we shall ask him to answer the following two questions: (1) "Do the philosophers "really" understand the q.c.c.? If so, what is the criterion?" (2) "By which procedure do you want to discern "real" understanding from the kind of understanding discussed here?"

Sect. 64. The Aim and Scope of a List of A- and B-formulations (AFf1).

— In the introduction, we expressed that the first purpose of our monograph is to lead persons to react with statements analogous to what in philosophical literature is called "opinions on the truth-notion", "views of the nature of truth", or "theories of truth". Our plan proved to be realizable: By asking the test questions of the type called q.c.c., a large number of answers was collected, and embedded in them we discovered formulations of the kind found in the professional theories of truth. In chapter II we have analysed the contents of some of these formulations — the A- and B-formulation-roots — for their own sake, using a selection of them as a fair sample of our total material.

Our next purpose is to analyse the answers to the q.c.c. as verbalized behaviour-wholes. A- and B-formulation-roots have been treated as if they expressed answers to the *same* question, and as if they were all statements of the same thing. The standardization and generalization carried out in this way serve very definite statistical purposes. Detaching the formulations from their context, we gained some insight into their symptomatic value as indicator of the age and education of the ps and into the factors that conditioned the individual choice of answers. To obtain 300 ABf dealing with just the same subject (for instance "statements which are absolutely correct") it is reasonable to suppose that 300 ps would not be sufficient. Perhaps 1500 or 2500 would do, but it is in no way certain.

The professional truth-theories and especially those formulations of them which were used as prototypes of our so-called "A- and B-formulations" — the "definitions" — do not concern the same thing. A short glance at any list of professional A-formulations shows this. Examples: A. Aall defines "to be true and right" and "the opposite", Acton says "our belief is true when —", Aliotta speaks about "il criterio della validità obiettiva delle conosanza". Aristotle states what "falsehood is" and what "truth is", Agustinus defines "what is true", Ayer speaks about the term 'true' and 'false' " and their function etc., etc. Some philosophers speak about "what is called true" others about "what ought to be called true" and so on. In spite of the differences, these formulations are constantly referred to in philosophic discussion *as if* they were concerned with the same, i. e. an Af concerning "what has *been called true*" may be attacked from the view-point that it is incompatible with the Af of the critic, which happens to concern "what *is* true". If a philosopher states that the word "*correct*" ought to be used as his Af shows, another may reply that this usage cannot be formulated as this Af, etc. A philosopher may attack the definition of what "is *true*", saying that the adoption of the definition would cause many things to be called true which are not "*certain*". And this he does even if the definition does not identify that which "is true" with that which "is certain".

Most of the differences of subject-matter thus found in philosophic discussion, occur in the answers to the q. c. c. given by our ps and many others. They should consequently be analyzed as relevant features of these answers. But the types of "whole answers to a. c. c." include a manifold number of variables incomparably greater than that of the A- and B-formulations. An answer may concern the "c. c. of", the "essence of", the "definition of", the "criterion of" what is true. An answer may concern what "is", what "is called", what "ought to be called" true or with "the meaning of the word true". Further, an answer may concern what is true, false, correct, certain, adequate, wrong, erroneous or be concerned with the Truth. Some ps define absolute truth, others everyday, scientific, mathematical, historical, subjective, objective, truth. Finally, some speak about true judgment whereas others speak of true things, and some speak neither about true things nor about true judgment, but simply about truths. It would be rash to say that all statements "on the whole mean the same". In many cases the change of formulation is apparently carried out with such care, and some differences are lively commented upon. This holds good both as regards amateur, and as regards professional, theories of truth. Among professionals the following differences are often made the centre of acute disputes: "x is criterion of — —" and "x may be defined as — —", "x is true" and "x is called true", "x is true" and "one ought to call x true", ""truth-falsity" as a logical relation is —" and "in every-day life we call true — —", "subjective truth" and "objective truth", "metaphysical truth" and "empirical truth".

Do the differences in subject-matter condition differences in the contents of the Af? Do the ps on the whole define "absolute truth" otherwise than "truth", do they define "true statements" otherwise than "true things" etc.? In which cases are differences of subject-matter connected with differences of relative frequency of Gr1-groups? Are, for instance, Af containing the formulation-root "agreement with reality" (Gr1.1) considerably more frequent in answers dealing with "that which is absolutely true" than in answers dealing simply with "that which is true"? Which correlations (if any) obtain between frequency-distribution of Gr1-types of Afr and subject matter?

To carry out the analysis of whole answers to q. c. c. it was necessary to make a list of the individual ABf and their different characteristics. This list is 5 times as long as the ABfrl and cannot be reproduced in extenso. In the following section the classification of Af worked out in the list is described.[1]

The computations involved by the adopted method are simple, but require much time. It might be asked if results could not be obtained by easier methods. Actually, the ps offer the l much direct material with bearing on the differences of meaning between "*the* truth", "true statements", "right things" etc. A vocabulary and one's own "feeling" (Sprachgefühl) constitute another source of information. But these sources of information are deceptive. They give for instance no material with bearing on problems of this kind: (1) "A person A states: "I follow the rule r_1, using the expression "is true", the rule r_2 using the expression "is called true". (a) Does the person A use the rules r_1 and r_2? To what extent has the eventual use of the rules effects that can be established observing acts of speech?" (b) (If A is of the opinion that other people use or ought to use r_1 and r_2 as he himself does:) To what extent are the rules r_1 and r_2 obeyed?"" (2) A person A states: "The meaning of the expression "E_1", is M_1, and not M_2. The meaning of "E_2" is M_2 and not M_1". What differences of function — if any — can be observed by systematic observations of acts of speech including the use of E_1 and E_2? If investigations of this kind had been carried out on a sufficiently great scale, one would probably be in possession of accurate knowledge about (1) the value of rules as symptoms of actual functions of speech and (2) the value of statements on meanings (and differences of meanings) as symptoms of actual differences in function of the expressions, the meanings of which were intended. The work of philologists seems to indicate that the power to describe the functions of expressions is very limited and that rules are to a high degree deceptive as symptoms of actual speech. If this is the case one has to choose between three alternatives: (1) to rely upon the "Sprachgefühl" and take the statements on differences of meaning seriously as symptoms of difference of function or (2) to express one's doubt in "Sprachgefühl" and statements on meaning[2] and leave questions on function open; (3) to try by systematic observation and statistical analysis, to arrive at reliable statements on differences of function — however *incomplete* the results may be. This third alternative is adopted by us below. Considering the strong tendency to adopt (1) — it is apparent in all philosophical attacks on problems of speech and language — and the importance of the functional aspect of speech behaviour, we think that we are forced to adopt the third alternative.

---

[1] Complete typewritten copies of the ABfl may be obtained from the author together with complete statistical analysis of the different types of ABf.

[2] i. e. statements of meaning as they must be conceived to have any bearing on the problems at issue — not whatever statements on meaning as they occur, for instance, in translations (Tisch "*means*" table etc.).

Sect. 65. Classification of Fundamental Formulations. — In this section we will classify the answers to q. c. c. according to the subject they deal with. In practice, this means the complete contents of answers excepting the bare A- B- formulation-roots contained in them. If, e. g., a p answers "c. c. of what is called erroneous is its opposition to facts" (imaginary answer), "its opposition to facts" is a group of words of the type reproduced in the ABfrl, whereas all other words may be said to deal with the subject of the answer. Our aim is to classify the subjects indicated by these words.

If the ps' answers dealt with just the same subject as the question put, only such subjects would be found in the answers that are represented in the q. c. c. of our qts. Now, 15% of the answers are — at least verbally — concerned with other matters, or matters, which we *beforehand* cannot regard as identical. It is therefore necessary to construct classifying principles applicable to a greater variety of answers than preconceived in the questions.

Some answers concern "truth", others concern things or statements "known with certainty". Differences of this kind are, we will say, such of "S-expressions" to make use of a short word. We are below concerned only with S-expressions contained in the replies of the ps. We may therefore define those differences which are caused by a difference as regards S-expression thus: A difference is a difference of S-expression if (and only if) it coincides with a difference between two expressions of the "List of S-expressions". In this list each S-expression gets its two-figured number (yz).

List of S-expressions.

yz No.		yz No.	
11	true	44	know with certainty, know for certain
12	truth, the true		
13	the Truth, the truth	51	certain, (sure)
14	the truest	52	certainty
15	not true	61	false
21	right	71	wrong
23	true or right	81	erroneous
31	correct	82	not erroneous
41	know	87	opposite of error(s)
42	known	92	fact(s)
		96	opposite of fact(s)

When, below, we speak of "the notions true (a. s. n.)" we imply "true" and all the other expressions in the list. Similar abbreviations are mentioned on p. 7. The list enables us to say that *all individual answers to q. c. c. containing A- and B- formulations, concern one of the notions true (o. s. n.).*

To the notions true (a. s. n.) the ps often added a qualifying word. Some of these, e. g. "absolute", "subjective", are well known from philosophic discussions. There are professionals who do not give any definitions of what is true (o. so. s.), but only of, let us say, *subjective* truth. Expressions that serve to indicate the implied kind of truth (etc.) we shall refer to as "delimiting expressions". Not all delimiting expressions are relevant in this connection. Some of them, the "ethical" qualifications, are left out because answers containing them involve no A- or B-formulations. (Cf. the definition of A- and B-formulations, sect. 13). Others are considered unimportant and are therefore left out, e. g. "quite", "completely", "obvious", "immediate", "actual", "very". The remaining, delimiting, expressions all occurring in the q. c. c. of p 1—250 are reproduced in the following list.

List of delimiting expressions or wx-list.

wx No.	
11	absolute(ly), unconditional(ly)
12	relative, conditional
21	objective
22	subjective, personal
23	real, actual

As to the technique of reference, similar remarks may be made as in connection with the "list of S-expressions".

Differences of S-expressions and delimiting expressions constitute the most easily classifiable differences between the subject matters of individual answers. We shall now analyze some rather complex kinds of divergences. For this purpose it is expedient to introduce a sort of coordination system, a "prototype" answer in relation to which all subject matters may be defined. Consider the answer:

$$\underbrace{qr}\quad\underbrace{s}\quad\underbrace{tuv}\quad\underbrace{wx}\quad\underbrace{yz}$$
"The c.c. of *that which* is *absolutely* true is *comformity to laws of nature*".

The part of this answer written in italics indicates its subject matter. By systematic substitutions inside this part, all types of answers are easily defined. Any expressions of the S-list may be substituted for "true" and any expression of the wx-list may be substituted for "absolutely". (All answers concerned with "absolutely true" are characterized by yz. wx=11.11.) We then arrive at the expression "is". Considerable parts of the literature on the notion of truth deal with the difference between "what *is called* true and what *is* true or what *ought to be called true*. A philosopher finds, for instance, that the definitions of his opponents hold as regards *what is called* true but not as regards what *is* true. Another philosopher finds that there is no difference, a third that the whole discussion on the truth-notion is spoiled by the constant neglect of the difference etc. Similar standpoints are found among the amateurs. It is therefore of importance to study the *main* types of expressions substituted for "is" in the prototype. They are contained in the list of "tuv-expressions" or "modes":

List of modes or of tuv-expressions.

Tuv	
111	is(are)
117	should be
118	ought to be
119	must be
121	is called, one calls
124	may be called
128	ought to be called, one ought to call
134	may be said to be
211	to me is (is yz to me)
221	I call
241	I mean is

It is a very much discussed question whether truth is a characteristic of statements or of things, of both, or of none of them. Lively philosophic interest also exists in the question whether truth *ought to be defined* as a term expressing a relation between statements or between things etc. We shall accordingly pay attention to the formulations of the bearing on these points and differentiate between the following three classes of expressions reproduced in the "list of types". They are easily defined as expressions substitutable for the unspecified expression "that" of the prototype.

List of types or s-expressions.

s	
1	what, something, cases (unspecified)
2	things
3	statements, opinions, views, thoughts, beliefs, replies, convictions, words, notions, inferences, cognitions.

Finally, we arrive at expressions occurring instead of "the c. c. of" in the prototype-answer. The most important are reproduced in the following list.

List of expressions of defining or qr-list.

qr	
11	(the) common characteristic(s) of
12	the distinctive (distinguishing) feature of, the characteristic of
13	the criterion of, the criteria of
21	the difference between — — and — —, I (we, one) distinguish(es) — — from — —
31	the expression (word) — — means — —, by — — is meant (we mean etc.) — —, the expression — — is used when — —, by saying that — — we (I) mean — —, "— —" means (that) — —
41	definition of — — :

The subject matter of each answer may be defined giving the numbers yz. wz. tuv. s. qr. characteristic of it. They are "located" by the coordination-system represented by the prototype-answers. This answer itself receives the numbers 11.11.111.1.11

Example: q (question of the leader): describe the c. c. of what you call "true" or "right".

a (answer of the p): the c. c. is an agreement between something I have thought (beforehand or afterwards) and the result of observation.

Here yz. wx. tuv. s. must be 25.00.221.1. The expression "the c. c. is an agreement" we interprete as "The c. c. of what I call "true" or "right" is an agreement — — ", because a direct answer to the question is clearly intended. The whole answer is therefore characterized as follows

25.00.211.1.11.A.

Very few, 12 or 2,4 % of the answers to q. c. c. involving A- or B-formulations belong *directly* to the prototype of the form qr. s. tuv. wx. yz. A great many answers contain no delimiting expression ("absolute", relative" etc.). They belong to the prototype if the wx-place is left empty. Thus conceived, 207 or 41,6 % of the answers belong to the prototype. Many more answers are brought back to the prototype form leaving different places of it empty. "The expression (word) true means — —" for inst., is viewed as a qr. s. tuv. wx. yz-form leaving tuv. wx., undetermined. We will express this lack of modes and of delimiting expressions by putting "oo.oo" at the place of wx and yz; this order of the numbers is found convenient. The adjoined letter A further characterizes the answer, denoting that it is a direct answer to the question set; B denotes that the answer does not deal with just the same as the question, i. e. that there is a difference of yz- or wx- or any other type of expression.

As a matter of course, by establishing a set of conventional rules for classifying general statements of truth, we do not claim to set forth a method whereby every such statement may be grouped without ambiguity. If we invited 10 psychologists, explained our classification principles and 9 out of 10 of them classed at least 450 out of 500 in the same manner as we do (using the same rules), we would be satisfied with the rules. Taking the aim of the classification into account, it is not difficult to see that a decrease of ambiguity to such a degree that 470 out of 500 (94 per cent.) were classed identically would *not* imply the possibility of great corrections in our theses based on the classification. If we take 20 of 500 general statements and classify them in 10 different ways, all of which may be more or less tenable on account of the ambiguity of our classifying rules, we find that the probability of the rearrangements implying changes in our conclusions is very small. Now, it is practically certain that an increase of unambiguity of our rules corresponding to that mentioned above, would imply severe complications. The description of the rules would perhaps grow to twice the length. For very practical considerations we decide to leave the rules as they are: investigators studying greater fields and equipped with bulkier protocols will need more complicated and unambiguous rules; we do *not*.

Sect. 66. Quotations from the ABfl.

11.11.111.1.11.A

12,3 q: C.c. of what is absolutely true.
   a: No one will be able to change it.

11.11.111.1.00.A

46,4 q: Is there anything absolutely true?
   a: If it agrees with one's own feelings and sense impressions.

11.11.111.2.11.A

125,3 q: C.c. of things that are absolutely true.
   a: What cannot be otherwise.

11.11.000.3.00.B

93,3 q: You use the expression unconditionally true?
   a: Yes, what appears never to change.

21.00.111.1.11.B

36,2 q: C.c. of all things that are right.
   a: In practical life means what is right, what is expedient.

21.00.111.2.31.A

77,1 q: What is meant by saying that a thing is right?
   a: That is to say that no one can challenge it.

21.00.111.3.31.A

158 q: What is meant by saying that the statement is right?
   a: That the objects, people, or things about which one is speaking have the form, the qualities one attributes to them.

44.00.000.1.11.A

137,1 q: You mean, consequently, that nothing is common (to what one knows with certainty)?
   a: It might be that it appears to us as immediately obvious.

Sect. 67. The Subject-Matter of Fundamental Formulation Roots. —
In this section we shall deal with results of statistical computations concerning possible differences in frequency of Gr1-, Gr2-, Gr3-, and Gr4-types

of fundamental formulations due to differences as regards subject matter of these formulations. If, for instance, certain Gr1-groups of definitions occur rather as definitions of (the subject-matter) "true statements" than as definitions of "true things", the size of the individual Gr1-groups (i. e. the frequency of individual types of ABfr) will diverge systematically from the average (relative) size of the Gr1-groups obtained, taking all formulations into consideration. The average percentage deviation of the frequency distribution of a certain class of ABf (defined by their subject-matter) from the average percentage frequencies of each Gr1-group, is a sensitive measure of the importance of changes of subject-matter to the "contents of the definitions" (i. e. to the "ABfr"). Lack of space forbids us to describe the properties of the statistical material at length. Computation shows that the distribution of Af over the main Gr1, Gr2, Gr3, and Gr4-groups is closely similar for all S-expressions chosen. Exceptions are few (less than 10%) and occur generally in connection with groups with relatively few Af. The average percentual difference from the average frequency distribution is but c. 30. Correlations as regards number of Af in each group cannot be interpreted but as evidence of close but perhaps partial functional inter-relationship between the S-expressions. The expression "the Truth" constitutes the sole conspicuous exception. The average deviations from the mean relative frequency of the different groups (with more than 3 Af) is so small that one may state: *"very frequent types of Afr are very frequent among "definitions" of "true" as well as among "definitions" of "right", less frequent types of Afr are less frequent among "definitions" of "true" as well as among "definitions" of "right" etc. etc.* The few exceptions cannot change these statistical conclusions.

As regards wx-expressions, the correlation with average frequency-distribution is even greater than as regards S-expressions. — There are no systematical differences between tuv-expressions as far as can be judged from the Af frequency-distributions. Inspection of the ABfl and other parts of the protocols confirms this conclusion. Here as in other connections there are exceptions, being perhaps very interesting but without any value of their own as long as our aim is *a general survey*.

Sometimes the discussion between l and p leads to direct questions on the possible difference between "what is true" and "what is *called* true". The majority of ps putting forward opinions on this point declared that no "real" difference existed. What they meant by "real" in this connection may be obscure, but they were probably willing to say that the difference could not justly influence their answers on q.c.c. The same fluctuations of terminology are found among ps as among philosophers, except in numerically very few cases in which attention is deliberately fixed upon a difference of formulation. Summing up our impression we may conclude (cf. our initial statement of problem): *The ps behave as philosophers.*

It might be expected that "true (o. so. s.) *statements*" should be characterised systematically different from just "truths", "true things" or "true somethings". This expectation is not supported by our statistics. There *may* be systematical differences, but there is no evidence in support of it — whereas there is *some evidence in support of lack of systematical deviations*.

The study of possible differences due to different qr-expression was carried out mainly to verify our presumption that the choice of "common characteristic" as the most important qr-terminus was "neutral". By "neutral" we mean here the following: The choice of "common characteristic" is "neutral" if there is no evidence in favour of the view that answers to q.c. in cases of "c.c." being adopted, differ systematically and by a considerable amount from cases in which other qr-expressions are adopted. Computation supports the expectation that the desired "neutrality" exists: the average percentage deviation from average frequency-distribution is but c. 20. (More precise estimates are meaningless as long as space forbids us to describe exactly our method of computation.)

Sect. 68. Expressions Used as Synonyms. — From the behaviour of the ps one may in most cases safely infer that the answers classed as B-answers in the ABfl are put forward as answers to the question of the I. They are judged by the ps to be direct answers in spite of their change of expressions. This cannot but indicate a *marked functional interconnectedness of the expressions*. We analyse below some of the most frequent changes open to inspection in the ABfl. They are instructive and show the same character as the changes found in philosophic discussion.

Concentrating the ps' attention on possible difference between yz-notions, one may expect other results than if one merely notes the fluctuations in terminology: If it is asked "What is the difference between x and y?" etc., the p will have a tendency to emphazise some differences. Such differences are not, however, very important to the study of the function of yz-notions: our question is not whether there are differences in function, but just what inter-connections hold between various yz-notions. To this purpose direct questions as "Is there any difference between x and y?" are no more valuable or, perhaps, less valuable, than observations of acts of functional identifications.

The fluctuations in terminology support the expectation that the following yz-notions are functionally closely inter-connected: true, truth, right, correct, known, know, certain, known with certainty, certainty, fact. There is no evidence in favour of the assumption that the rest of the yz-notions are not equally closely inter-connected — with the exception of "the Truth". Of much more importance, however, are the conclusions as regards expressions not included in the yz-list (for instance "it is the case") but occurring as ABfr: a great deal of them occur as functional synonyms. The definitions of the ps may consequently to some extent be regarded as symptoms of actual speech-habits.

Most frequently, s-expressions (not to be confounded with S-expressions) are changed. If the question of the leader concerns "true *statements*" he may obtain answers concerning "true *things*". If the subject matter of the question is (indefinite) "truths" he may obtain answers concerning any of the s-expressions and so on. The assumption that "the" non-philosopher distinguishes (functionally) between truth as property of statement and truth as property of things, and that he favours the latter, seems therefore quite unsupported. The expressions "what", "that", "things", "statements", "words" etc., are used promiscuously whenever misconceptions are out of sight. Directly asked if "truth" is a property of this or that, it is noticeable, however, that the view according to which "truth" is primarily and properly a property of statements is represented (p. 66, age 16, for instance). The most frequent changes of yz-expression are from "right" to "true" and from "true" to "certain".

The exceedingly complicated picture of *functional* interconnectedness between yz-expressions, s-expressions etc., convince us that it is impossible to trace the "meanings" and "uses" of these terms by the method of introspection.

The statistics showing that *the distribution of types of definitions is approximately invariable to changes of subject-matter* (as long as the main s-expressions are considered) cannot *directly* be regarded as an argument in favour of *general functional* similarity between these expressions. The statistics show that in certain situations — situations characterized by the questions of the leader and the disposition of the p to answer — tend q.c.c. to call forth similar verbalized reactions of the p, i. e. similar "definitions". This means that these expressions are closely connected in the reaction-system of the p. But "functional identity" of the s-expressions require a special very far-reaching connectedness in this reaction-system. The required connection cannot be established without extensive direct observation of the use of the expressions *in systematically varied situations*. The not-statistically analyzed portions of the protocols — the whole discussions between l and p seem to support the view of extensive functional similarity — if not identity — between several s-expressions. The extensive occurrence of changes of expression, fluctuations of terminology of the p (as well as of the philosophers) is one of many arguments in favour of this view. To obtain exact knowledge about the possible functional relationships, we would, among other procedure, construct discussions. An example illustrating what is intended:

The ps are invited to discuss (for instance) whether Holberg is a Dane or a Norwegian. The l adopts the standpoint that he is a Dane and for each proof he puts forward, he concludes with a systematic variation of S-expressions and Af. Calling the proofs A, B, C etc., the concluding remarks of the l can be written thus: "A, consequently my standpoint is *true*", "B, consequently *it is so* that Holberg is a Dane, — —". Observing the reactions of the ps, it can be established which expressions are functional synonyms and to how great a percentage of ps.

If no accurate knowledge of the functional relationships is aimed at, the procedure would be much too complicated. There are much easier methods: meditations on the "meaning" of the terms, their "essence", "contents", "proper use", abstracted from every concrete application of them. A contemplative and introspective method is easily justified by the emphasis on the difference between *notions* ("Begriffe") and *terms*: "the use of this or that term does not indicate anything about the real meaning ("Bedeutung") of the *notions* which happen to be expressed by that *term*.[1] The latter is an invariant to casual acts of speech or even divergencies of definitions." But adopting this attitude towards the problems, they are left over to the mercy of vain and quasi-profound gymnastics with "essences". To the hundreds of theories of the "meaning of truth" other hundreds may by this method be added. Each generation and each ideologically independent group has its favourite general notions and categories which are used as banners. It is demanded that "all" problems are solved using them, and the "solution" of the "truth-problem" has consequently to be restated by each group. — Suppose that S-expressions other than those treated statistically in this monograph were taken into consideration, and tests of the kind illustrated above were carried out. To get an adequate picture of the functional interconnectedness thus obtained by means of an "operational behaviourism" — to use two favoured terms of today — we propose the following advice:

Denote 500 S-expressions $S_1, S_2, \ldots S_{500}$. Let a point in a plane be indicated by (x, y) using Cartesian coordinates. A one-to-one correspondance between pairs of S-expressions is established as follows: If the two S-expressions (S_i, S_j) are found to be functional synonyms in z_k per cent of cases this is represented by the point (i, j, k) in the three dimensional space. The functional interconnectedness of all 500 S-expressions may be represented by a surface on which all such points are located. The verbal behaviour-units indicated by uniform habits using S-expressions are pictured by the large number of points in the above mentioned surface with a distance from the xy-plane approximating 100. By suitable rearrangements of the order of S-expressions, one may obtain surfaces which indicate more ele-

---

[1] The introspective and deductive method has been "rationalized" by the adoption of extremely "intellectualistic" views on speech and language. We have in the monograph "Erkenntnis und wissenschaftliches Verhalten" § 28 ff tried to point out that theoreticians of knowledge, and logicians, have had a tendency to stick to the views on speech and language which were common in former centuries. The functional attitude of modern philologists has not as yet made much impression on those who deal with language from a "philosophic" point of view.

gantly the degree of tightness with which any collection of S-expressions is knitted functionally together.

No doubt the study of functional synonymity between S-expressions will always remain incomplete. The effort to sharpen the expressions indicating weight of statements cannot be supposed to yield any results, however, without such studies. Some S-expressions must be picked out and their use standardized by means of simple rules. The majority of the expressions have to be discarded.

The number of different Gr1-types of elementary Afr may serve as a symptom of the *variability of functionally interconnected S-expressions*. According to our statistical data, the ratio of decrease of new types of Afr with increasing number of ps is surprisingly small. For every 15,4 elementary Afr (on an average), 10 belong to different Gr1-groups. Counting the number of elementary Afr which must be collected to obtain Afr of 20 different Gr1-groups, one arrives at a surprisingly small number, namely 32,7 (on an average). To obtain x different Gr1-groups ($10 < x < 110$), less than $(x/10)^3 + x + 9$ elementary Afr are needed.

It is a great goal of scientific methodology to standardize the use of S-expressions. As yet almost nothing positively is done: the logic of the manuals only deals with "true", "false" and occasionally some few others. In modern logic a greater number of S-expressions, for instance, "probable" have been subjected to profound analysis; but of a rather formal character. References to actual function of these expressions are generally as inadequate as those found in the philosophic discussion on the notion of truth. The same can be said about references to the standardized use, in cases in which the text is not written according to a formalized scheme of language. No systematical observations how S-expressions function in science have been carried out. It is of great importance to the development of a realistic, non-formal attitude towards the problems relating to "weight of statements" that the actual, very complex situation inside science is realized and the consequences drawn. Ostwald, to take an instance, uses S-expressions 480 times in his discussion of atomic weights. (Cf. his "Grundriss d. allg. Chemie", 5. Aufl. p. 140—166). Of these expressions, about 100 are different.[1] Ostwald discusses every element apart and concludes each time by the adoption of a certain value as the "best" value indicating its atomic weight. It may be safely assumed that most of these concluding statements fulfil the same achievement, i. e. that they are intended functionally to be synonyms. In spite of this, the most various S-expressions are chosen to indicate the weight of the conclusions: "besonders *zuverlässig*", "die *richtige* Zahl",

---

[1] We operate here with the broader definition of the term "S-expression". It denotes the expressions of the "list of S-expressions" of sect. 65 and expressions, which presumably are highly functionally interconnected with these. The term "expressions indicating the weight of statements and estimates" may serve as a good name for most of them.

"mit großer *Sicherheit* zu *setzen*", "der *wirkliche Wert*", "wir *setzen* Pd 106,7" etc. etc. It is apparent that the requirements of style are often considered more important than the consistent use of S-expressions. Whether a man uses this or that expression to denote the weight of a statement is in the main judged to be irrelevant. S-expressions are thus even in the exact sciences bad symptoms of weight-evaluations. Further development of scientific speech habits will change this situation.

Sect 69. Frequency of the Different Standpoints towards Absolutes. — Are there absolute truths, someth ingone can trust perfectly, something that holds good in all conceivable cases, something unconditionally certain? The simple question on "absolutes" (i. e. on absolute true statements, absolute certainty etc.) in our qts, causes the ps almost immediately to take up a great range of problems of the kind just indicated. The main positions of philosophers as regards these problems are all refound among the amateurs.

Earnest classification of the ps' standpoints towards absolute must be carried out, several points of view being adopted. From each point of view the standpoints fall into separate groups. Lack of space forbids us to carry out more than two classifications. The first, — the Gar-classification — leads to 5 main types of standpoints and 18 smaller groups defined by combinations of the 5 main groups.

Ga1.1. This group comprises the most frequent standpoint among professionals as well as amateurs: "belief in the existence of something absolute". Persons stating that there is something absolute or that they call something absolute, and giving at least one example of this.

Group Ga1.1. also comprises persons who give examples of something absolutely true (o. so. s.) without definitely expressing that they think something of this kind *exists*.

Ga1.2. includes persons who explicitly accept the existence of absolutes but do not give any examples at all. They either ignore the requests for examples or refuse to answer them unambiguously, or they say that it is difficult, practically impossible, or theoretically impossible, to find examples.

Ga1.3. includes persons who deny the existence of absolutes. Their denial may be in the form of a positive statement: "There is nothing absolutely true (o. so. s.)". Such a statement is regarded as a necessary, as well as a sufficient, proof that they belong to Ga1.3. Persons who accept the statement "there is nothing absolutely true (o. so. s.)" as absolutely true are accordingly grouped together in Ga1.3.

Ga1.4 comprises persons accepting the existence of absolutes, but only with certain reservations. The reservations may take the form of (1) explicitly stated conditions, or (2), attempts to weaken the "mode" (cf. sect. 65) of the question put. Examples of the first alternative: "*If* 'absolutely true' means what all agree on', then something is absolutely true"; "*in practice* much is absolutely true, but I do not pretend to know if these things are also theoretically true". Examples of the second alternative: 1: "*Is there something absolutely true?*" p: "It is absolutely true *to me* that — — —" or p: "People call absolutely true what — —".

Ga1.5 comprises persons refusing to take a specified view of the problem of the existence of something absolutely true (o. so. s.) or of any other questions about "absolutes". These persons state the reason for their refusal by saying that this is impossible to know, or that it is impossible to answer the question at issue or that the question is meaningless.

Ga1.6 comprises persons that first adopt a view justifying us in arranging them in the group (Ga1.1., but being further examined they leave their standpoint and take the specified view of Ga1.3. They may be said to "become sceptics", this being formulated below thus: "Ga1.1→3".)

All the remaining standpoints are defined in a way corresponding to Gr1.6. The frequency of the different views are shown by Table 69.1.

Table 69.1. *Size of the different Ga1-groups.*

Ga. No.	Ps.	Per cent ps.	Ga. No.	Ps.	Per cent ps.	Ga. No.	Ps.	Per cent ps.
1	80	54.4	Gal. 1→3	3	2.0	Gal. 5→2	1	0.7
2	17	11.6	Gal. 1→4	2	1.4	Gal. 4→1	1	0.7
3	23	15.6	Gal. 1→5	1	0.7	Gal. 4→3	1	0.7
4	10	6.8	Gal. 2→3	1	0.7	Gal 3→1	3	2.0
5	2	1.4				the rest	0	0.0

The second grouping-principle — Ga2 — is closely connected with Ga1. In Ga2.1 we place all persons in Ga1.2 *and* persons arriving at specified views belonging to these groups after first having held other opinions. Ps. belong to Ga2.1, for instance, if they initially think that nothing is absolutely true, but ultimately find that "the earth is round" fulfils the conditions required. In Ga2.2 we place persons who think that "there is nothing absolutely true" as well as persons who think this statement is the only one which is absolutely true. In Ga2.2 ps are placed who belong to Ga1.3 or adopt Ga1.3 as their ultimate opinion. Persons, whose standpoint towards the existence of absolutes is known, but who cannot be placed in Ga2.1 or Ga2.1, are put in Ga2.3.

Table 69.2. *Size of the Ga2-groups.*

Ga2. No.	Ps.	Per cent ps.
1	103	70.1
2	29	19.3
3	15	10.2

According to the tabulated values, one may with great confidence entertain the opinion that *belief in "absolute" is much more frequent than disbelief*. Not all ps are, however, willing to give an example of something absolute. — Only two ps think the question of the existence of absolutes to be "meaningless", and of these two, the former originally adhered to the standpoint that there are absolutes.

It might be expected that ps who drop their first standpoints adopted and then entertain a new opinion on the existence of absolutes, would change their view according to simple laws. The examination-technique did not favour any regularity, however. If a p first declared that there is nothing "absolute", the l tested the deepness of his conviction by asking, for instance, "Not even mathematical statements?". If, on the other hand, he declared this or that to be absolutely true, the l systematically asked for "reasons". This was often interpreted as "scepticism" of the l, and it was thus indirectly suggested to the p to drop his example. *If he did drop it, the technique was reversed.* In cases of prolonged discussion *there was a tendency of the ps to adopt a certain standpoint as the ultimate one.* Personally, I expected that it would turn out easier to a p to drop the belief in absolutes than to adopt it after first having doubted or denied the existence of anything absolute. Actually, the same number of ps dropped Ga1.1 and adopted Ga1.3 as the number which dropped Gal. 3 and adopted Ga1.1. This means, that of the ps believing in absolutes, a smaller percentage radically changes its view than of the ps denying the existence of anything absolute.

Interpreting the numerical values of table 69.1 and 69.2 it should be remembered that only explicitly and thoroughly stated views are represented in the statistics. Some ps seemed to oscillate between several views to none of which they adhered long enough to express themselves clearly.

The main standpoints towards absolutes occurring in philosophic literature are — as already mentioned — refound among the ps. Attention deserves to be called to the following refound standpoints:

(a) There is no difference between truths and absolute truths. Something is either a truth or it is not a truth. There are no degress.

(b) There is a difference between truths, some being absolute, others being not-absolutes. (Absolute, relative, unconditioned, conditioned, timeless, changing with time, mathematical, physical, ultimate, etc., are all expressions used by the ps.) Truth is susceptible to degrees. Something is more or less true.

(c) Truth is relative in the sense of changing with time.

(d) The conceptions of the notion of truth is changing with time.

(e) Something is true independent of all relations to human beings.

(f) "Absolute truths" is a religious expression. It has to do with faith, not with knowledge.

(g) One ought not to use the expression "absolutely".

(h) All truths are created by man. So far they are absolute: they are absolute as conceived by man.

(i) Only postulated truths or truths created by man are absolute.

(j) Nothing is absolutely true except that there is no absolute truth.

(k) Nothing is absolutely true, even not the statement "there is nothing absolutely true".

(l) One cannot know whether there is any absolute truth or not.

(m) There is but one kind of absolute truth: the mathematical.

Sect. 70. Standpoints towards Different Types of Absolutes. Until now we have not distinguished between the belief in the existence of something absolutely *true* and belief in something absolutely *right* etc. This we have done, because we expect that most persons holding that there are absolutely truths also hold that there is something absolutely right, something absolutely certain, etc. The most direct way to test the correlation between beliefs in various absolutes is to ask the p direct. This method was seldom used (for technical reasons). One may, however, test the correlation indirectly by computing the relative frequency of Ga2-groups in relation to type of absolutes. It is found that the belief in the existence of an absolute Truth is much less frequent than the belief in other types of absolutes (absolutely true statements, something absolutely certain, for instance). Neglecting the S-expression "the Truth" and the more rare ones, we find that the frequency distributions of standpoints towards absolutes is closely similar whatever yz-notion is chosen. The average deviation from the mean percentage frequency of the different standpoints is but 6.5 %.

There is some evidence in favour of the reality of the high deviations which characterize the yz-expression "the Truth". We conjecture that mainly one factor is here operating to give such results: "an absolute Truth" is an expression very often found in religious and ethical literature and the question "Do you think that there exists an absolute Truth? is consequently regarded as a question about religious and ethical convictions. "Something absolutely true", on the other hand, is an expression which is found in all sorts of discussions and is therefore *less* intimately bound up with any special ideology. There may consequently be a certain percentage of ps willing to admit the existence of something absolute, but is checked by the expression "an absolute Truth". The substantiation seems in this case as in so many others to have a distinctive ideological relevancy.

Sect. 71. Standpoints towards Absolutes, Correlations with Age, Education. — The tables 71,1 and 71,2 give evidence of the close correlation between belief in absolutes and age and education in spite of the small number of ps in each class.

Table 71.1. Relation between Ga1-groups and age.

Ga1 No.	Number of p Age cl. 1	Per cent	Age cl. 2	Per cent	Age cl. 3	Per cent	Age cl. 4	Per cent
1	7	63.6	28	63.6	38	53.5	7	33.3
2	2	18.2	5	11.4	7	9.9	3	14.3
3	0	0.0	5	11.4	12	16.9	6	28.6
4	0	0.0	3	6.8	4	5.6	3	14.3
5	0	0.0	2	2.3	0	0.0	0	0.0

Table 71.2. Relation between Ga1-groups and education.

Ga1 No.	Number of p Ed. cl. 1	Per cent	Ed. cl. 2	Per cent	Ed. cl. 3	Per cent	Ed. cl. 4	Per cent	Ed. cl. 5	Per cent
1	10	66.7	34	66.7	14	58.3	21	38.2	1	50.0
2	3	20.0	4	7.8	2	8.3	8	14.5	0	0.0
3	0	0.0	6	11.8	3	12.5	13	23.6	1	50.0
4	0	0.0	3	5.9	5	20.8	2	3.6	0	0.0
5	0	0.0	2	1.9	0	0.0	0	0.0	0	0.0

Ps of low age and education classes show a strong tendency to believe in absolutes. This correlation belongs to the most certain of our statistically obtained results. There may also be a tendency of the less aged and educated to avoid other answers to the questions on the existence of absolutes than "yes" and "no". With 4 exceptions, all ps of age or education class 1 answer "yes", i. e. they believe in the existence of something absolute, and with 2 exceptions all of them either consistently answer "yes" or "no". The effect of age and education seems to be quite of the same order and direction. In our tables this is enhanced, however, because of the relatively small number of ps of class 3 and 4 with education 1 or 2. The correlation between the effects of age and education is probably real, but less marked than indicated above.

Here as otherwise, our statements on the effects of age are only meant to be valid for persons aged 13 or more. It may be expected that as soon as a person arrives at the stage of development at which he takes the questions on absolutes into consideration, or at which he is capable of discussion on these questions, he then favours the belief in those absolutes.

About half of all ps can be expected to entertain the opinion that the question of the existence of absolutes coincides with those on the existence of something true (o. so. s.) There is in the majority of cases no question as to the value of the standpoints as expressions of actually held opinions. But just the expressions "absolute", "unconditional" etc. of the formulations on absolutes, condition an increased variability with various factors as age, education, milieu, time, religious confessions etc. Factors as nationality, type of government, may indirectly play a rôle, and family constellations a direct role. An elucidation of the genesis of the standpoints towards absolutes, would require a psychoanalysis of the ps. With less direct material almost nothing can be said of this genesis. We think it worth while, however, to indicate some difficulties connected with the interpretation of a belief or disbelief in absolute truths. Our aim is thereby only to call attention to the essential ambiguity of "abstract" views in the following respect: *One and the same standpoint may serve as a symptom of diametrically opposite traits of the emotional reaction-system of different ps.*

It is a commonplace in psychology to view the tendency to participate in strong beliefs as a function of age and education. As long as one refers to actual discussions carried out by the persons and does not include "implicit" beliefs (beliefs said to be adhered to if a definite non-verbal behaviour is manifested), we think that our statistics support this view. The elder or more educated ps are (in discussions) "sceptical" compared with the younger or less educated. But the views *discussed* are but a small fraction of all statements made by the ps and the scepticism subjected to statistical analysis is primarily one of expression — one of "style". As soon as one tries to interpret the scepticism as deep-rooted tendencies of the reaction-system of their adherents, a host of difficulties appear. These cannot be overcome without further analyses and increased material.

Suppose, for instance, that we arrive at the following conclusion: Persons of age 15 to 18 are more liable to be convinced of something than persons of age 30 to 40. Very superficial inspection of this statement reveals its extreme vagueness. It seems reasonable to us to expect that a large percentage of beliefs adhered to by a person of 15, is doubted at the age of 40. But the tendency to feel more sceptical at 40 may only picture the tendency to retrospection: one does not count with beliefs *actually* held: They are rather felt as "facts" than as "beliefs". As the rate of change of beliefs probably decreases after 40, there are less people who look (retrospectively) at their beliefs held at 40 with general scepticism. This may particularly be the case if certain beliefs, beliefs in ideologies, religious, metaphysical, or political, are emphazised. To this comes the important change in technique of controversy, probably going on as age and education increase. The types of expressions are modified, old types of expressions obtain modified functions. We do not pretend to *know* anything about these factors. It is important to us only to warn against "interesting" theories in these fields. They are necessarily over-simplifications caused by lack of serious observations.

Scepticism as an attitude towards verbally expressed beliefs may be a superficial reaction towards very definite events which may be completely unmentioned by the adherent of sceptism at the time when occupied with a justification of his attitude. The justification may be of a highly differentiated and esteemed type, for instance, a justification by means of arguments touching different groups of statements all of which by suitable choice of viewpoints are proved to support the sceptical attitude. Philosophic doctrines of scepticisms are the best instances of such justification. There are also valuable instances among the protocols of our ps, but they alone do not, to any appreciable degree, support the view that the factors held as causes of the attitude by its adherents, are actually found to be causes on closer investigation. In most cases there is not the slightest reason to expect that the "insight" in this or that property of beliefs caused a person to adopt scepticism and not any other standpoint towards the subject. It may be just the reverse: The p may find himself already accepting scepticism and proceeds to justify it. The *motives invoked* by the p taking his beliefs into consideration may be a function of age and education, whereas *the nucleus of the sceptical doctrine, the disbelief in absolutes, is retained unchanged*. Scepticism of this sort is general enough to be viewed from several different points of view. It can be interpreted in sufficient contradictory ways to turn almost anything into an argument in favour of or against the doctrine.

We emphazize that our last statements are but conjectures. It is in no way our pretention that data reproduced in this work support them to any appreciable degree. Our aim is to call attention to all the open questions in the field under investigation. Almost nothing has been done as yet. Our ps do not give sufficient material towards answering any of the current problems on the psychology of scepticism and on the genesis of abstract doctrines in general.

Sect. 72. Standpoints towards Absolutes and Sex. — Correlation with 132 ps of the group who answered questions on absolutes, adhere either to Ga2.1 or Ga2.2. 72.5% of the masculine and 86.5% of the feminine ps adhere to Ga2.1. 27.5% of the masculine and 13.5% of the feminine adhere to Ga2.2. This indicates that feminine persons have a greater tendency to believe in absolutes than masculine. Taking the statistical properties of the material into account, we arrive at the conclusion that the correlation between sex and Ga2-groups is probably *real*.

Sect. 73. Standpoint towards Absolutes. Gr1-groups. — Reading philosophic discussions on the notion of truth, one gets into the habit of expecting advocates of this or that type of definition to adhere to belief in absolute truth, whereas advocates of a different type of definition is expected to doubt or deny the existence of absolutes. Statistical investigations support the assumption that there are correlations between types of "fundamental formulations" and the author's standpoint towards the existence of absolutes. Unfortunately, the number of our ps is not 5000, but only about 300. Detailed statistical analysis of possible correlations between types of fundamental formulations and standpoints towards absolutes is, therefore, out of our reach. Some groups of closely similar formulations are, however, large enough to throw some light on possible correlations.

Computing the values for 28 groups, it appears that the individual deviations of percentage fr.p. for Ga2. 1 and Ga2. 2 from the mean are much greater than could be expected with some reason on account of the small number of items in each group. Consequently it is to be expected that some of the deviations express real correlations between Af groups and standpoint towards absolutes. Before entering the detailed exposition of these possible correlations, we would draw attention to some conclusions with can be made without further argument:

There is no evidence in support of the assumption that ps by "logical necessity" combine certain definitions of truth (o. so. s.) with a certain view of the existence of absolutes. There are ps explicitly adhering to the opinion that a certain definition, implies, if adopted, the existence of absolute truths, and one may expect many others to entertain analogous opinions if they are asked about the matter. But the number of groups of Af containing members associated with positive, *as well as* members associated with negative, standpoints towards the existence of absolutes is so great, that itwould be quite gratuitous to invoke "logics" or "reason" to explain the correlation between Af-groups and Ga-groups. One *might feel inclined* to add that the ps have not considered the "truth-problems" long enough to feel the necessity of combining certain definitions of truth with the standpoint Ga2. 1 and certain others with Ga2. 2 — the ps have not the qualities one may expect from the real "connoisseur". They are dilettantes and their opinions are dilettantic, capricious and not bound to the logic of the material they deal with. We do *not* add this for the sole reason that it would imply a group of people that makes the impression not to be "dilettantic" (*in the sense in which the ps could be said to be so on account of the contents of the protocols*) in their truth-theories. No group of professionals makes that impression. Taking the fundamental vagueness and ambiguity of the statement "there is an absolute truth" etc., into account, it seems reasonable to expect that philosophers choose their standpoints on alogical grounds.

Ps adhering to Gr1. 1 all believe in the existence of something absolutely true (o. so. s.). This means that one may with a relatively high degree of certainty forecast a tendency to combine Gr1. 1 with Ga2. 1 rather than Gr1. 1 and Ga2. 2. We anticipate that professionals adhering to Gr1. 1 also show a marked tendency to prefer Ga2. 1 (belief in absolute truth). The combination Gr1. 11 and Ga2. 1 may (with about the same degree of certainty) hold. There are many other correlations which probably are real, but lack of space forbids us taking them into consideration. It is of some importance to note how extremely difficult it is to forecast whether a p holding the view v, as regards existence of absolute, tends to believe in a special group g of definitions of truth. There is no room for profound deductions in these complicated matters.

Sect. 74. The Confidence-Test. — Introduction. — How can the contents of amateur-theories on the notion of truth be forecast? This great problem can be attacked from various points of view. Until now, we have studied some statistical relations holding (1) between certain features of the theories and (2) between these features and age, education, sex of their authors. These relations can be used to forecast properties of the truth theories if we decide to include new ps in our material together with other relations, which we have not dealt with statistically, but which can be expected from general psychological principles or from our every-day knowledge. It is, for instance, to be expected that difficult words as "transcendency" will not occur in Af put forward by test persons of age class 1. In the following sections we discuss some very difficult questions which cannot be treated adequately without much experimental work. What we have done is only an experiment "pour voir" — nothing more.

People are more or less *confident* as regards their own faculty to comprehend and judge things. If two test persons are requested to solve a problem, they will comment on the possibility of this, some claiming that they cannot, others that they are sceptical as regards their capacity, whereas others think it overwhelmingly easy. People are also more or less *confident* when requested to decide whether something is true or not. Some people think that it is absolutely certain that two multiplied by two gives four, some think that it is open to doubt, others think that it certainly is *not* true. (Only one of our 300 ps thinks so). Some ps mistrust *all* statements, claiming that no statement is perfectly certain. Of these sceptics, some are very confident as regards the non-existence of perfectly certain things. Of the ps claiming that there does exist something worthy of full confidence in as much as it is "perfectly certain" some are not very confident that what they say is right, i. e. they actually are not very confident in making their judgment. *Are there any marked correlations between important features of the amateur-theories and different kinds of confidence characteristic of the test-persons?* If we were to try to measure confidence or to classify test persons in *more or less* confident test-persons, and compare the results with the adopted type or truth-theory, we would have to distinguish between many kinds of confidence. We do not expect that a person tested would be very confident in the sense A would be very confident in the sense B. If our work were one belonging to the psychology of character, the question as to correlations between the results of various tests would be very important. Out work does not, however, belong to the psychology of character any more than it belongs to any other psychological branch. Below, we call a test "a test of confidence": but what is tested by the experiment performed, will be carefully discussed without presuming that there is a unique relation between our "operational" concept of confidence as pictured by our experimental conditions, and the concept of confidence as used by psychologists or by "the" lay man. We could equally well have called our test "test of x" or "test of dogmatism with which certain persons entertain opinions as regards odours". It is to be hoped that psychologists will carry out other tests analogous to ours and measure the correlations of the results. Only after a long series of observations will it be worth while to consider *to which degree* the obtained values are symptomatic of of the person tested. To us only one relation is of direct interest in this connection: correlations between the type of truth-theory adopted and opinions entertained under the experimental conditions now to be described:

Sect. 75. Description of apparatus: 12 test-tubes placed in a holder are filled with distilled water with the exception of three containing strong solutions of (respectively) pineapple ether, wintergreen oil and peppermint oil. — Introduction to experiment: A test-person is confronted with the test-tubes and the l says: "Here you have some test-tubes with solutions of different spirits". After this the test-tubes are placed in such a way that they are unobservable to the test-person. Experiment: The leader takes the first test-tube saying "This is a strong solution of pineapple ether" and hands it to the test-person, who is allowed to smell but not longer than 15—20 seconds. The l. then takes the test-tubes with wintergreen oil and peppermint oil, behaving in the same manner and informing the test-person of the actual contents. l: Now you will get 5 test-tubes with weak solutions of the three spirits you already have smelt. (the l hands a test-tube filled with distilled water to the test-person). l: Do you smell anything? (The p is allowed to smell for 10 seconds if he wants to smell so long). l: If you smell something write "yes" here on this paper. (A form is explained to the p.) If the p "smells nothing", he is requested to write "no". If he answers yes: l: How sure are you that you smell something? Write it down here using your own words or these expressions. (The l gives the test-person a slip of paper containing a series of expressions like "perfectly sure", "tolerably sure" etc. etc.). (If the p claims to have smelt something) l: What do you smell? — — l: How sure are you that this is what you smell? (The p is requested to write it down using his own words or some expression on the list. The l takes the next test-tube, the second, said to be a weak solution, and proceeds as in the previous case. After the 5. test-tube: l: Now you will get 5 test-tubes with weak solution of pineapple ether, wintergreen oil and peppermint oil or with clean water. Do you smell anything? — The leader hands successively to the p, 5 test-tubes containing distilled water. The same questions are put as in the former cases. After the 5. test-tube: l: Finally, you will get 5 test-tubes with weak solutions of pineapple, wintergreen or peppermint. (The same procedure, test-tubes with distilled water are used as in the fôrmer cases).

60 persons performed the test, 56 under satisfactory circumstances. The results were worked out as follows:

Sect. 76. The Q and C. — The so-called tests of suggestibility are carried out in such a way that the difference in confidence expressed by the test-persons is not taken into account. One person may think "perhaps I may state that this smells, perhaps not: there may be many circumstances which work against a reliable judgment in this case" and then he decides to answer that he smells something. Another person thinks it evident that he smells something quite distinctly. He answers the same as the first person. Both get the same index of suggestibility. Whatever can be said to be measured by the so-called suggestibility-tests, we think it desirable to try to take *the confidence of the ps in their own judgment* into account. We do this by correlating confidence-points (cp) to the answers to the question "How sure are you?" As a standard, the answers of the list of expressions mentioned above was used. "Perfectly sure" implied 100 cp, "Rather sure" 50 cp etc.

Other answers — rather few in number — were estimated so as to agree with this standard. We call the average amount of cp per test-tube (i. e. per answer of a specific kind) Na, if only affirmative answers to the question "Do you smell something", Nb if only affirmative answers to the question "What do you smell?" are taken into account. The sum $Na + 2Nb$ we call Q (a sort of *weighted* percentage cases of suggestibility). Q can theoretically vary from 0 to 200 and so it also does in connection with our 56 ps. The average Na is 59 and the average Nb 42. From the difference it may be inferred that there is an tendency to be less sure in cases of requests to state *what* one smells — but that the average degree of certainty is in both cases of the same order, ranging from "not quite sure" to "rather sure".

As a measure of confidence — or "brute" confidence, disregarding the difference between expressed certainty of affirmative and of denying answers, we use the arithmetical average number of cp per answer (C). This quantity ranges (in theory as well as in practice) from 0 to 100.

Sect. 77. Q, C and Standpoints towards Absolutes. — Our account of the "confidence test" is placed in close connection with our statistics on the standpoints towards absolutes as we have expected that the statistically obtained relation between "confidence" and "belief in absolutes" should throw some light on the problem "theory versus practice" as it appears in connection with philosophic opinions. Can the theory of a p be forecast from his general behaviour? Are philosophic opinions symptomatic of this behaviour?

At the first moment one expects the "sceptically minded" persons to be the most reserved in stating their conclusions in problem-solving tests as well as so-called "tests of suggestibility". One expects at least a tendency to evade expressions of great confidence and to comment on the experimental conditions. Carrying out the test described in sect. 75 and similar tests, left unmentioned on account on the small number of ps tested, one is, however, constantly reminded of the great variety of factors probably influencing the choice of expressions as well as the choice of "no" or "yes". We shall pay attention to some of these factors.

Sceptical ps are more frequent among the philosophically interested than among the uninterested. The choice of a sceptical sounding manner of speech seems to be a symptom of a predisposition to relatively high interest in questions of the type found in our questionnaires. After having answered the questionnaires, our sceptical ps were confronted with the experimental test above described. They knew that the test served the same inquiry as the questionnaires. Some of their interest, and some of the positive "Übertragung" towards the leader (as a leader of the test) was naturally transferred into the new situation. But a sympathetic attitude as well as ambition favours positive answers to the question of the l. Just the ps consistently answering *negatively* and with the greatest amount of reservations become the smallest Q and C. It is to be expected that many of the test-persons with a small Q have distrusted the honesty of the information of the l. The possibility that all tubes contained water has probably had some influence on their attitude. But a positive "Übertragung" towards the l tends to minimize distrust and favour a straight-forward interpretation of the test. Q and C therefore "measure" to some extent the confidence towards the leader — persons with greatest Q (perhaps also persons with greatest C) being the most confident. Q and C also "measure" the ambition, willingness to be a *good* test-person, willingness to include the l among the authorities deserving some obedience and to include the test among the activities deserving respect. — In some cases the influence of a negative attitude towards testing was very apparent: The ps had to be persuaded to sit down and give up their work in order to take part in activities they looked upon with obvious unwillingness. As an outlet of such an attitude, the reserved answers as well as the confident negative answers are perfectly common symptoms. Persons looking at the *test* with good-will and confidence are consequently more likely be classified as "non-sceptics" — in spite of the circumstance that their good-will is a direct symptom of sceptical attitudes in other situations.

With these difficulties in mind, we are not inclined to draw any conclusions as regards possible connections between Q and the general behaviour of our ps. Correlating belief (and disbelief, resp.) in absolutes with the average size of Q, we find very striking values, however. No one sceptical towards the existence of absolutes has a Q greater than the average. This means that *there is a positive correlation between belief in absolutes and suggestibility-confidence as defined operationally by the quantity Q*: ps doubting or denying the existence of absolute truth (o. so. s.) tend to obtain small Q, i. e. he avoids statements expressing great certainty in cases of problematic situations of a definite type. Similarly, the adherents of absolute truths congregate in the upper regions of the confidence scale. They are, however, more widely scattered than sceptics. What one at the first moment expects — perhaps for perfectly untenable reasons — is supported by the statistical analysis. We think the number of ps tested is sufficient to justify the view that this *general tendency* of the variations of Q are "*real*": We may expect that a tenfold group of tested ps would obtain Q's obeying the same (statistical) law of variation, and we may expect this with a certainty great enough to be of a practical significance.

The relatively great dispersion of the individual Q's is of a kind indicating that there are many "exceptions", and that a doubling of the statistical population is desirable. (We do not mean that there are exceptions to the statistical law just formulated: the concept of "exception" has no meaning in connection with statistical laws. We mean that the expectability of verification of the (non-statistical) statement "Ps adhering to Ga2.2 have a P smaller than a" in individual cases is not much greater than 0,5).

We have called our experimental test "suggestibility-confidence test". By this we mean but the following: Some sort of confidence is investigated together with a type of behaviour commonly called "suggestion". In our experiment the following features are called attention to by the term "suggestion": The observer expects with considerable certainty that the ps would answer "no" (or, more, general "negatively"), to the questions if he had given the following instruction: "In these test-tubes there is only distilled water. Do you smell anything? —" It is a usual, normal reaction to smell nothing (or the same each time) being confronted with three portions of water. The observer consequently expects that the above mentioned instruction would exclude direct answers to the question "What do you smell?" When therefore other than the expected types of answers are obtained, the test-tubes containing the same (according to the criteria of the observer), but the instruction being otherwise, one infers that differences in answers can be forecast if differences in instruction are known. Exactly *what* features of the instruction favour "odours being reported by ps confronted with distilled water" is a perfectly unsolvable — and perhaps meaningless — question as long as no systematic change of instruction is carried out. Such systematic variation has not been tried by any experimental psychologist as far as we know. The theories as to which features of the experimental conditions cause the law-directed occurrence of positive answers, can therefore be disregarded with a good conscience. According to a theory having wide acceptance, the ps "actually think that they smell X because of the leader having postulated the possibility of X being smelt. Actually there is no stimulus of X and the ps are therefore liable to an error". All difficulties are hidden in the expressions "*think* that they smell X". "*stimulus* of X" and "liable to *error*". We mention these things to warn against keen interpretations of possible correlations between suggestibility-confidence and belief in absolutes (i. e. absolute confidence in something).

The exact relation between "suggestibility-confidence" (Q) and general confidence (C) being unknown, it is of interest to investigate the relation between the latter and Ga2. 1, Ga2. 2.

Sect. 78. Size of C ("General Confidence") and Standpoints towards Absolutes. — In Table 78,1, the ps are grouped according to their C, "a" denoting the average size of C. The definition of Ga1 is given in sect. 69.

Table 78,1. Relation between C and Ga2. 1, Ga2. 2.

	Number of ps	Number of ps with classified standpoints towards abs.	Per cent Ga2. 1	Per cent Ga2. 2
Ps with $C < \frac{2}{3} a$	4	2	0	50,0
Ps with $a > C > \frac{2}{3} a$	23	21	76,2	19,0
Ps with $\frac{3}{2} a > C > a$	23	19	89,5	0,0
Ps with $C > \frac{3}{2} a$	6	5	100,0	0,0

The general tendency of the values is probably real. Comparing the correlation between Q and Ga2, and between C and Ga2 we find that the latter is much the more marked. This supports the assumption that *one may with greater justification expect believers in absolutes to express themselves* with great certainty than expect them to show a high suggestibility-confidence (according to the definition adopted for this term in sect. 76.)

Sect. 79. Originally, the test described in sect. 75 was intended to provide material bearing on the question "Do the contents of truth-theories vary with the traits commonly investigated in the science of character, and, if this is the case, to what degree may tests of the usual psychological kind be valuable to forecast the type of these contents?"

Let us take the standpoints towards absolutes as a typical feature of a truth-theory. The correlations discovered in the foregoing sections convince us that our index of "suggestibility-confidence" and of "confidence" is as valuable to the prognoses required as are the traits "age" and "school-training". A great number of other tests and close inspection of every p would be necessary, however, to obtain results of any general character. Sweeping psychological theories of philosophic production — as, for inst., the various psycho-analytical ones, which offer *complete solutions* by deduction from general maxims — are worthless if they do not stimulate to the treatment of particular cases. Their function is "programmatical".

Sect. 80. Introduction to the Statistical Analysis of the Examples of Something True (o. so. s.). — Nearly all the 250 ps requested to give examples did so. We thus obtained as many as 974 "truths", varying from each other in a most astonishing way. Examples suiting the general theories and affording tests as to how the theories are to be handled in concrete cases, may be classed as the typical features of truth-theories among professionals — in spite of the common (and perhaps not unjust) accusation against philosophers for neglect of examples. The cardinal point is the manner in which the example is presented: whether straightforward or with reservations and comments of abstract and misleading character. It may be said to the honour of the ps — excepting perhaps the sophisticated ones of education class 4 and 5 — that they deliver their beliefs in the most straightforward way possible.

It would be an interesting inquiry to estimate the percentage of the protocolled examples which any given percentage of the ps accept as adequate. One might take 100 examples chosen at random among those actually delivered and find out how many of them were found adequate by, say 100 %, 90 %, 80 % etc. of (say) 50 ps. We have not carried out such an experiment, but a comparison of the given examples convinces us that no example (or perhaps 1 example in every 5. group of 50 ps) would be accepted by 100 % and very few by as much as 90 %. Among these few the "mathematical" and "the earth is round" would presumably range. Neglecting the examples which most ps would declare to be uncontrollable to them because of the lack of knowledge (which could be easily obtained, however, by common types of information), the number of examples accepted by 90 % or more would be no greater. The examples which would be omitted as uncontrollable would on the whole be a statement of birthdays, and similar personalia, statements on the colour of the room in which the p happens to be examined, on the weather at the time of examination etc. Concrete relations, in short, as regards which it is easy to find "experts" with first-hand knowledge. There are, however, many ps, whose scepticism touches upon such relations if they appear in statements claiming "truth" (o. so. s.) A comparison of the examples given by the ps convinces us (further) that very few, if any, examples, would be accepted by less than 10 %.

Sect. 81. To get an impression of the types of examples put forth by ps, it is necessary to inspect the protocols. The following examples are picked at random from our general lists.[1]

(p 7 age 15, ed. cl. 1)
1. It is true that I am now sitting and writing.
2. It is true that I go at school.
3. (Neg.) that I have been to Berlin.
4. Oslo is the capital of Norway. Abs.

---

[1] "Abs." to the right of the examples means: The example is maintained as an *absolute* truth (o. so. + s.), "(Neg.)" to the left of an example means: The example is of something wrong (o. so. + s.)

5. Henrik Ibsen is dead. Abs.
6. That I am a boy. Abs.
7. (Neg.) that King Haakon is of Norwegian birth.

    (p 8 age 30 ed. cl. 4)
1. The law of gravity.
2. That I am living.
3. That I receive impressions.

    (p 11 age 32, ed. cl. 1)
1. To abuse our abilities for selfish purposes.

    (p 12 age 28, ed. cl. 2)
1. To be honest.
2. That I am sitting on the boat.
3. That we live.

— — —

    (p 21 age 26, ed. c. 4)
1. Mathematical proofs.
2. Death.

    (p 19 age 20, ed. cl. 1)
1. That I am sitting here. Abs.
2. That the earth exists. Abs.
3. That I arrive in England. Abs.

P 19, together with some others, was examined on board a ship going from Sweden to England. It is interesting to note that a large percentage of them declared as true — or even absolutely true — that they would arrive in London. Testing the arguments in favour of their hypothesis, they received the impression that the I did not believe that they would reach England. One of them was even on the point of questioning the captain whether they were going in the right direction. They were slightly ironical at the railway station in London as if their arrival must have been a great deception to the "sceptical" I. The incident is very instructive as it shows how an impartial examination of opinions of opinions is mostly interpreted as doubt. Such an examination may therefore be expected actually to be an expression of doubt in most cases of everyday life. Only such an inference can explain the deep rooted character of the interpretation. It is often observable how impartial examinations create doubt in the ps: they give up statements almost certainly of value as predictions, because of very sophisticated argument of the I showing that in, say, 1 in 1 000 000 cases, the statement perhaps will be wrong. It is not necessary that the I postulates that there are such cases. It is generally amply sufficient to ask the p whether the statement holds or not in the imagined cases. One may indicate the attitude of these ps saying that they do not "operate with a continuous scale of probabilities". If there are arguments against a statement, this is judged bad, irrespectively of the character of the arguments as regards strength. This presumably reflects the earnestness with which arguments most often are put forward in everyday life and more specifically if their function is to facilitate cooperation during small everyday tasks. An argument against a statement is put forward to weaken it to a degree which is of *practical* importance. Arguments without practical importance or which are not supposed to have any practical importance by their exponents, are completely lacking. The "philosophic play" is little known, as are the analyses of opinions for their own sake.

A person imbued with philosophic scepticism would presumably say that p 5 (cf. the list) is incautious in stating that it is absolutely true that Ibsen is dead. Many persons have been more than 100 years old and many persons on record have been judged dead in spite of their living in the best of health. Consequently there are some chances that Ibsen lives. The philosophic sceptic would perhaps declare that P 5 is in *error* and that it is only *probable* that Ibsen is dead. We think that such arguments against the ps are beyond the mark. The p 5 may be perfectly acquainted with the "fact" that some persons are more than 100 years old etc. He may even agree with the sceptic, that one may be mistaken in declaring a man "dead", and that such mistakes certainly will occur in the future as often as in the past. But ps are not always disposed to take such possibilities *seriously*. P5 thinks it is nonsensical to give up or doubt the statement "Henrik Ibsen is dead" unless there are *serious* arguments against his statement. Such arguments are lacking, as far as we know, and the probability of mistake derived from the above arguments is much too small to be taken seriously. The statement "Ibsen is probably dead" seems generally to imply that there is a chance of practical importance that Ibsen is still going strong. If one wishes to make a calculation of probabilities as does Reichenbach, one may deliberately adopt other interpretations. But this private spreeh habit does not affect the normal functions of statements of probability in every-day life. Consequently, we think that the p cannot be said to be in error.

(p 29 age 21, ed. cl. 2)
1. The historical facts I myself have experienced.
2. The political development in Austria during the last two years.
3. The revolt among us in May 33.
4. The imprisonment of certain comrades.
5. The "Entlassung" of certain comrades.
6. (Neg.) Certain newspaper articles.
7. (Neg.) Something in the teaching of catholicism: the priest is consciously saying something false.

(p 34 age 21, ed. cl. 4)
1. That Cesar has lived.
2. You shall not break the marriage.
3. There is a hell.

4. That the electric tramway passes by.

— — — —

(p 197 age 28, ed. cl. 4)
1. God is good.
2. If a=b, b=c, then a=c.
3. The straight line is the shortest between two points.
4. (Neg.) White is black.
5. (Neg.) A peacock can crow, Per Degn can crow, consequently Per Degn is a peacock.

(p 234 age 25, ed. cl. 3)
1. A stone.
2. A man.
3. A thought.
4. ⅓.

(p 242 age 31, ed. cl. 2)
1. Das Sein.
2. Sonne.
3. Gestirne.

(p 247 age 21, ed. cl. 3)
1. An axiom.
2. If a=b, and b=c, it must be viewed as probable that a=c.

These examples make many comments unnecessary. We would, however, draw attention to the fact that the following standpoints (among others) are represented among ps:

(a) The standpoint that no example is statable is refound among amateurs. (p 84 for instance.)

(b) The standpoint that there is but one truth is refound (p 59 for inst.)

(c) The standpoint that only "conventions", "axioms", "mathematical statements" are true, is refound.

(d) The standpoint that the type of example is determined by what is meant by "true" is refound.

It is tempting to examine the individual types of examples as they occurred in the *discussion* between p and l. There is much to say about the influence of various factors during the discussion, the degree of tenacity with which the statements are maintained, the variability of opinions on one and the same subject, the different views on truths as something lofty, eternal, non-human etc. etc. We shall neglect these points, however, to get a clearer view of the statistical properties of the material.

Sect. 82. **Classification of Examples.** — There are a great many methods to group the examples, all being of some interest. The number of points of view is scarcely less than in connection with classifications of Af. Only one classification is here carried out. We call its underlying principle "Ge1", and the resulting groups Ge1-groups. The standard type of example runs as follows: "x is an example of something absolutely true". Instead of "is" any expression of the tuv-list may occur, instead of "something", any expression of the list of s-expressions and so on. Disregarding the differences of S-expressions, we arrive at groups of "example-roots" in the sense we have often spoken of fundamental formulation roots. It is the part of the examples corresponding to the "roots" we are to classify.

Som examples refer to events connected with the person who states the example. In many cases philosophers as well as amateurs emphasize that events of this kind have qualities not found in connection with other events. We have therefore decided to take the examples apart in which such reference or a reference to "we" is found and call them examples belonging to Ge1,1. In Ge1.2 we place examples referring to other persons, excepting "persons of historical importance according to school books and newspapers" which are grouped into Ge1.4.

In Ge1.3 we place all sorts of trivialities put forward as examples. A short inspection of the list of examples would convince the reader that such a group can be constructed without much casualty. Positively, we class as trivialities statements without any general interest according to the standards of measurement found in one milieu of the ps. Negatively, examples are gathered under Ge1.3, which do not refer to any person, which contain what is taught anywhere (as far as I know), and which does not sound philosophic. The examples 1, 2, 3 and 6 of p 7 reproduced in sect. 81 are, for instance, examples belonging to Ge1.3 according to our estimation. We thought it worth while to try to group "trivialities" together in one group because of the importance of these examples as regards the following questions: What is the emotional colour of the notion of truth if it has any? To what degree do people associate solemn, important or in any other sense, outstanding, things with "truths" (o. so. s.)? To what degree do they think of trivialities, *ideologically neutral happenings* and relations?

Group Ge1.4 consists of all sorts of statements which are taught or supposed to be gathered as significant and as laws of nature. The whole department of scientific knowledge is arranged under Ge1.4. (If a person put forward as example a statement supposed to be a law of nature, but according to the l only means a misapprehension of some such law, the statement is nevertheless arranged under Ge1.4. The l does not adopt any standpoint towards the "truth" of the "truths".) The rest of the Ge1-groups are less frequent.

Sect. 83. Frequency of the Different Ge1-groups. — Table 83,1 shows the relative frequency. To get an impression of the *remarkable small divergencies* from average frequency distributions we have divided our material into two classes: Examples put forward by ps 1—150 and examples by ps 151—250. It should be remembered that there are great differences in type of questionnaires and that the external situations during the examination have also varied to some degree. Both percentage frequency points and percentage of total number of examples are computed. If a p has 5 examples belonging to Ge1. 1 and 6 others belonging to various other Ge1-groups, Ge1. 1 becomes ⁵/₁₁ fr. p.

Table 83,1. Size of the Ge1-groups

Ge1. No.	Per cent p 1—150	Per cent p 151—250	Per cent p 1—250	fr. p. p 1—150	fr. p. p 151—250	fr. p. p 1—250
1	27,1	14,3	23,0	26,7	11,0	20,4
2	4,5	6,4	5,1	4,7	4,0	4,4
3	30,0	32,4	30,8	25,3	25,0	25,2
4	26,3	39,0	30,4	26,0	32,0	28,4

Table 83.1 together with not-reproduced tables dealing with the more rare types, show that less than 1 out of 20 examples are normative — all the rest are "matter of fact" statements. If data concerning one's own person are regarded as trivialities, about 60 % of all statements may be looked upon as concerning "unimportant", in no way "outstanding" things. Only about 7 % have direct ideological relevancy brought from ethical, religious or philosophic quarters. This may be interpreted as a symptom of *"logical" conception of the notion of truth in contrast to an "ideological" conception*. (Conceptions most likely to be ideological: "the Truth", "Truth for me", "the great Certainty", "truthful", "the true life", etc.) There are, however, pure ideological conceptions of truth represented among ps of all classes of education. There are also ps who could be classed as adherents of the truth notion as a formal notion, "true" being but attributed to statements often called "tautologies".

Sect. 84. Thing-Examples. — Some of the ps put forward "things" (in contrast to statements) as examples of something true (o. so. s.). Compared with the number of Af characterized by s=2, this is a very small number. If a p states, for instance, that truths are *things* having the quality x, one may consequently expect that he will give *statements* as examples of *things*. This throws some light on the notion of "thing" among non-philosophers: *statements are generally conceived as a kind of thing*. (Cf. the philosophical discussions on this point). Comparing examples given by ps identifying truth (o. so. s.) with a r- or f-factor (cf. sect. 36) with those adhering to the view that truths merely correspond, agree with, or can be brought to harmony with a r- or f-factor, we find that the tendency to choose thing-examples is no more marked among the former than among the latter.

Sect. 85. Age, Education, and Ge1. — The tendency to choose examples dealing with one's own affairs or experiences weakens with increasing age and education, perhaps most marked with education. It has been our impression that the ps do not select examples dealing with their own ego because of the (sometimes supposed) greater certainty with which this can be known. One has often the impression that the supposed greater egocentricity of the younger ps makes them occupy themselves with their own affairs also during the examination. Concluding, we think that computation indicates a rather *close correlation between type of examples and age, education* — a correlation which is considerably closer than that between age, education and choice of Af. This result is of theoretical interest. It underlines the far-reaching independence of types of definitions of truth: factors which condition the types of answers to requests for examples and question absolutes are in no way important to the choice of type of definition. The difference is — as all statistically obtained results — one of degree, but this does not make it less important. If we conceive the group of standpoints gathered under the name of "truth-theory" as *traits* of the person who adopts the theory, it may be said that they are *more or less apt to correlate with other traits of the person in a relatively easy traceable way*. The *definitions* of truth — the most important of the traits gathered under the name "truth-theory" — are less apt to correlate with traits as age and education, whereas traits as choice of examples and standpoints towards absolutes correlate highly with those traits.

Age and education tend to cluster with the majority — if not all — of the traits investigated in the science of character. The amount of correlation with those traits is therefore highly symptomatic of the "depth" of the traits.

There is no systematic difference between types of examples of something "absolutely true" (o. so. s.) and of something "true" (o. so. s.). The frequency distribution of examples supports strongly the assumption that the "notion of truth", which has been favoured as an object of speculation in philosophy and logic, does not have any property in the speech of every-day, which does not also belong to a great number of other "notions" — those expressed by S-expressions (yz-expressions).

Sect. 86. Choice of Examples and External Surroundings during the Examination. — It is very difficult to estimate the influence of external surroundings during our examinations. There is no direct way in which the possible influence of the choice of Af could be investigated — a sort of psycho-analysis excepted. The same difficulties are found as regards other features of the amateur theories of truth, with perhaps one exception: the choice of examples. We had the impression that external surroundings had no appreciable influence on choice of Af, standpoint towards existence of absolutes and similar abstract subjects, but that the search for examples very often led to statements on some feature of the room, objects seen through the window etc. As it was not possible always to examine in the same room, we decided to make a control. A curious result of this control was the following: Placing a globe in a conspicuous position in the room during the examination the frequency of the example "the earth is round" doubled.

Sect. 87. Certainty of Mathematical Statements in the Eyes of the Ps. — The number of mathematical examples is considerable. There are 72 of them in total. This means that 7,4 % of all examples are mathematical and that there is more than one example for every fourth person. The rôle of mathematics in the amateur theories of truth is no less interesting than its position among professional. Many ps, the scepticism of whom embraces all sorts of "truths", are suddenly sceptical as regards their own scepticism as soon as the I alludes to mathematical propositions. It seems as if school mathematics has cured many souls of doubts: "If nothing is perfectly true and trustworthy the world is bad. Mathematics are absolutely true. Consequently also other things may be true. The world may be good." The belief in absolutes based on the existence of (supposed) absolute true mathematical propositions seems to be as common among amateurs as among professionals. It is perhaps easy to over-estimate the originality of the amateur theories on this point. Text-books of mathematics contain many platonic elements, and the teachers of mathematics may generally be faithful to tradition.

Concluding, we wish to call attention to the following standpoints refound among ps, and which have not been mentioned when discussing their standpoints towards "absolutes":

(1) Statements on which mathematics are based cannot be proved.

(2) They cannot be proved, but are self-evident.

(3) There is but one type of true statement, namely the mathematical, based logically on its premises.

(4) Mathematical truths are created by man.

(5) Mathematical statements are based on experience.

Sect. 88. Introduction to the Discussion of the Ps' Attitude towards the Afr of Others. — Various aims made it highly desirable to investigate the reactions of one p towards the statements of others. It is, for instance, impossible to find out to what degree the Afr of a p is conceived as unique and the best alternative to this p without investigation of his reactions towards the Afr of others. The Afr of a p may be "isolated" formulations of his reaction-system in the following sense: confronted with various formulations similar but not identical with his own Afr, he will never react in the same way towards any one of them as he will towards his own. Or, the Afr may be a member of a group or complex of formulations, towards which he will tend to react in a similar way. He will in this case find a great percentage of the Afr of others adequate. One may investigate the degree of isolation of his Afr by confronting him systematically with other Afr, counting the number of Afr he may be expected to be willing to substitute for his own. In this way the boundaries of functional behaviour-units can be traced with some precision. One sort of "isolation" of formulations is of the kind attributed to "solutions". Afr are put forward as solutious of problems. It may be that a p propounding x as a solution will also be willing to accept y — another Afr — as a solution. The fraction a/r obtained by dividing the number of Afr he accepts with the number of Afr he rejects will, for instance, measure the degree of "*uniqueness* as solution" which he attributes to his own solution. If he rejects 100 Afr with which he is confronted, this is a symptom of far-reaching "uniqueness" of his own Afr (according to his own estimation) as a solution of particular problems. If he accepts 90 and rejects 10 one may infer that his own Afr belongs to a group of formulations to which at least 90 others belong and which has the property that the p will on certain occasions react with statements all classifiable under the name "acceptance of the formulation at issue".

We have already described some material bearing upon these problems. The phenomena labelled "multiple formulation" (cf. sect. 22) throws some light on them and indicate that perfect "uniqueness" is uncommon, if it exists at all. Below, some quantitative statements about these matters are given.

We shall first examine the results of some qts worked out to test the attitude of ps towards Afr of their colleagues, i. e. put forward by other ps under similar experimental conditions. The contents of the qts are roughly indicated in sect. 10.

Sect. 89. The qt DA. — To get the best statistical material with with the least effort, we decided to let some ps read the Afr of others, declaring what is reproduced in sect. 10 under the heading qt DA. After some experiment we decided to let the ps take standpoint to the Afr as if they were all answers to the question "What is the c. c. of that which is true". Introducing different yz-notions, the ps were easily mislead or spoiled much time by fixing their attention to the differences between the words "true", "right", "correct" etc. We accordingly retained the expression "true" everywhere.

The qt DA was answered by 23 ps. It was found inconvenient to force the ps to adopt any standpoint to a *definite* number of Afr. Some ps use half an hour to comment on one single Afr, whereas others find it easy to make up their mind towards a dozen within the same lapse of time. On an average, the attitude of a p towards 20 Afr was tested. The total number of evaluations or "tested attitude" amounts to 456 distributed on 102 different Afr. Some Afr were considered by as many as 9 ps. On an average each Afr were considered by 4 to 5 ps. None of the 102 Afr (on which our statistical conclusions are based) are evaluated by less than three different ps. The ps were not permitted to pick out the Afr they wanted to consider; they had to follow the order of the list. The unequal number of ps who have considered each of the 102 Afr is partly caused by some answers having to be rejected, containing formal errors or being too scanty etc. The reader may get an impression from the protocols (mostly obtained by the writing method and by inspecting the following examples of answers chosen at random.

Some answers of p 55, age 15, ed. cl. 2.

"Afr 52,3 (That I know it.) What is knowledge? Is it subjective or objective? That I *know* a thing, does that mean that I possess, and am aware of the "facts" (truth)? Or that I am perfectly convinced of the correctness of my own thought?

Afr 53 (the statements of scientists). The problem is only pushed over to the scientists: what determines that which they call "facts"?

Afr 54,1 (What people say when they are convinced of it) I. e. "*subjective*" truth. Cf. 52,3.

Afr 54,2 (That I have learnt it.) Of whom? The all-knowing? Cf. 52,3.

Afr 55,1 (What one is convinced is the case.) As 54,1. I have the impression that the author, giving this answer, was overwhelmed by the feeling of the ethical and moral value attached to the sincere conviction." —

Commenting Afr 55,1, p 55 comments his *own* Afr. The question of the l was "What is the c. c. of what you call true." This is by p 55 called "subjective" truth.

Some answers of p 66, 15 years old, ed. cl. 1.

"Afr 1,1 (That it agrees with reality.) A good answer.

Afr 7,5 (That it cannot be challenged.) A good answer.

Afr 9,1 (Agreement between something I have imagined (beforehand or afterwards) and the result of observation.) As an example contradicting this answer, we may take the movement of the earth around the sun.

Afr 9,2 (My own conviction.) This conviction does not need to agree with reality.

Afr 46,1 (One cannot suppose the things to be otherwise.) There is much one cannot imagine which is nevertheless true.

Afr 59,1 (It serves life.) "Lies also serve life (may be it is deeper than I can understand)." — The answer of p 66 reads "what agrees with reality".

Some answers of p 207, 16 years old, ed. cl. 2:

"Afr 1,1 (That it agrees with reality.) The word reality can be substituted by the word truth. Because of this I think the answer is bad.

Afr 2,1 (the fact of the case.) I cannot accept it because it explains truth just as if one would prove that the shortest path between two points is the straight path, *because* this is — the straight path.

Afr 2,2 (Agreement with the facts of the case.) The same as 2,1.

Afr 7,5 (That it cannot be challenged.) Accepted." —

P 207 arrives ultimately at the conclusion that there is no sense in asking for a c. c. of what is true. His original answer was a definition: "From whatever point of view it is contested, it has no influence on it."

Some answers of p 210, 16 years old, ed. cl. 2.

"Afr 1,1 (That it agrees with reality). Bad. Many false things can have that property.

Afr 2,1 (The fact of the case.) Vague.

Afr 2,2 (Agreement with the facts of the case.) Vague.

Afr 7,5 (That it cannot be challenged.) Tolerable. One does not *have means* to contradict it.

Afr 108,3 (That all mean that it is so.) No perfect answer. "All" can be in error.

Afr 111 (What we react to quite naturally and do not think about.) False and imperfect. What is quite natural to us human beings — with our senses — cannot tell whether a thing is true."

After having inspected a great deal of the Afr of his colleagues, p 210 writes: "I have the impression that no one has answered with these statements being asked what truth is." Actually, the ps thought their colleagues had much the same opinions as they themselves.

Sect. 90. Assenting, Neutral and Critical Evaluations (ae, ne, and ce). — The examples of sect. 89 give but an inadequate impression of the far-reaching heterogeneity of the answers of the p. It is, however, possible to divide them into three categories: remarks expressing rejection of the Af at issue, such expressing acceptance, and remarks which can be interpreted both as expressing rejection and acceptance or which do not seem to have a bearing on either acceptance or rejection. The first category of remarks are "critical", the second "assenting" and the third "neutral". We shall abbreviate them below as follows: By "ae" we mean "assenting evaluating reaction" or, shorter, "assenting evaluation", by "ne" we mean a "neutral evaluation" and "ce" we mean a "critical evaluation". Most remarks are easily and unambiguously classifiable, the rest leave room for doubt. By means of some examples we shall illustrate roughly how we deal with doubtful cases:

Some answers of p 131, 18 years, 2. cl. of ed.

Afr 52,3 (That I know it.) This being the case, presumably very few truths would exist. [Taken literally, this answer is "neutral", taken in its context we think it the best to classify it as critical].[1]

---

[1] Our comments are enclosed within "[" — brackets.

Afr 53.1 (Scientists' statements). There is, I dare say, nobody disagreeing more than they are. [Literally as ne. Classed as ce].

Afr 54.1. (What people say when they are convinced of it). In past ages one believed in goblinry. [Afr 53.1].

Afr 55.2. (Agreement between statement and facts.) Inane. [Some ps think that answers to the q.c.c. may be adequate, but *must* be inane. This p does not (probably!) mean this. His answer is consequently classed as a ce.]

Afr 58.4. (What one knows that is a fact.) How does one know this! [The p demands some further explanation: He is dissatisfied with the formulation. We have not in all similar cases classed the answer as ce. In this case we *have* and for the following reasons: (1) p 171 writes "!" instead of "?" after his "question", (2) as exclamation it is usually used critically by 131.]

Afr 59.1. (It serves life.) Consequently, accidents are fictions. [Literally a ne. No traits of p 171 seem, however, to indicate that he entertains the opinion that accidents *are* fictions. We class his answer as a ce.]

Afr 60.1. (It sounds natural, as a rule.) Usually. Not always. [From other answers of p 171, it may be expected that this is an expression of criticism.]

There are dozens of answers which give rise to doubt. The majority of these doubts vanish as soon as one has got a clear impression of the context in which the answers occur. The rest are too small in number to make any considerable difference to the results. We have in some cases directly asked the ps whether an answer is meant as critical or not. As a result of such inquiries we think it justifiable to view some answers classed as ne, and occasionally as ce, as belonging to the class ce. As in most cases when judging professional truth-theories, one has to do with written products of the authors and cannot use the direct method to *ask* what they mean, the classifications based on the written products of the ps are, consequently, from many points of view, much the more valuable for the sake of comparison than the direct more "introspective" method.

Sect. 91. Statistical Results of qt DA. — Table 91.1 shows the relative frequency of ae, ne and ce.

Table 91.1. Evaluations of Afr. Relative frequency of ae, ne and ce. QtDA.

	ae	ne	ce	total
Number of e	66	39	351	456
Per cent	14.5	8.6	77.0	100.1

It appears that critical statements are more than five times as frequent as those assenting. This result has very far-reaching consequences. It means, for instance, that the ps are in no way indifferent to modifications of their Af: *they do not generally tolerate other solutions than their own.* They *"mean"* something fairly definite in so far as they protest against most suggestions of formulating the solutions otherwise than they have done it themselves. In other and more precise words: one may expect that two or more ps each stating an Af are unwilling to substitute their own for the Af of others in discussion; they would try to prove that the "alien" Af falls short of their own.

The similarity of this general behaviour with that of professionals will be dealt with properly in other connections.

There are, of course, exceptions to this behaviour among the professionals as well as among the ps. It is not uncommon, for instance, that ps having been confronted with great lists of Af, also judge their own Af with critical eyes.

As might be expected, the different critics were unequally severe on their colleagues. The most severe critics reject all Afr with which they are confronted. The standard deviations of percentage ac, ne and ce are great.

Sect. 92. Critics and Type of Afr. — Are some of the Af constantly critizised, others constantly agreed with, or in general, what differences does the type of Af make to the critic?

Table 92,1 shows Afr of different classes: in class 1 Afr are placed which are agreed to by all (100% of the) ps taking it into account. In class 2, those are placed which are not agreed to by all, but by more than 75% etc. Tables 92.2 and 92.3 show the similar relations connected with neutral and critical comments.

Table 92,1. Assenting comments and type of Afr. QtDA.

	Class 1 (100% ae)	Class 2 (100 > ae ≧ 75)	Class 3 (75 > ae ≧ 50)	Class 4 (50 > ae ≧ 25)	Class 5 (25 > ae ≧ 0)	Class 6 (ae = 0)
Number of Af	1	2	7	22	12	58
Per cent Af	0.98	1.96	6.86	21.57	11.76	56.86

The table gives a vivid impression of the rareness of accepted Afr. The average numbers of ps who evaluated each Afr of DA is but 4.5, but in spite of this, only one of 102 is accepted by all (4) evaluating ps. If (on an average) 20 ps had judged the Afr, the number of 100% accepted ones would probably not exceed 1 per thousand.

Sect. 93. Below, we pick out some Afr of special interest to see how they look in the eyes of the ps. (1). The Afr 1.1 (agreement with reality) is agreed to by 3, criticised by 4 and made the object of neutral comments by no ps. Examples:

P 207: The word "reality" can be substituted for the word "truth". For this reason I find the answer bad.

P 120: This is obvious. — I do not think this is a definition: it is the same (said twice).

P 234: Not satisfactory. Reality is only a part of truth.

The ps 120 and 207 expect from a definition that it shall *explain* something. According to the terminology of Dubislav, they work with the notion of a "Wesendefinition". Philosophers criticising the "agreement with reality" formula Dewey, for instance, argue in the same way.

The formula 40.3 "it rains now" is true if it actually rains now, is accepted by p l, finding it even useful in practice. Some months later on p 1 a rejects the formula: "It says truth is truth! A definition must be otherwise: one cannot use the same expression. It explains nothing. The same is said twice."

P 55 says: "This *seems* to turn round in circles. Example: I observe an event. To me the event is a fact, because my senses have convinced me of it. But if the whole should be due to sense-illusion, the proof (of this) would be furnished in the same way. But this time a false assumption is made. (Literally: But if the whole is due to sense-illusion, the proof will be once more furnished on the same false basis, and, consequently, it can be of no decisive importance.) — But "viewed from outside", judged automatically by the thing itself, independent of any person, the formula is all right. A thing, an event, "something", is true if it exists in reality. —

The p (15 years old) is completely ignorant of any sort of philosophy and logics, but it is interesting to find a certain connection between his views and current arguments among contemporary thinkers. —

(2). The pragmatical formulation Afr 59.1 ("it serves life") is met with the prosaic argument "much may be true, which does not serve life" by p 1. P 55 says: "Here we have an answer touching the nucleus of the notion of truth. But the answer is rather unclear and vague. One must be permitted to break into the poetical sphere surrounding it with an objection as practical and commonplace as: A violent accident has happened. Many people are killed. The event is in spite of this a truth. Does it serve life? — The answer is not scientific enough."

It is remarkable to note how similar these arguments are to those most often put forward in anti-pragmatic literature.

(3.) The Afr 101.1 "that it really exists", is judged to be "vague" by p 1, who also puts the question "Do mathematical statements exist?". P 55 comments: "What is existence and what is that which is? This answer (Afr 101.1) does not suit statements of history." The metaphysician p 189 says: "But is it certain that something exists? I would rather

propose (the following formulation): If something existed, it would be true."
P 210: "None, or at least a very unclear answer."

Sect. 94. The qt DB. — The qt DB (cf. sect. 10) was given up very soon as we had the impression that it did not lead to results distinctly different from qt DA. The adoption of the term "definition" did not change the results. We were accordingly justified in retaining the term "common-characteristics". The percentage ae turns out to be 13.3, ne 8.3 and ce 78.3. The divergence from the results of DA is smaller than might be expected.

Sect. 95. The qt DC. — Two problems caused the working out of qt DC. The number of different Af produced by our ps is very great. It is an open question how many different Af would be accepted by at least (say) 1 p out of 5. To solve this question we think it desirable not only to make ps criticise the Af of their colleagues, but to write down formulations which have not been put forward by any amateur (or professional) and then observe how much more severely by these fancied Af would be judged by the ps. By this means, one may gradually discover the types of Af which are practically certain not to be accepted by as much as 20% of the ps. Preliminary experiments convinced us, however, of the big material necessary to carry out such a test. We consequently decided to simplify it: sitting down for some three hours we wrote 72 answers to the questions "what is the c.c. of that which is true?", which at that time we had neither observed among the ps nor among professionals. 64 of these answers are Af. Some of them are very complicated, others are simple. We are convinced that anybody working with "experimental truth-theories" would have been able to produce the same or even a greater number of Af during the same interval of time. We have since found a few of the "72 fancied Af" among ps or professionals but in spite of this they were retained in the list (abbreviated: "list of fancied Af").

As in connection with qt DA and qt DB, we find much more critical, comments than appraisals: as many as 116 were critical 29 neutral and only 24 assenting. This means 68.6% against 77.4% ce in connection with DA and DB (the material of both qts put together), 17.2% ne against 8,2% ne, and 14,2% ae against 14,4 ae in connection with DA and DB. The larger amount of ne in DC-material presumably reflects the greater complexity of the statements in the list of fancied Af than in other lists. In so far, we must conclude that the ps behaved as if the 72 Af were *opinions*, for instance, of colleagues. The frequency-distribution of percentage ae, ne and ce for the individual Af is closely similar to what one found when inspecting the material of DA and DB.

To give an adequate picture of the statistical results of DC, we shall examine the degree of severity of the 18 ps evaluating the 72 Af. Four ps each producing four evaluating are "100% critical"; 4 ps are critical in more than 80% of the cases, 7 are critical in 50% to 80%, and 2 in less than 50% but more than 40% of the cases. These values are similar to those found in connection with DA and DB.

They and many others support our general conclusion that *the ps react in a similar fashion towards "fancied" as towards "real" Af*, and that the total number of possible Af, which satisfy at least one p out of five, must be very great.

Sect. 96. The qt DD. — As explained in sect. 10, the DD consist of a list of professional Af together with a short instruction. The test was carried out, following the same rules as those involved in qt DA, DB and DC. In this connection, we shall limit ourselves to a short description of the list.

More than two thirds of the Af of the list were gathered by using old references in our manuscripts dealing with the truth-problem. The rest was gathered to fill up holes in the presentation to get a *fair sample of "definitions of the notion of truth" put forward by professionals*. By "definition" we here mean formulations being Af and concerning the S-expressions true, truth, correct, adequate, right ("richtig"), false, falsity and a few others. The expressions "certain", "sure", "fact", and some others of the list of S-expressions (cf. sect. 65) we decided to leave out of consideration. Formulations from all major epochs of philosophic thought were included. Most of the authors are professional philosophers and logicians, some are philosophers *and* poets or "merely" poets — the terminology is certainly vague — and some are (philosophizing) scientists. Most of the Af are picked out of papers in which the discussion of the truth-problem occupies no unimportant place, others are found in contexts foreign to the truth-discussion. If the *immediate* context of the formulation was found highly important to the understanding of it, it was reproduced in the list. One may point out that the ps ought to have read the whole broad context to understand them: this may be so or it may not be so. What is important to us is to construct "experimental conditions" of the same sort as in connection with DA, DB and DC. It would not be possible if the ps were permitted to inspect the papers of the professionals: Ps were not permitted to inspect the papers of the amateurs.

170 PAf (professional definitions of truth) were evaluated by 16 ps, producing, in total, 393 evaluations. This makes 10,6 PAf per p, 24,6 evaluations per p and 2,3 evaluations per PAf. None of the 170 Af was evaluated by less than two ps.

Sect. 97. Attitude of the ps towards the Products of Professionals as Reflected by the Relative Frequency of ae, ne and ce.

Table 97.1 shows the amount of ae, ne and ce compared with the results obtained by examination of DA + DB and of DC.

Table 97,1. Comparison of attitude towards professional Af and other Af.

	DD	Diff. from DA + DB	Diff. from DC
ae	26,2	+ 11,8	+ 12,0
ne	14,8	+ 6,6	÷ 2,4
ce	59,0	÷ 18,4	÷ 9,6

Table 97,1 indicates that ps are more liable to agree with the professional Af than with those of their colleagues. But the majority of evaluations are in both cases critical; only 1 in 4 definitions is on an average accepted.

We pick out below some PAf and see how they look in the eyes of the ps. The ps "100 %, agree" with many PAf. Because of the small number of ps evaluating each PAf this is not astonishing, however. One PAf is evaluated by three ps all of which agree with them: PAf 16 of Goethe "Ich halte die Gedanken für wahr, die für mich fruchtbar sind, die sich suf eine natürliche Weise meinem übrigen Denken anschließen und die mich fördern". Some PAf are evaluated by two ps, both of which agree with them: PAf 21, truth is "adequatio rei et intellectus" of various authors; PAf 52, Truth has "die mit Erfahrung und Denken harmonierenden Urteile, — —" of Richter; PAf 110, "true means true for a given purpose. Any "truth" 'actually' enunciated should be conceived as the best (i. e. most valuable) alternative its asserter could think of, of F. C. S. Schiller and so on. As is seen from this small enumeration, the taste of the ps is susceptible to great individual differences. This impression is enforced taking into account PAf which are *universally* rejected by the ps evaluating them: PAf 42 is rejected by four ps: "Das Wahre ist das Ganze" of various authors, Hegel, for instance. Some PAf are rejected by three ps: PAf 2, truth is "agreement of some sort between judgment and fact" of Dewey; PAf 7, "A true thought is assent given when the object has had time or opportunity itself to determine the contents of the thought," of Walker — and many others.

PAf 148, ""p" ist wahr, wenn p" of Tarski received much criticism as well as appraisal.[1] Some arguments for and against the formula are quoted in sect. 93.

---

[1] Special questionnaires were used to establish the willingness to substitute "p" for "p is true". Suitable examples were listed in qts. The results cannot be stated in a few words and must be omitted in this work. — The "PAf 148" (Tarski) is not to be identified with the so-called "semantic notion of truth". To construct this notion the method of formalization is essential. There is, however, a tendency to look at PAf 148 as a definition of non-formal truth. It was therefore included in our lists.

Sect. 98. The ps' Arguments against Professional Af. Examples.
— The following examples or arguments are meant to illustrate some typical traits of the ps' points of view. They are by no means meant to offer a systematical review of types of argument: Such a review would be no less complicated than a review of argument among philosophers. The following list results from choice at random. *We have not picked out instances of "clever" criticisms in cur eyes.* What we aim at is a fair picture of the the total material. The reader may judge the material from his own point of view.

Some answers of p 16, age 25, ed. cl. 3.

Af 1. (Truth involves "the relations between two physical things, between speech reactions and the things to which they refer.")[1]

Evasion.

Af 2. (Truth is "agreement of some sort between judgment and fact.")

Evasion.

Af 7. ("A true thought is assent given when the object has had time or opportunity itself to determine the contents of the thought.")

An object may have the occasion to determine many thoughts which are not "true". All thoughts are determined by objects. Are they therefore all true?

Af 10. ("I hold that the true and the false are respectively the real and the unreal, considered as objects of a possible belief or judgment.")

Unclear to me. — — This definition defines something more simple by means of something more complicated.

Af 14. ("When we say: something is true, we mean that it agrees with statements denoting observed facts.")

False. Many statements about observed facts are false.

Some answers of p 28, age 21, ed. cl. 4.

Af 89—114. I cannot agree that any of these are criteria. They elucidate the problem. — One cannot put forth any criterion. To try to answer such a question: 10 years must necessarily be spent to elucidate the problem. — To operate with the word "reality" is a subreption.

Af 98. ("Unsere Erkenntnis ist *gewiß*, wenn sie sich gründet auf Evidenz (1) des äußeren b) und inneren c) Sinne, (2) des Gedächtnisses und (3) richtiger Schlußerfolgerungen von den Wirkungen auf die Ursache.")

"True" must be "true *to* someone" — in relation to something perceiving.

Af 106. ("The opinion which is fated to be ultimately agreed to by all who investigate it, is what we mean by the truth.")

There can be no opinion which is predetermined to be the ultimate — —. Truth is relative to time, place and man.

---

[1] The names of the authors were not given to the ps.

114. ("Truth is founded by evidence. Every judgment that limits itself to establish the intention or meaning that is at issue, is evident.")

He does not say anything about the meaning of "evidence." — The problem is: "What is evident to the individual and to the mass" — Cheap!

143. ("The true is the name of whatever proves itself to be good in the way of belief, and good, too, for definite, assignable reasons.")

I agree, if "good" is not taken in a moral sense, or as an individual evaluation of the desirable or undesirable. "Good" means consequently something as "lasting worth" and does say much more than "true".

Af 144. ("Falsehood is saying of that which *is* that it is not, or of that which is not that it is; truth is saying of that which is that it is, or of that which is not that it is not.")

Word-definition and even unnecessarily unclear.

Af 145. ("Das Kriterium der Wahrheit eines Satzes ist seine Bewahrung im konkreten Leben.")

Yes — and then. The very point is just what is expressed thereby that a statement is "bewährt" and what are the conditions for this.

Af 51. ("Truth for me is that which I cannot help believing.")

Does not say anything. Naturally the truth is in this way compelling. And it is gives a good picture — but does in no way explain the conditions that something is compelling as true.

Af 4. (Test of truth: "Conformity to an external reality, to things out there, so to speak — — and complete consistence with itself.")

This may be a good definition of the common general use of the word. But it explains nothing — shows nothing about the functional significance to mankind — and is, therefore, a bad criterion. One must try to give an answer to what it is to say that one feels something as agreeing with the external reality. — — If the statement (i. e. Af 4) is to be used as a criterion, the notion "external reality" must at least be determined in relation to the individuals in a way that conveys something, as an impression of a definite worth and effect.

In a certain percentage of the cases the ps clearly do not understand the professional Af. It is, however, very difficult to find out in which cases the answers seem to be as far from the mark as is necessary to to justify the judgment: "he has not understood". The difficulty is just as great interpreting amateur critics as interpreting professional critics: "Has Bradley understood James?" "Has James understod Bradley? "Has Schlick understood Neurath?" "Has Neurath understood Schlick?" Such questions are no more difficult than the following: "Has p 16 understood Bradley?" "Has p 29 understood Neurath?" "Has p 1 understood p 232?" etc. Fortunately, the ps seem on the whole to be less ambitious than philosophers on this point: they are more willing to admit that they do not understand. They have nothing to lose admitting that.

Sect. 99. qt DE. — A considerable fraction of the ps confronted with PAfl reacted spontaneously with statements like the following: "But this I do not understand." They were unwilling and hesitating on account of the difficult language of the professionals — perhaps not so much on account of the contents. They felt distinctly more capable of criticising the the amateur Af, which are on an average, expressed in simple language. To minimize the linguistic difficulties of the ps we decided to translate 90 PAf into Norwegian and to avoid technicalities as far as possible without distorting the (eventual) meaning of the PAf. 13 ps answering qt DE made 283 evaluations of these 90 translated PAf. This makes 21,8 evulations per p and 3,1 evolutions per PAf.

Statistical computation reveals a remarkably more sympathetic attitude of the ps towards translated PAf than towards untranslated. The percentage ae; ne; ce was 41,0; 17,7; 41,3 resp.

Sect. 100. Are the ps More Critical towards Afr of ps of Low Education than towards Those of ps of High Education? — We have found that the ps are, on the average, less critical towards professional than towards amateur Af. It is to be expected that an analogous difference may be found between criticism towards Af of ps of high education and Af of ps of low education. At least one factor favours the acceptance of Af of highly educated ps: their authors are much more able to *express* their opinions and to choose an agreeable style. It is of importance to estimate the difference in attitude as a function of the education of the authors. Computing the percentage ae, ne and ce attached to Afr of ps of various classes of education, the assumption is supported that Afr of ps with high education are, on the whole, less criticised than Afr of ps with low education. 13,7 % of the evaluations of low-educational Af are assenting, whereas the corresponding number for high-educational Af is 19,1 %. But the values do not support the assumption that the difference is marked. It is highly improbable that further material would reveal a difference as, say, 50 %. It is to be noted that the inclination to accept Af of highly educated ps is not determined by the occurrence of new Gri- or other types of Af among them. We have shown that there is no conspicuous development of types of Af with increasing education. The result reflects to some degree the fact that we have not classified the Af according to to their style and complexity. It can be shown that complex formulations are less criticised than simple.

Sect. 101. General Comparison between Attitude towards Professional and Attitude towards Amateur-Af. — Our material — 1361 evaluations — justifies, we think, the following conclusions without further argument:

(1) The majority of Af is rejected by the ps, irrespective of it being the product of professionals or amateurs.

(2) The ps think better of the professional solutions of the "truth problem" than the Af of amateurs, especially if the former are translated into simple language.

(3) The types of argument put forward judging the Af, are found in connection with amateur Af as well as in connection with professional Af.

(4) The difference in attitude towards amateur and professional Af makes itself apparent only if great samples of Af are taken into account. It cannot be inferred with any reasonable amount of probability from a single evalution or a small number of evalutions (1—50) whether the evaluated Af is a professional or an amateur one.

(5) Af of ps of high education or age are nearly as vividly criticised as Af produced by ps of low education or age (the difference being about $^1/_3$).

(6) Many trends of arguments found among the professionals are refound among the amateurs. The same types of arguments are put forward in connection with the same types of truth-theories.

(7) The statement (6) supports the view that the majority of the truth-theories are 'understood' by the majority of the ps to a degree comparable with the degree of 'understanding' which philosophers exhibit discussing the sames truth-theories.

Sect. 102. It has not been possible for us to let the ps discuss and criticise the whole answers of their colleagues. Such an experiment would undoubtedly give interesting results, but would, if one did not wish to spend a year or two of work on it, give no results of statistical value. This, we think, is a great drawback and we have consequently limited ourselves to the consideration of one single point of the answers: The Afr. It may be asked of how great symptomatic value the attitude of the ps towards the Afr of their colleagues is of the attitude expected to be observed (by suitable experiments) towards other parts of the amateur-theories. The opinions of the ps diverge to a very high degree as regards all main features of a truth-theory. It is therefore to be expected that the amount of criticism would be very high if by means of lists we let the ps judge the opinions of others as regards all these features.

We expect, on the other hand, a smaller amount of criticism if the ps were permitted to read through the whole of their colleagues' answers. Seeing the different opinions in their full context many misinterpretations and misconceptions would be avoided. *It is interesting, however, to note that the arguments put forward against Afr which are completely thrown out of their context correspond to a conspicuous degree with the arguments of philosophers put forward in connection with the same subjects.* The amount of correspondence cannot be estimated in this work; suffice, to call attention to its existence.

Sect. 103. Amount of Labour Necessary to Improve the Reliability of the Statistical Results of This Work. — One of our main conclusions may be formulated thus: If one is seriously interested in the discovery of amateur-theories of truth, the amount of knowledge secured will be roughly proportional to the labour spent in collecting and analyzing material obtained by questioning the ps and by observing their behaviour. Mediations and deductions from general principles will not do — just as little in this field of research as in botany.

Generalizing, we find it reasonable that the method must be one of patient observation on statistical analysis dealing with questions about other general attitudes (ideologies, doctrines, tendencies). The so-called "meaning" of a term, statement, theory and the realization of "norms" (whether logical, mathematical, grammatical, vocabular or ethical) belongs to the subjects appropriate to this method. Deductions from general principles, from supposed "categories" or "laws of thought" and similar constructions *may* occasionally be of worth — today, however, the amount of speculations perfectly cripple any attempt whatever to *observe* and abstain from speculative generalisations and inferences. The title "Physics" or "Geology" does not occur today except as a title of textbooks — not of original papers. The attempt to discover not merely a new physical theory, but a new body of knowledge comparable with the whole science of physics would be judged insane. Not so as regards the huge fields lying at the cross-sections of the sciences or being but imperfectly grasped by any existing sciences. The problems of these fields are attacked wholesale. Most often the attempts are found in books titled "Philosophy", "Metaphysics", "Theory of Knowledge", "Erkenntnislehre", but they are also found in monographs explicitly rejecting philosophic speculation as method. Under titles as, for instance, "Scientific method", "Logics" one may find attempts to solve hundreds of questions just as complicated and just as untouched by serious efforts to *observe* and *see* as the questions discussed in this monograph. One may say that the "solutions" put forward are not so seriously meant as it may seem to the reader. This is no justification of the "solutions", however. To take an instance: in our own monograph called "Erkenntnis u. wiss. Verhalten" a great number of general statements occur about subjects we really do not know anything about. The more incomplete our knowledge, the more sweeping, elegant and cocksure our statements. A monograph touching those few things in "Erkenntnis und wissenschaftliches Verhalten" we seriously we know anything about, would lack statements comparable in abstractedness believe and elegance with statements of the kind *expected to occur* in these fields of research. The constant feeling that if one does not throw new solutions" of the problems which by the tradition are attacked wholesale, one's contribution is immaterial — this feeling must invariably lead to intellectual dishonesty. If a certain amount of intellectual dishonesty is tolerated in a field of research, this has the effect that it is no longer seen and that the stimulus to improvement vanishes.

In the case of the question "what are the opinions held by non-philosophers on truth?", the amount of knowledge obtained is roughly proportional to the amount of observation and analysis of observational data. This conclusion is very common-place but has some important consequences. It says that our results may be viewed as a function of labour spent on their establishment. By "our results" we mean primarily those supported by our statistical inquiries plus some minor unreported results discussed in the original manuscript. In this section we shall try to give an estimate of the labour required to improve the results, (1) by increasing the reliability of the already stated results and (2) by attacking some of the questions on different lines. During the collection and interpretation of our material, we often calculated how much time and money we would have to spend if we decided to improve our technique at some points or to strengthen weak points of our argument. Our calculations were often (but not generally) wrong and it should be unnecessary to add that a great deal of improvement is realizable by magnified "power of thought". One's powers are regrettably constant, however, during the performance of a task. The individual worker is therefore forced to take other factors into account.

The labour spent in the establishment of our results may be estimated to c. 6000 hours. Time spent in making lists and mnemotechnic advice is included. Such work is essential if one wishes to have more than a dozen truth-theories in mind and not only rely on "intuition" constructing classes and types. — *Problem: how many hours may be expected to be required to double the extent and reliability of our results?* — The word "doubled" is here not meant literally except in connection with purely statistical results. This is an improvement which is radical enough to be clearly perceived at every point and from every point of view.

To begin with, we would wish to examine 100 new ps orally and without using any questionnaire. Then we would wish to systematize the following experiment now and then already carried out by us: several ps are brought together and invited to discuss the notion of truth. Shorthand reviews of their arguments have to be worked out. Then we would wish to increase the minimum number of ps answering a questionnnaire from 8 to 20; this would require no considerable amount of work if the writing-method were employed. Finally, we would wish to inquire systematically into possible changes of opinions in ps examined as long as two years ago. The amount of work necessary to carry out these collections, we estimate at about 400 hours.

New lists of Af, Bf, Df, and other types of fundamental formulations should be carried out and the classifications adapted to an increased standard number of ps from 250 to 750. By this increase of ps, the estimates of relative frequency of different types of fundamental formulations and their relation to age and education could be formulated with doubled reliability (using the familiar statistical theorems on doubling "probability" by increasing the statistical population). From the outset of the work new ps of age cl. 4 and ed. cl. 1 should have been primarily chosen to eliminate a weak point in our selection of ps. New tables of correlations have to be constructed. Estimate of necessary labour: 4500 hours.

Further requirements: a new ABfl and analysis of the functional interconnectedness of different yz-notions as revealed by this list. New expressions should be included in the list. Questionnaires of cl. A and B ought to be constructed in which instead of "true" the most frequent Afr were made central expressions. Question 1 of qt AA should, for inst., read, "What is c. c. of what is in agreement with reality". 20 new questionnaires each answered by 20 ps; about 2500 hours.

Some more ps should be tested by "confidence-tests" to study the scope and significance of the characteriological correlations stated in sect. 75 et seq. As many as 50 sceptics would be required, also to construct some new tests. To double the reliability of our tentative statements about relation between choice of definition of truth and belief in absolutes we should have to increase the number of ps tested. About 2000 hours.

The intelligence-quotient ought to be taken into account. It should at least be known for every third p. Possible correlations should be worked out between intelligence-quotient and type of Afr, standpoint towards absolutes, choice of examples, confidence, standpoint towards importance and scope of the "truth problem". Correlations between the obtained results and those obtained by us classifying the ps into 4 classes of education should be analysed. These inquiries seem to us to be of great importance to the problem of possible development of truth-theories from the age of 15—16 to mature age, if the person steadily gets a more philosophic and general education. About 3000 hours.

Revised analyses of examples of something true including the new ps. Use should be made of some questionnaires containing standard types of statements (religious, philosophic, mathematical, physical etc.). The ps ought to be invited to adopt a standpoint towards these examples. Some of the most frequent examples discussed, in amateur as well as professional theories of truth, ought to be included. The results should be tabulated; about 5000 hours.

In sect. 88 et seq., we have based our statistical results on the evaluations of a small number of ps. The number of Afr evaluated has been very great. Requirements: Control of the results by letting a great number of ps evaluate a small number of Afr, 50 amateur definitions, 50 fancied definitions and 50 professional definitions, for instance. Further control: 50 ps should be permitted to read the protocols if they wished to know the context of the Afr. In this manner it should be possible to consider the amount of criticism as a function of the amount of first-hand knowledge of the opinion criticised; 4000 hours.

For the purpose of comparison we have hitherto worked with a standard number of professional truth-theories produced by 160—170 philosophers. For the sake of ameliorated comparison, new studies of these theories should be made. (The products of previous studies are thought available, of course.) Important points of the truth-theories, as attitude towards tertium non datur and towards other subjects should be compared with greater care with the attitudes of the ps. Some new qts would probably have to be constructed; about 3000 hours.

Finally, the proposed improvement of our results would demand a closer coordination of the individual statistical results reproduced in our tables. The statistical properties of the new material ought to be studied using statistical calculations to a somewhat higher degree than is already done. — Some inquiries to find systems of correlated values should be carried out to find possible "types of amateur-theories" by purely statistical means. These inquiries ought to be done during the direct work with the ps to find the relations between impressions of the l and statistically obtained results; about 3000 hours.

These improvements may perhaps be said to double the extent and reliability of the statistical results stated in this work. The solution of the self-imposed problem is therefore: About 30000 hours work is necessary to carry out the required revision. — In the following section we shall point to some consequences of these estimates. The important thing is not the fact that "30000 hours" is the solution of the problem of this section, but that *calculations of this sort always seem possible* — at least in the fields of research touched upon in this monograph.

Sect. 104. Problems Solved Wholesale to Avoid a Closer Touch with Facts. — There are fields of research which are favoured by tradition in the sense that a single subject is thought worth while to study a whole lifetime — and for its own sake. There are fields of research less favoured. In the latter fields one expects problems — irrespective of degree of complication — to be solved by a single stroke of the pen. No real study seems worth while: consequently, one states one's "solutions" or avoids mentioning the problems. An investigator of traditionally favoured fields seems on an average to know how to express himself cautiously: he knows that other workers may inquire with an extreme degree of endurance into just the same problems and that the amount of empirical data continuously increases. The worker in other fields has no reason to express himself with caution: one may expect others to give wholesale solutions without any more argument than oneself. This is good tradition. It is a commonplace that to "solve" *all* riddles of the universe costs much less time and labour than to compile observational material bearing upon the solution of *any single one* of them. Given a field of research without long scientific traditions, it is therefore more likely to find "complete solutions" than any single argument based on observations reported, however, simple. To report observations does not pay, especially when they only can afford more or less scanty material in favour of statements on special problems and colleagues in the fields at issue report complete solutions of general problems.

To avoid misunderstandings, we emphasize that by "tradition" we do not mean "bad and stupid tradition". We wish by that word only to indicate an aggregate of factors operating together and influencing the choice of work by a student, for instance; or, more generally, by the young generation of research workers. Something is found more "important", "prospective", than something else. *Some sort of equilibrium is expected to hold between the amount of work and the "importance" of results.* The more out of the way a subject lies, the more "complete and elegant solutions" are necessary to reach the equilibrium. "How non-philosophers define truth" is a problem far out of the way of traditionally favoured subjects of earnest research: there are no institutes promoting its cultivation. No difficult title ending with "ologist" decorates its devotees. It seems to us misleading to say that the reason for this status is the *speciality* ("smallness") of the problem. We think that the contrary better illustrates the causal connection: the problem is conceived as a special one because of the lack of institutes, -ologies etc. A great deal of examples from the history of science and technology shows how problems are classified in relation to the existing groups of *cultivated* subjects, i. e. in relation to the niveau of development of the different studies. — As a *consequence* of the place of the problem "How non-philosophers define truth" the authors mentioning it produce only "complete solutions" and avoid reference to possible observations or working hypotheses. It is further a consequence of tradition what weight is attributed to the solutions. "Hypothetical solutions", "working hypotheses" are not offered, i. e. do not exist, because the equilibrium above mentioned would not be reached by means of them. There is no "demand" strong enough. And yet it should be plain to everyone that even tentative hypotheses bearing upon the problems, imply observational work. It may even roughly be calculated how much labour it costs to obtain material with a given scope and a given degree of reliability. Why, in spite of this, is observation systematically neglected and sweeping, vague, general statements being offered the reader without preliminary argument? It seems as if this situation could be predicted by means of hypotheses of the sort just propounded: A sort of equilibrium between effort and social demand is maintained. The demand is in the case at issue minimal and, consequently, the "producing cost" must also be minimal. Observation costs much time and its result is uncertain and open to control. Wholesale solutions pressed into one or a few sentences can be "deduced" from one's philosophical opinions and cost almost no time, whatever. Neglecting comments on the method by which they are arrived at, they are not easily controlled and refuted. As long as the demand is minimal, speculation has to flourish — as it does in the discussion about the notion of truth among non-philosophers.

To make out more clearly what we mean by this equilibrium hypothesis, we shall discuss some objections which might be made against it:

(1) ""Basic" problems of the different sciences need much logical analysis, much purely theoretical treatement before the typical methods of observation can offer any results. There may in scientific quarters be a strong demand for observational evidence. If the equilibrium hypothesis is taken seriously this demand cannot be accounted for." Answer: The hypothesis deals with questions which can be formulated so as to be attacked in an efficient way on mainly observational lines, and which have been discussed for a considerable time. The subject ""truth" as conceived by common-sense" has been discussed for centuries without observational evidence. If there are problems in these fields, they are observational.

(2) "Ask some people working with questions touched upon by your hypothesis *why* they do it and why they do not mention any systematical observations in their publications. You will find that they can account for this in a rational manner and you will see that they follow the demands of their intellect. They search for a solution of *their* problems, not for the satisfaction of the demands of social groups." Answers: There is much evidence showing how verbal reports on motivation ere misleading. Any act can be "rationalized" in the sense that it can be made compatible with the ideology of one's group. — One may follow one's "intellect", but what the "intellect" follows is another problem. One does not consciously choose a question as something worth while because there is a tendency in one's surroundings to accept the question as "important", "subtile" etc. But it can be shown that there are deep lying correlations between the choice and social estimations.

3) "Your hypothesis sounds so strange, why you do not make any difference between social groups as, for instance, "agrarians" or "clericals" and the group "scientists". The choice of problem and method of attack are partly determined by "social estimations" of the scientists. This does not mean anything else than that they are determined wholly on intellectual grounds." Answer: The actions of scientists (including their socially operative estimations) cannot be supposed to be derived from special laws. If the laws are called "intellectual" this ought not to mean that they are tabu and the label neither weakens nor supports our equilibrium hypothesis. We do not deny "intellectual motivation", but whatever may be reasonably intended by that expression, we deny that such motivation does not interact with the whole reaction-system of man.

(4) "You boast that you have carried out systematic observation to determine the notion of truth among non-philosophers. This means to distort the equilibrium between demand and effort, which you just have postulated."

Answer: Our systematic observations are carried out to study professional truth-theories. According to our opinion, such theories can be studied in statu nascendi among non-philosophers by means of questionnaires of the type quoted in this monograph. To study the use of the word "true" other types of qts and more indirect methods would have been necessary. — A question deemed important and central among certain groups of scientists and philosophers is to determine the consequences of scientific methods on the "Fragestellungen" of philosophers. "Truth-theories" are typical products of so-called "scientific philosophy" ("theory of cognition") and, studying them, I do not distort — as far as I know — the equilibrium just mentioned. The relation "science — philosophy" I feel as "*my* problem" and I motivate its importance on purely "intellectual" grounds. But this does not mean to me that my choice of work is not partly determined by the estimates of the group with which I sympathise. On the contrary: I think it relatively easy to trace factors of social origin determining the choice, method and type of conclusions put forward. The knowledge of these factors can be used to forecast the structure of future statements of mine.

Reading one's own works, I think everyone has observed that main subjects or subjects studied earnestly are luted together by statements (with the character of theses) of obscure origin: statements made by the pen without any conscious effort from our side. Analysing this framework, we find that the more cocksure theses deal with subjects which tradition allows to treat in this way. Most of these subjects belong to "No-man's-land" — vast fields, which have not been cultivated for their own sake. One stops a moment, puts down a thesis and hurries on to arrive at the central subjects of one's attention.

To this No-man's-land the subject "common-sense and truth" belongs: philosophers and philosophizing scientists have for centuries stepped in here only to hasten on to their central subject: what *is* "truth". The demand for earnest work in these fields is so small that observational methods are ruled out — to maintain the equilibrium.

Sect. 105. Programmes for Future Inquiry Formulated as Theories. — One cannot from the following statements expect any information of the exact relation between observation and theory. This relation and the consequent weight and reliability of our statements have been a subject of discussion in the previous sections. We shall try to indicate which attitude towards the main questions discussed in this monograph is (according to our opinion) the most appropriate by the planning of future inquiry:

1. Non-philosophers have no theory of truth, no general opinion on the notion of truth, neither explicit nor implicit, which distinguishes them — as a group — from philosophers.

II. The misconception that non-philosophers adhere — explicitly or implicitly — to a definite type of opinion on the notion of truth is primarily due to an ignorance of the extreme diversity of opinion found among non-philosophers as soon as they are invited to speak about the notion of truth. Secondarily, the misconception is due to belief in intuitively obtained information as to the "essence" of the philosophic attitude towards things in general. The attitude of non-philosophers towards the notion of truth has been *deduced* from alleged knowledge of their character and ideology. A deduction of this kind is meaningless and impossible, even if such knowledge should be available.

III. All the main standpoints advocated in truth-theories as they are met with in philosophic literature (excluding theories on "formal truth") can be refound among persons without any philosophic education. All the main opinions on the possibility of defining truth, its definition, its verification, its existence, on the existence of absolute truths, on the eventual meaning of this problem, on the law of excluded middle etc. are refound.

IV. School children at the age of puberty are capable of discussion of these subjects and form their opinions accordingly. They may be said to be *philosophers by occasion*, and the types and variability of their standpoints correspond to those of the *philosophers by profession*.

V. Basic formulations as regards definition of truth and other subjects closely related with it, undergo but little change with increasing age and education. They are generally retained, whereas arguments change.

VI. When basic formulations are subjected to prolonged discussion, they lose their original character of tentatively propounded solutions of a problem, or of mere "Einfälle", and obtain the character of strongly held opinions and convictions. The majority of the formulations — not so much the ways, by which formulations are justified and made acceptable to reason and the moral claims of the person — are retained more or less unmodified by influence of milieu (and occupation). The majority of basic formulations of other persons are rejected.

VII. Certain standpoints, as, for instance, those towards the existence of absolute truths seem very often to generate in discussions of a special kind with ethical bearing. The genesis of other standpoints, as, for instance, adopted definitions of truth, cannot be traced without very close inspection of the ideology of the person as well as his daily occupations.

VIII. In the light of our observations, opinions on philosophical and metaphysical subjects (as tested by a definite kind of them, the "truth-theories") can be conceived as retained pubertic formulations remodelled and deepened under the influence of formulations transmitted by tradition.

By saying that they are "pubertic" we mean: (1) the inclination to adopt and develop philosophic opinions as well as the apparent passionateness and depth of belief, shows a maximum at the age of late puberty, and (2) the formulations — not so much the ways, by which formulations are justified and made acceptable to reason and the moral claims of the person — are retained more or less unmodified by the influence of milieu (and occupation). Of the types of opinions presumably showing a different development, we think those should be mentioned which concern detailed scientific subject-matter: we expect these opinions to be essentially plastic and under more or less continuous differentiation and new-building. — The expression "opinions on philosophic and metaphysical subjects" deserves some comments: we do not thereby refer to whatever statements are found in philosophic literature. The central statements, the conclusions of trends of arguments are intended — excluding, for instance, scientific doctrines advanced in support of such basic formulations.

The diversity and consistency of amateur theories of truth, point to the possibility of an "experimental philosophy". By this expression we do not mean more than in other cases in which "experimental" is used as a characteristic, for instance, "experimental biology". If the oecology of pine forests is studied by means of planting pines in new areas and under systematically changing conditions, the behaviour of the pines throws some light on the dynamics of pine woods in general. The fact that one cannot build up a pine synthetically corresponds to the fact that we cannot *experiment* with milieu in which truth-theories grow spontaneously. Just as an expert on experimental forestry may infer something of the conditions of woods in past ages with the aid of the fossils of the paleontologist, the student of dynamics of amateur theories of truth may, by means of philosophic literature study the dynamics of truth-theories of the past.

The fact that specific formal theories of truth involving theories of deduction and logical calculus are not easily re-created by amateurs, points to the difference between speculative theories of a primitive character and other theories. By "primitive" we here mean the opposite of "elaborated", "consciously developed", "resulting from a succession of trial-and-error processes". Comparing the amateur and professional theories, there is a difference between learned commentaries and doctrines associated with, but not constituting, the professional truth-theories and the mainly primitive comments of the ps. The occasionally profound analysis of history of thought connected with professional truth-theories is, for instance, quite absent among our ps. Adopting the above-explained expression "primitive" for what is easily reproduceable among ps, it coincides with the *speculative core of philosophy*. The coincidence is a "hypothesis" which is fairly well supported by our protocols which contain many philosophic amateur theories in addition to truth-theories.

The question arises how far speculations other than those centring around the essence of "truth" can be investigated on the same lines as those adopted in this paper. No problem of speculative philosophy seems to be as easily dealt with statistically as the truth-problem. This was a reason for us to emphasize the method at the cost of more subtle characteriological analyses, which surely would imply an enormous series of experiments. Work with qts not reproduced in this paper, convinced me, however, that much preliminary work on philosophic speculation can be successfully carried out by adopting *the differential method of questionnaires in connection with the method of "free association"*. There are scarcely any of the traditional philosophic problems which are not suitable for this procedure. Characteriological analyses demand coordinated work of experimental psychologists and psychoanalysts (and evidently presuppose an intimate knowledge of philosophic literature.) We suspect, however, that such analyses are apt to favour hasty and "profound" conclusions if no carefully elaborated statistical material is already available.

CHAPTER V

The Theories of Philosophers on the Opinions of Non-Philosophers.

Sect. 106. Introduction. — In the introduction we have described the cs-theories very superficially. In this chapter they are more amply discussed. The theories to be described in the following sections concern various groups of non-philosophers. From one point of view the theories deal with subjects which do not overlap. What unifies the theories is largely their discussional aspect. Philosophers refute or comment on them as though they all were concerned with the same subjects.

Here as in the following sections our statements are based on a knowledge of only a fraction of all philosophic theories concerned with the view of non-philosophers. The uniformity of the material, however, speaks in favour of our assumption that the fraction familiar to us is *a fair sample of all theories* — at least, as regards those features referred to in our statements.

In the cs-theory of Heinroth, the non-philosophers at issue are called "das Volk an sich", "das Volk", "der große Haufen". A "Volkswahrheit" and also a "Wahrheit des Kindes" is mentioned. Lenzen speaks about "uneducated minds", Walker about "the ordinary man". Reininger speaks about "die mit der natürlichen Betrachtungsweise Übereinstimmende Auffassung der Wahrheit".

Some philosophers postulate an all pervasive kind of truth: Leroux speaks about "la notion commune que la conscience humaine se fait de la vérité", Hoernlé about "the usual view" and "criterion", Dewey about "the common and undeniable assumption". Beatti mentions truth as it is "viewed by all people". Similar reference is found by Nichols. Other philosophers refer to non-philosophers indirectly, stating something about "the popular use of "truth"" or "ways in which the word truth is commonly used", (Brandt, Paulhan, and Pratt). Pratt also mentions "the real commonsense theory" of truth. Carnap speaks more carefully about ""Wahrheit" in üblicher Bedeutung" and in the "Umgangssprache". Husserl mentions what is supposed to lie "in dem blossen Sinn der Worte wahr und falsch", and he may therefore propose something as "the right conception of evidence and truth". Finally, there are philosophers who describe truth as it reveals itself "wenn man einen Bauer fragen wollte" (Lossius) or "if common sense had been asked to formulate" it (Marhenke). This type of reference sometimes is very short as by Boas: "ask a man — —". We think it astonishing how accurate, unambiguous and "straight on" these references of the philosophers are. One should consequently expect that it is relatively easy to control statements based on them.

Sect. 107. General Views Imputed to the Amateurs. — At first we shall quote some statements without A-formulations. — Some philosophers think that non-philosophers under-estimate the difficulties of trying to find out what "truth" is. To common sense, says Paulhan[1], the question "what is truth" seems very simple. Marhenke[2] declares that "the definition of the truth and falsity of beliefs is not quite so simple as common sense and Mc Taggart suppose".

Comparing the explicit and implicit views of amateurs and philosophers on the difficulties in question, we think that no serious difference is traceable. Certainly, some ps are very optimistic, but this is also the case with some of the philosophers. Descartes[3] declares: "Il (Herbert of Cherbury) examine ce que c'est que la vérité; et pour moi, je n'en ai jamais douté, ne semblant que c'est une notion si transscendentalement claire, qu'il est impossible de l'ignorer". Nobody entertains the opinion that e. g. Brentano[4] is no philosopher or that he does not work seriously. He thinks, nevertheless, that the clearing up of the discussion on truth is no serious task: having brought his A-formulation and formulated what is gained by his argumentation, he says: "Das also dürfte etwa unser Lohn und Gewinn sein, gewiß genug bei einer so bescheidenen Frage, wie die von uns gewählte, bei der es sich ja um nichts als um die Erklärung eines durch alltäglichen Gebrauch jedem geläufigen Ausdruckes handelt." There are optimistic philosophers and there are pessimistic ps, ps with deep "Problemgefühl". Such ps take the question on the notion of truth extremely seriously and the view that it is impossible, or practically impossible, to arrive at any definition is not very uncommon.

Some philosophers indirectly take standpoint to what the non-philosophers mean, stating that the theories of truth adhered to by their opponents contradict the basic structure of truth revealed among the non-philosophers. Pragmatists often hear this from antipragmatists, cf. the statement of Leroux[5] according to whom the pragmatic definition is not only "mal fondeé en raison" but "se trouve, par surcroit contredire la notion commune que la conscience humaine se fait de la vérité".

---

[1] Revue philos. 75, 1913, I, p. 225.
[2] Publ. Univ. Calif. 11, p. 169.
[3] Cit. from Cassirer, Theoria 1937 p. 163 anm.
[4] Wahrheit und Evidenz, p. 29.
[5] Le pragmatisme americain et anglais, p. 302.

Does the pragmatic theory contradict "la notion commune", yes or no? — This question, like so many others, is altogether unanswerable. The idea to compare a certain philosophic theory with something as vague as "the common notion of truth", is impossible. There is no answer to such questions. What may be stated and controlled is the relative frequency of ABſs and other formulations of the ps showing more or less similarity with pragmatic formulations. To some degree, views on the value of the amateur formulations as expressions of "opinion" may also be controlled in the sense in which the pragmatists may be said to hold their theories as opinions. But no bridge of scientific investigations seems to lead from statements on such matters to general and sweeping statements as those quoted.

It is not impossible that Leroux means to refer to the *use* of the word as *observable* among non-philosophers. In this case his formulation is clearly misleading and the lack of reference to what sort of observation is carried out makes the theory worthless. Nelson, on the other hand, entertains a similar opinion, but explicitly refers to the use of the *word* "truth": "Will der Pragmatismus nicht anderes als eine Wortdefiniton der Wahrheit, so läſst sich gegen ihn vom logischen Standpunkt nichts einwenden. Nur wird der Begriff, der nach dem bisher üblichen Sprachgebrauch mit dem Wort Wahrheit verbunden wird, nicht aus der Welt geschafft."[1] Here it is implicitly assumed (1) that there exists something worthy of the name "hitherto common usage of the word "truth"", which may be hit upon so easily that no further description how to find this something is needed, (2) that this something is expressible as a notion and (3) that the notion constructed in this way is directly *comparable* with "the definition" characterized as "pragmatism". None of these assumptions seems to us to be easily tenable. We need not repeat why.

In this connection may be mentioned the very common reference of the philosophers to the "meaning" ("Sinn" und "Bedeutung") of terms like "true" and "false". They usually do not intend the "dictionary meaning" of these words. Or, to put it somewhat more definitely, one can seldom find symptoms that a philosopher would consent to substitute the term "expression of the meaning of truth" as it stands in his writings with the expression "what may be found in the place p in the dictionary or encyclopedia e, article "Truth"". The statements of the type "a is the meaning of truth" do not seem to be controllable in this way. We dare to say that in the majority of cases no description is available of the technique to control such statements, and no hints are given how to repeat the (eventual) researches which were carried out to establish them and that, if a description of the technique is available, it is so vague and abstruse, that effective control is consequently out of reach. This is disastrous in these matters,

---

[1] Nelson, L. Atti del 4. congr. philos., I, p. 155.

because one may with remarkable security forecast: if the philosopher A states "a and not b is the meaning of truth" one may find a philosopher B who states that "b and not a is the meaning of truth". What sort of knowledge can such statements secure, if no indications are made, how they were arrived at? If A had said "Sitting down and asking myself what the meaning of truth is, the Einfall A occurs, if any", and B that under similar circumstances he gets the Einfall B, we think that their contribution to human knowledge would have been greater — however small it may be judged. It would have been greater because it makes reference to a kind of "test", a questionnaire-method with one test-person. — How is it, for instance, possible to control a subtle thesis of Husserl[1] concerning the notion of truth if it is argued that "This lies in the mere meaning of the words true and false"? If someone dared to contest it or to consider it humbug, how could it be possible to get a pupil of Husserl to prove that it *is* profound without giving any hints how to decide between the statements "a and not b lies in the mere meaning of the word true" and "b and not a lies in the mere meaning of the word true"? — The search for the "mere" or "common" or "popular" meaning of a term — *especially if something more than dictionary synonyms is aimed at* — cannot, in our opinion, be carried out contemplatively and introspectively, but only by observation.

We will now leave the vague statements on meaning and take a glance at some very clear and easily controllable statements on the notion of truth. The following forecasts of Lossius[2] are perhaps the most instructive: "Wenn man einen Bauer fragen wollte, warum er glaube, daß seine Wiesen grün, seine Kühe roth und seine Pferde schwarz sind, so würde er ohne Zweifel zur Antwort geben: "will ich's sehe", und wollte man weiter fragen, warum er glaube, daß dasjenige wahr sei, was er sieht, so würde er diese Frage entweder keiner Antwort wert halten, oder sagen: "weil alle Menschen dies tun"." It would be out of place to complain of Lossius that he is vague and is afraid that his statements might be too easily controllable — provided we take his statements verbally and not allegorically. The extremely low probability that the first and best peasant we meet would answer as forecast by Lossius makes it a duty, however, to interpret him allegorically. We may assume that he means: the peasant will answer *something like that*. He may e. g. entertain the opinion that the "ordinary" man in contrast to philosophers sticks to sense-data. It is instructive that utterances of non-philosophers are often thought to be unambiguously interpretable as showing more connection with a certain philosophic truth-theory than with any other. This view is untenable. The immense variety of answers of truth-theories and the frequent divergence among philosophers when they

---

[1] Cf. Logische Untersuchungen, I, p. 117.
[2] Lossius, Ursachen des Wahren. Gotha 1775, p. 194.

interpret examples of something true in the light of truth-theories make such a treatment of the utterances worthless. We shall in sect. 109 illustrate the conviction of some philosophers that the behaviour of the non-philosopher must be interpreted rather in the light of one philosophic theory than of any other, that he implicitly "adheres" to this, not that, "theory".

Is it so that the non-philosopher *knows* what he means by "true", has he an "idea" of truth? Heinroth[1] thinks that "das Volk besitzt seine bestimmte Vorstellung von der Wahrheit, ohne dieser Vorstellung diesen Namen zu geben." Such an opinion is very difficult to control: if it is found that inside every class of education and every class of age, the formulations of the non-philosophers diverge, how are we to interpret the existence of a common "idea of truth"? Perhaps by the "common use" of the word true. But must a man who uses a word some hundred times a day have an "idea" of this use? Our material cannot be said to disfavour or to favour the opinion that "something is in common". It is so vague that it allows several incongruent interpretations. "Man weiß im alltäglichen Leben was unter Wahrheit zu verstehen ist", says Pozniansky and also other professionals, but they do not explain how they know this or what is meant by "verstehen". In certain discussions we would agree with him, in others, we would not: If one's disposition at the moment is benevolent one declares that one agrees, if not, one protests. What may easily be observed is that people very often use the words true and false, that their hearers seldom comment upon their use of the word, argue against the use etc. This sociological material may be interpreted in various ways. One of these, we think, is very dangerous: it is implicitly argued that the material implies the possibility of arriving at a statement — let us call it "p" — of moderate complexity with the following property: it shall express or describe the use of the word true, so that future examples of usage of this word can be forecast with reasonable certainty or in such a manner that it is "explained" by the statement. — From the possibility of arriving at the statement p the existence of a definite "meaning" ("Sinn") and ("Bedeutung") of the word "true" is inferred. This "meaning" should, according to the interpretation under treatment, be expressible by a statement. Specimens of such statements show that there are philosophers who expect this statement to be short and easily handled. That is all illusion, we think. If more than dictionary synonyms for the word "true" are aimed at, if it is seriously intended to describe the (eventual) "specific" function (Leistung) of sentences in which "true" occurs, very laborious investigations have to be carried out.[2] We forecast that the result of these investigations is not expressible by a statement of the sort of p above mentioned. It would have to be extremely complex. The indications of function must

---

[1] Heinroth, Über die Wahrheit, Lpz. 1824, p. 73.
[2] On the notion of "specific" function, cf. Arne Ness: Erkenntnis und wissenschaftliches Verhalten, § 8 et seq.

vary with the design of the indications. It is not to be expected that a single group of indications can be said to be "*the* description of function", or the logical product (or sum) of all indications arrived at. One may construct a metaphysical ideal limit towards which all descriptions shall converge, or which expresses all possible designs, but this does not improve the *practially obtainable* indications of function. —

Is the "truth" conceived by non-philosophers as something eternal or something transient? Beatti[1] thinks that the former is the case: "Die Wahrheit wird wie erscheint, von allen Menschen als etwas festes, als etwas unveränderliches und Ewiges angesehen." Among as few as 250 ps we found the views conflicting severely with this theory and it is therefore untenable. The same may be said of the very similar, but better controllable statement of Carnap: ""Wahr" (in der üblichen Bedeutung) ist ein zeitunabhängiger Begriff, d. h. er wird ohne Angabe einer Zeitbestimmung prädiziert."[2] It is perhaps open to discussion if the ps may be said to ""*predicate*" the *notion* "true"" at all, but *if* we allow this expression, we must admit that time-indications are often met with. Expressions like the following "true then, but not now" are frequent. The view that a statement can be true at the time t_1 and false at the time t_2 is also found. Carnap might perhaps object that he does not mean that time-indications *never* occur, but that they seldom occur — compared with the number of times in which "true" without time-indications occur. We think this is a reasonable assumption. It must be remembered, however, that this does not necessarily mean that ""true" is conceived as a notion independent of time". Why should a "notion" which occurs in 90 per cent of cases without time-indication be "independent"? —

The opinion that uneducated persons rather than educated ones are absolutists is very common. As we have seen, there is a remarkable decrease in the number of ps favouring absolutistic views on "truth" with increasing education. Educated ps favour moderate expressions: they seem to know better than less educated "how to behave" in discussions. There may also be said much in favour of the opinion, that, on the whole, the tendency to *declare* something as absolutely certain follows the same law. It is, on the other hand, very difficult to decide if the *acts* of educated persons are less rigid than the acts of uneducated. An inquiry into such subjects would be interesting. As long as nothing is done, let us admit our ignorance. In this connection it may be mentioned how often absolutistic attitudes of a stupid and degrading character are attributed to those who do not publish any opinion on philosophic questions — and how this is done without the slightest reason. Philosophical doctrines are made more clever by making

---

[1] Beatti, J., Versuch über die Natur der Unveränderlichkeit der Wahrheit, p. 23.

[2] Carnap, R., Actes du Congrès International de Philosophie Scientifique. Sorbonne, Paris 1935 IV, 1.

non-philosophers (sometimes called "naive realists") stupid. The naive realist, says Müller-Freienfels (to quote at random) "ahnt nichts von den mannigfachen Trübungen unseres Wahrnehmens und Denkens durch die abnormitäten der Sinne, Einfluß von Gefühlen und Vorurteilen, — —".[1] If such things were said about an African tribe last time observed in 1820, it would be pardonable. But actually, the majority of philosophers' fellow-citizens are intended.

Sect. 108. Alleged Truth-Theories of the Non-Philosopher. — Before we begin to quote from the long list of philosophic truth-theories imputed to the non-philosopher, we think it is worth while to mention that philosophers exist who declare non-philosophers and common sense to be immune from *any* philosophic tendency: Lenzen[2] for instance thinks that realism and subjectivism are sophisticated standpoints — common sense is prior to distinctions of that sort. It is very plausible that ps of the education-classes 1, 2 or 3 only extremely seldom develop standpoints *identifiable* with those of philosophic realism, idealism or subjectivism. They certainly do not use the philosophic vocabulary. But there is no doubt that they are capable of entertaining opinions on the truth-notion, which may be said to be more than embryonic theories of knowledge: they are philosophical standpoints translated into untechnical language. Their ABf and other general statements convince us thereof. An example of a not infrequent type of subjectivism among non-philosophers: "Perhaps the world is but a dream — —". What is lacking is the conscious elaborations of theories, the technical language and the sharpening of standpoints as a result of prolonged discussion. The truth-theories of professionals are products of centuries of discussion and other causes of mutual influence. It would be a miracle if a p answered to qts with a truth-theory endowed with just those characteristics which prolonged philosophic discussions are apt to favour. We have seen, however, that by steadily increasing the duration of examinations, the views of the ps tend to show those characteristics. Letting a group of ps discuss their views, the same can be shown.

As already mentioned, philosophers show a strong inclination to identify the non-philosophic view of truth with formulations expressed by A-formulation of Gr1.1 and Gr1.2. Before entering into the philosophic discussion on truth, Dewey,[3] for instance, declares that "agreement of some sort between judgment and fact", is "the common and undeniable assumption". The same declaration is made by James. "— — de beaucoup les plus nombreux traducteurs fidèles du sens commun, charactérisent la vérité comme un accord de l'idée et de la réalité, une relation de correspondance entre notre

---

[1] Müller-Freienfels, Psychologie der Wissenschaft. Lpz. 1936. p. 219.
[2] Lenzen, University of California. Publications in Philosophy. Berkeley 1929, vol. 11, p. 153.
[3] Dewey, J.: Essays in experimental Logic, p. 231.

pensée et son objet —", says Leroux.[1] The shortcomings of this formulation are consequently explained as characteristics of a primitive and naive conception: Kozlowski[2] e. g. speaks about "a naive phase" according to which "la connaissance correspond a une réalité exterieure". Goedeckemeyer[3] comments on the "truth of the transcendent truth-notion", "der seinen Namen daher hat, daß er die Wahrheit bestimmt als die in der ganzen bisherigen Philosophie der vorherrschende gewesen ist, und daß er auch das ausdrückt, was der *sogenannte philosophisch Ungebildete* wenn auch meistens ohne klares Bewußtsein, unter Wahrheit versteht." Reiniger[4] (and with him Stern[5] diverge somewhat from this type of formulation: according to "the natural point of view" means "Objektivität (Wahrheit) der Erkenntnis ihre Übereinstimmung mit dem erkannten Sachverhalt". The list of A-formulations put forward by our ps shows most convincingly that the formulations of Gr1.1, Gr1.2 or Gr1.3 are in no way more characteristic of non-philosophers than a great deal of other formulations. It seems as if philosophers have a stronger tendency to accept Afr belonging to Gr2.1 than non-philosophers. Against this, some philosophers may object that (1) non-philosophers — also when they formulate their Afs otherwise — "mean" "agreement with reality" or (2) that other formulations have the same meaning as those of Gr2.1 or (3) that non-philosophers use the word true in such a way that one may identify "true" (to non-philosophers) with "agreeing with reality (to non-philosophers)". Such statements are largely speculative. We have already pointed out why they cannot convince us.

According to Richter[6] there are some characteristics of truth which are fundamental and generally accepted. These are — among others — "Unveränderlichkeit der Wahrheit und deren Evidenz für alle Subjecte," Richter[7] thinks that all people really find the same things evident — but only "bei gesteigerterter Selbstbesinnung". This statement is very difficult to control. What would he object against the opinion that people "bei *herab*gesetzer Selbstbesinnung" have a tendency to accept the same things? We are afraid that the criterion put into practice would be identical in its effects with the following "true is what according to Richter *ought* to be evident to everybody".

Le Roys says: "Le sens commun appelle *vraie* toute idée conforme à la chose qu'elle représente. Le vrai de ce point de vue réaliste, c'est donc l'être même. La notion de vérité repond alors à la formule scolastique: adequatio rei et intellectus." Without saying how he has arrived at the

---

[1] Leroux, op. cit, p. 302.
[2] Kongressber., 3. Int. Kongress f. Philosophie p. 728.
[3] Der Begriff der Wahrheit, Zeitsch. f. Philos. u. philos. Kritik, Bd. 120, p. 186 f.
[4] Philosophie der Erkenntnis, p. 373.
[5] Die philosophischen Grundlagen von Wahrheit, Wirklichkeit, Wert, p. 54.
[6] Der Skeptizismus, II, p. 19.
[7] Op. cit. II, p. 352.

conclusion, le Roy declares that the non-philosopher's theory implies a "realistic ontology" and "the criterion of fact".[1]

Walker[2] finds that objective evidence is the criterion of truth and "the only criterion which the ordinary man uses". "Objective evidence" he explains thus: "We assent because we are forced to do so by the object itself, because it is the object itself and not some other object or cause which seems to have manifested itself to our mind. We assent because that to which we assent is *obvious* and we cannot help assenting".

As a last definite theory concerning "truth" among non-philosophers we will quote that of Pratt,[3] who is one of the few philosophers known to us who explicitly attribute more than two distinct formulateable meanings to the word "truth" as it is commonly used. The tendency to clarify the meaning by a group of synonyms is refound among philologists. The difference between philologists and philosophers on this point can be formulated thus: The "dictionary-synonyms" of the philologists are (1) greater in number and (2) illustrated by phrases actually found in literature and conversation. The reader may control our statement inspecting the large observational material collected in the articles "true", "truth" etc. of the best dictionaries. The description of Pratt reads thus: "The three different ways in which the word truth is commonly used are, then, the following: (1) As a synonym for "reality", (2) As a synonym for known "fact" or verified and accepted belief, (3) As the relation or quality belonging to an "idea" which makes it "true" — its "trueness."

Sect. 109. **Alleged Philosophies of the Non-Philosopher.** — We will finally quote some philosophers who describe the standpoint of non-philosophers by very general philosophic notions — without mentioning A-formulations. "My account of truth is realistic" says James,[4] "and follows the epstemological dualism of common sense". Asked about what he means by this expression, James would — if we permit ourselves to take the contents of his writings as symptoms of his opinions — probably answer in such a way that a *denial* of what he in the quoted passage has stated would be highly difficult to defend. James fights against philosophic views, however, which he maintains are not in agreement with *common sense*. The weak point in his argument is clearly perceived if his opponents are asked whether their views are or are not in agreement with common sense and how they think about the relation between James' epistemology and common sense. One may expect a considerable fraction of the opponents to maintain that *they* and not James follow the "epistemology of common sense". A *denial* of their statements turns out equally difficult to defend.

---

[1] Le Roy. La pensée intuitive, II, p. 182.
[2] Walker, Theory of knowledge, p. 641.
[3] What is pragmatism?, p. 51.
[4] The meaning of truth, p. 267.

This means *that one may, as philosophers, interpret common sense largely as is convenient for one's philosophic purposes* — one may feel confident that the controllability of one's statements is so doubtful that they are easy to defend against the attacks of opponents.

To say that the common sense view of truth is "realistic" is in no sense a more or less tenable position than the opposite — to maintain that it is not "realistic". If, on the other hand, we tried to infer from our material that common sense is "realistic", our arguments would be easily destroyed by counter arguments as the following: "You take the behaviour B as a symptom of a realistic attitude. I cannot allow this. B is a symptom of non-realism, or it is at least inessential to the distinction between realism and views opposed to realism (for instance, idealism)". Just the same would happen if we chose to interpret our material in favour of views opposed to "realism": this word is sufficiently vague and the controllability of statements based on the distinction "epistemological realism" — "epistemological non-realism" — sufficiently small to make it an easy task to defend whatever standpoint needed during one's whole lifetime.

Another instance: in the discussion between Pratt and the pragmatists on the notion of truth, Pratt[1] states that "this belief, in fact, is very much older than "philosophy" and is one of the fundamental principles of common sense — as Professor James himself would doubtless tell you. It is, in short, simply the belief that you can mean something which is entirely outside your own experience". Of what worth is this statement, if, as is the case, no attempt is made to base it on arguments whatsoever? If the statement does not interest you, you leave it unattacked. If Pratt, on the other hand, infers something from it which you do not like — nothing is easier than to interpret the expressions "entirely", "outside" or "your own experience" in such a way as to make your own standpoint untouchable in the eyes of your friends. You may invoke "fundamental principles of common sense" at any point of your theories you will. *Who knows anything about these principles, if there are any?*

Piaget puts forward a very suggestive theory on the ontogenesis of the truth-notion. As he maintains his view after very ingenious experiments with children, the theory is worthy of close consideration. We cannot, however, discuss is as closely as we would wish for the simple reason that our ps very seldom are younger than 12. — "Au point de vue l'élimination, le respect de l'enfant pour l'adulte", says Piaget,[2] "a pour effect de decleucher l'apparition d'une conception annonciatrice de la notion de vérité, la pensée cesse d'affirmer simplement ce que lui plait pour se conformer à l'opinion de l'entourage. Aussi prend naissance une distinction equivalente à celle du vrai et du faux." The child arrives at a notion of

---

[1] What is pragmatism? N. Y. 1909, p. 139.
[2] Le judgment moral chez l'enfant. Paris 1932, p. 467.

truth: "le vrai est ce qui est conforme a la parole adulte." How is this view to be understood? Perhaps the following formulation indicates the way in which it may be controlled; "Children behave — at a certain stage in their evolution — as if they would conceive that, and only that, true, which conforms to the sayings of the adults." But so formulated, we think it is a bad theory: it seems untenable to hold that the sayings of adults determine the whole range of the complex behaviour of children. We must assume that great unities of complex behaviour have no direct connection with adult sayings and that these unities — whether verbal or not — can be interpreted as symptoms of "hypothesis in children" (cf. for inst. Krechevsky "Hypothesis in rats"), which they acknowledge to be "true". Piaget himself, interprets the complex behaviour of children in this way. We think it is justifiable to state: "There are things accepted by children as true, which neither conform to, nor non-conform to, the sayings of adults." The sayings of Piaget may, of course, be interpreted otherwise on account of the ambiguous characteristic of the expression "notion of truth". Taking it for granted that Piaget does not try to support bad hypotheses about subjects he knows as few others do, we reformulate his theory as conceived by us: "Where the behaviour (speech-behaviour or other behaviour) of children (at a certain stage of their evolution) seems to be determined (partly or wholly) by the sayings of adults, the behaviour follows such patterns, that it may be said that the children implicitly or explicitly accept these sayings spontaneously." This theory will probably find almost universal recognition, but it has nothing to do with a *general* statement of what children accept as true, or with a *general* characterization of "the notion of truth among children".

Sect. 110. Taking a rapid glance at the collection of quotations of sect. 106—109 as a whole, we think it stands out very clearly that there is a disproportion between the keen, sweeping, and exceedingly vague statements found in them and the material put forward to strengthen or prove them: this material is "microscopic" in substance. If the statements are based on prosaic investigations as those habitual in psychology (tests, questionnaires etc.) or if they are inferred from ethnological records of some sort, why are not these investigations mentioned? We find no reason to assume they are concealed to the reading public and we are therefore forced to conclude that no such investigations are performed. It is most likely that the statements are obtained "intuitively" or by preparing and modelling impressions obtained in every-day life, "vorbewußte" (preconscious) impressions based on "anonymous" experiences, happenings undatable and unlocalizable, but perhaps very great in number. Even no rationalist of our time would deny that the overwhelming large part of the statements of all of us are based on this anonymous and ghostly authority. Personally, we consider this part not in any way less valuable than any other part.

But, if impressions of this sort occur in *print* verbalized as sweeping theories and the occurrence of these theories stimulate great *discussions and debates lasting for centuries*, the point is reached where it seems scientifically sound either to make the statements less sweeping, formulating them, for instance, as follows: "I — a respectable citizen and philosopher — have the *impression* that non-philosophers — — —" or actually *carry out some investigations or other* that can be repeated by others so as to make the statements controllable. What has been important to us is to show that, methodically, very simple investigations will probably force the discussion on the "notion of truth" (among non-philosophers) to follow new lines. Much pseudo-knowledge will have to be discarded and the pretentions of the theories somewhat moderated. Fruitful and sterile questions will be separated.

Sect. 111. Suppose some young man or other happens to be interested in the notion of truth and he decides to study this and similar notions as they occur in daily life and in science. He will find a literature crowded with attempts to define "truth" and to explain the use of this word in the light of the definitions. He will find that solutions of all problems connected with the use of the word "true" and similar words are recommended after brief argument. He finds the solutions stated in a few sentences, whereas their claims are enormous. This young man will tend to be influenced in the direction to take part in the competition of the truth-theory-market, throwing some new general formulation or other into it. Our material shows that at the age of 15—18, there is generally very small resistance of persons against general ideological, "cosmological" and philosophical formulations — at least among persons of the well-to-do-classes. Producing truth-theories he may consequently be said to follow the line of "least resistance" in his mental development. Partial solutions, working hypotheses or discussions of "minor" problems will not satisfy him. But just such theories and descriptions are worthy: they can be formulated so as to be controllable and there can be hope to verify them by means of prosaic methods. The necessary foundation for progress is thus provided. We think here of descriptions of the use of the word "true" (a. s. w.) in daily life, in popularizations of scientific results or in science itself; further, we think of sociological and logical analyses of the fight between different hypotheses in a particular science in a particular century, psychological descriptions of the function of the words "truth" and "reality" in philosophy or religion, proposals on the use of "S-expressions" like "true", "accepted", "probable", "untenable" in discussions of particularly nice questions etc. etc.

There are already a great many contributions to the treatment of questions like these quoted. Some of them seem to be based on acute scientific reasoning and long experience with scientific method. They are, however, on the whole, fully subordinated under the unlucky "theories of truth". *The valuable scientific contributions are pressed so as to appear relevant to vague, general opinions on "truth"* or to metaphysical systems claiming to solve all problems of the theory of knowledge. Discussion centres around the most general formulations of the theories of truth and *not* around the scientific contributions put forward to "prove" them. If the scientist A proposes a truth-theory t_1 and bases this partly on some statements s_1 concerning the evolution of theories in his branch of science, and the scientist B proposes t_2 partly based on s_2, the direction of the discussion will be largely determined by the standpoint of A and B towards t_1 and t_2 ignoring s_1 and s_2; t_1 and t_2 are expressed so as to exclude the possibility of sound discussion: The vagueness of truth-theories makes any attempt of A to correct t_2 by means of s_1 or of B to correct t_1 by means of s_2 futile. Consequently, the valuable contributions expressed by the series of statements s_1 and s_2 are neglected, the collaboration in the field of knowledge to which s_1 and s_2 belong, is made impossible: interest centres around the attempts to infer this or that general philosophic theory. An example: the incontestible contributions of Duhem ("A") to the history of physical hypotheses and to the logic of physical research (s_1) are mainly discussed in their relation to some extremely general and more than usually vague statements (t_1) inferred by him from his scientific investigations. Among these are also formulations formed as a "theory of truth". The yielding of the contributions expressed by the statements s_1 is — historically considered — greatly diminished thereby that the statements t_1 have been in the foreground in discussions — all other statements being viewed only in their worth of possible arguments for or against t_1. To prove the relevancy, data of the history of science have been circumscribed and re-interpreted in an arbitrary way. They have been tormented until they seemed to refute just those A-formations which the opponents have happened to choose and to prove their own A-formation.

Going back to the supposed student mentioned above, the consequences of his taking the formulations t_1 or t_2 au grand serieus are readly perceived: By doing that he will be able to contribute to the philosophic discussion about truth. He will also make an important step towards adjustment to the social group of philosophers, he will be "accepted" as a member of this group. He will, on the other hand, take part in the under-estimation of scientific work of the type s_1 and never find any reason to investigate the many problems of history and logic of science, the psychology and sociology of research for *their own sake*. He will not take part in the improvement of co-operation in the many fields of knowledge not yet investigated scientifically for lack of coordinated work of specialists. The standpoint to such problems will tend to be dictated by his ultimate ends: the construction of truth-theories and general theories concerning science. To the hundreds of theories already on the market, a new one will appear. From our protocols it most convincingly appears that persons as soon as they — perhaps mostly at the age of late puberty — have acquired the technique of manipulation of abstract and "difficult" words, in nearly all cases are ready to adopt a theory of truth as their opinion (resp. conviction) after very little discussion. The tendency to believe in sweeping, philosophic theories — whether "dogmatical" or "sceptical" — must be reckoned with as normal *before the person has begun his philosophical studies at the university*. The specific philosophic university studies as contrasted with scientific ones thus favour the cultivation and *fixation* of an already existing bent of mind.

The acquaintance with contributions to one or several of the subordinated questions of truth-debators, which does *not* culminate in truth-theories or general statements on the possibility of such theories, but is based on the acceptance of the (generally) subordinated questions as primary — we hope this acquaintance will make it easier for him to refrain from worthless playing with sweeping statements. His energy can be released and eventually absorbed in positive scientific investigations of some fields of problems or other until now only step-motherly treated. He will not be greatly imposed upon by the theories of truth, nor by the pseudo solutions of the problems that the function the notion of truth may be said to fulfil in everyday-life and science.

What at first may be felt as a narrowing of horizon will reveal itself as a clearing up of the field of vision. In the place of pseudo-knowledge and seemingly profound "Fragestellungen" one will find admitted ignorance on the one hand and sound hypotheses on the other.

Sect. 112. Philosophy versus Science. — The "theory of truth" is only a small department of philosophy. In denying the value of that department, we do not mean to deny the value of whatever occurs under the banner "philosophy". Problems falling outside the scope of any *particular* science existing, and problems touching the limits of *established* scientific principles, are often called philosophic. As a consequence of the development of science, the type of such problems is a function of time. "Philosophy" thus conceived cannot be a source of knowledge apart from science and concerning special problems. In spite of this, we esteem "philosophy" in that sense extremely important and attribute to it high cultural value. Unhappily, however, the prevalent conception of philosophy implies the existence of problems which cannot and shall not be treated as scientific problems, but as problems of a special, eternal and "higher" kind. The most vigorous group denying the existence of such problems, the "logical empiricists", are not — to take an instance — viewed as philosophers, but as "philosophoben". Those who cultivate most intensively the problems which according to us could justly be called "philosophic", do not offer their contributions as philosophic, but as scientific. Consequently, we think it most appropriate to the cultural situation to give up the term "philosophy" to denote genuine problems not belonging to any of the existing special sciences. Studying these problems, we think that the aim cannot be any other than to incorporate them in bodies of knowledge of the type called "sciences". Classifying them under the heading "philosophy", means to-day, to deny that this is the ultimate aim.

It is to be expected that the above-stated view of "philosophy" would be taken as an attack on *speculation*. This would be a misconception, however. Interest in the increase of human knowledge presupposes that knowledge is distinguished from *speculation with the pretentions of knowledge*, but the interest does not conflict with genuine interest in speculations *offered as such*. We cannot think of a man interested in basic scientific questions who has no need for completion of his general views. Taking phantasy to help, this completion may convey great satisfaction and delight. Utopian constructions of this kind centring around questions of the social sciences show that speculation properly is an art capable of high development. The need for artistic, speculative contributions is apparently less intense in connection with questions other than the social, or so it seems when inspecting the inconspicuous literature of this kind centring around physical, biological or psychological problems. Apart from the phantasies about beings endowed with a larger number of senses or with infinite powers of insight (the Laplacian spirit etc.), there are hardly any speculations worth mentioning which are not sullied by more or less clumsy claims to contribute knowledge. The ability found among painters or poets to put aside the informative attitude, has apparently not yet developed. One dares not offer the reader pure speculations, one suspects that he does not need them or doubts one's creative ability. A compromise is consequently made — both with the requirements of artistic creation and those of knowledge. Hybrid products deceiving both reader and author are brought to light. In the fight against speculations carrying false colours, the cultivator of the artistic, and the cultivator of the scientific bent of mind, keep together.

Sect. 113. Among the problems of scientific interest which only the force of tradition has connected with the traditional philosophic "problem of truth" the following are typical instances:

(1) Problems as regards the development of hypotheses in science. Why this or that theory was accepted etc. The function of scientific discussion, as revealed in a particular science in this or that period.

(2) Problems involved in the study of how opinions of groups come into existence and how they die out. The function of maxims and programmatical statements to ideological currents.

(3) Logistic problems related to the formalization (including axiomatization) of statements on weight of statements. Rôle of expressions as "imply", "prove", "decide", "true", "false", "impossible", "probable" in formalized systems.

(4) Linguistic means of expressing weight of statements: their function and occurrence in science. Practical proposals to standardize and sharpen these linguistic tools where great accuracy is thought desirable.

(5) The function of weighing statements in research behaviour. Its development studied in relation to general cultural development.

Each of these problems demands its specific type of approach but none of them seems to demand that the border-line of scientific methodology be transcended.

Printed July 27th, 1938.

www.ingramcontent.com/pod-product-compliance
Lightning Source LLC
LaVergne TN
LVHW061332060426
835512LV00013B/2608